THE
COLLECTED POETRY

AI
MÉ
CÉSAI
RE

The
Collected
Poetry

AIMÉ CÉSAIRE

Translated, with an Introduction and Notes by
CLAYTON ESHLEMAN
and
ANNETTE SMITH

UNIVERSITY OF CALIFORNIA PRESS • BERKELEY / LOS ANGELES / LONDON

The translators would like to express their gratitude to the following periodicals and newspapers in which many of these translations appeared: *Bachy, Bashiru, Butt, Callaloo, Coherence, Conjunctions, LA Weekly, Montemora, Network Africa, Obsidian, Oink* and *Sulfur*. "The Woman and the Knife" was published as a broadside by the Red Ozier Press. "Hail to Guinea," "The Time of Freedom," "Africa," and "A Salute to the Third World" made up an issue of the Munger *Africana Library Notes*. "The Virgin Forest," "Another Season," and "Day and Night" appeared in *A People's Grief*, edited by Robert Bensen. Nine poems from *Noria* appeared in *Mélanges offerts à Aimé Césaire à l'occasion de son soixante-dixième anniversaire, edited by Jacqueline Leiner*.

We are also grateful to the Pierre Matisse Gallery in New York City for permission to reproduce the artwork by Wifredo Lam.

Grateful acknowledgment is made for the following permissions: to Éditions du Seuil for *Cadastre* and *Ferrements*; to Présence Africaine for *Cahier d'un retour au pays natal*; to Éditions Gallimard for *Les Armes miraculeuses*.

University of California Press
Berkeley and Los Angeles, California

University of California Press, Ltd.
London, England

Library of Congress Cataloging in Publication Data

Césaire, Aimé.
   Aimé Césaire, the collected poetry

   1. Césaire, Aimé—Translations, English. I. Title.
PQ3949.C44A24   1983   841   82-17394
ISBN 0-520-05320-6

Printed in the United States of America

4   5   6   7   8   9

ACKNOWLEDGMENTS

Aimé Césaire's works form a vast and complex ensemble. We hope that our translation will be an incentive for additional contacts with them and with their numerous commentators. For the introduction as well as the translation, we have leaned heavily on several decades of Césairian studies. It is impossible here to give proper credit to everyone: the Césaire bibliography* is voluminous enough that to the many names that constitute its entries we can only express our gratitude collectively. Without the pioneering work of Lilyan Kesteloot, the dedication of a subsequent wave of scholars such as Thomas Hale, Jacqueline Leiner, Bernadette Cailler, and Georges M.aM. N'gal, without the precedent of Emile Snyder's translations (the first to make Césaire's poetry available to a large audience), and without A. James Arnold's excellent *mise au point*, *Modernism and Negritude*, our own task would have been a great deal more difficult.

Toward some individuals, our debt is more specific; professors Thomas A. Hale, A. James Arnold, and Gregson Davis read and responded to the penultimate draft of the translation with helpful and imaginative suggestions. In cases when the experts disagreed with us or with one another, the translators were faced with lonely decisions. In spite of the old saying that victory has many fathers and defeat is an orphan, we are the parents of any errors left in the text. In addition, Thomas Hale has contributed additional material for Césaire's biography; James Arnold has been all along a generous and perceptive critic and an authoritative source. Professor Marjorie Perloff and our colleague Professor George M. Pigman have advised us in the matter of the Introduction. Edith Taylor and Rosey Meiron have typed various parts of the manuscript with their usual competence and good grace. To all these people we express our deep gratitude.

Finally, we thank the National Endowment for the Humanities for a Translation Fellowship (1981), which facilitated the completion of this work; the Poetry Society of America for awarding us the Witter-Bynner Grant-in-Aid (1981); the California Institute of Technology for providing throughout the entire work the basic support that made this arduous project possible at all; and Aimé Césaire himself for agreeing several times to answer questions only he could answer.

TABLE

CONTENTS

INTRODUCTION

I

Here is a riddle about contemporary French literature: which maverick of French academe proudly refers to his cannibalistic ancestors? Which major surrealist poet has held a deputy's seat in the French Assembly for thirty-seven years? Which teacher of dead classical languages ended up creating a new one? What member of the world intelligentsia makes himself totally and directly accessible to a constituency of underprivileged blacks? Which major postwar poet is also a major playwright? Which French mayor and member of the parliament commutes to his municipality over the Atlantic? What well-known statesman periodically voices his skepticism about power? What apostle of decolonization once sought the status of a French department for his country? Although each of these questions might have more than one answer, together they could only receive one: Aimé Césaire. Over several decades, Césaire has worn many hats and has been many different things to many people. No wonder, then, that as late as 1965, Michel Leiris found it normal to open an essay on the Martinican writer with the question, "Who is Aimé Césaire?"[1] We shall attempt to answer this question in the present introduction.

Aimé Césaire was born in 1913 in Basse-Pointe, a small town on the northeast coast of Martinique which lies in the shadow of the volcano Mont Pelée. He was the second of six children. Aimé's mother was a dressmaker and his father a local tax inspector. Under the tutelage of his grandmother, Eugénie, Aimé learned to read and write French by the age of four. While the Césaire family did not belong to the class of illiterate agricultural laborers that made up the vast majority of black Martinicans, they were poor. Unlike most Martinicans, however, the family made an ongoing effort to inculcate French cultural norms. By the time Aimé was eleven, the Césaires had moved to Fort-de-France, the capital of Martinique, where Aimé was able to attend the Lycée Schoelcher, the only secondary school for all of Guadeloupe, French Guiana, and Martinique, until after the Second World War.

Creole is the first language of all black Martinicans but to be exclusively a Creole speaker shows an inferior social position. It is indicative of the Césaires' middle-class aspirations that Aimé's father read the children the French prose classics and the poetry of Victor Hugo instead of telling them stories in Creole. Césaire, as a matter of fact, has never to this day envisioned Creole as a vehicle for Martinican cultural expression.

The abundance of Martinican fauna and flora in his poetry probably has as its first cause the influence of a teacher he studied with at the Lycée Schoelcher. Eugène Revert taught geography and attempted to interest his students in the peculiar geographical characteristics of Martinique at a time when standard examination questions were based on mainland French history and geography. It was also Revert who identified Césaire as a candidate for France's highest liberal arts institution, the Ecole

Normale Supérieure in Paris, and recommended him as well for the Parisian Lycée Louis-le-Grand, at which, in September, 1931, he began to prepare for entrance to "Normale."

While at the Lycée Schoelcher in Fort-de-France, Césaire had met Léon-Gontran Damas from French Guiana, who would later join him in formulating the notion of negritude. At the Lycée Louis-le-Grand in Paris, he was befriended by Léopold Senghor from Sénégal. In 1934 Damas and Senghor started a newspaper, *L'Etudiant noir*, which intended to bring together students from Africa and those from the West Indies and was to be a matrix for the concept of negritude. The West Indians Léonard Sainville and Aristide Maugée and the Senegalese Birago Diop and Ousmane Socé also belonged to this *cénacle*. In the circle of *L'Etudiant noir*, Césaire met a young Martinican woman, Suzanne Roussy, whom he married in 1937 and who would later participate as a full partner in the magazine *Tropiques*. It is also during this period that Césaire took classes from Professor Le Senne at Ecole Normale. Le Senne's works on human and racial typology probably contributed to orienting Césaire and his friends toward the concept of a black cultural archetype which transcended geographical boundaries.

Whereas a concise appreciation of American black poetry was not to appear until the July 1941 issue of *Tropiques*, two years after the Césaires' return to Martinique, the Harlem Renaissance was well known to black students in Paris during the early thirties. Speaking of this period, Senghor, who went on to become a poet and the President of Sénégal, has written: "We were in contact with these black Americans [Claude McKay, Jean Toomer, Langston Hughes, and Countee Cullen] during the years 1929–1934, through Mademoiselle Paulette Nardal, who, with Dr. Sajous, a Haitian, had founded the *Revue du Monde Noir*. Mademoiselle Nardal kept a literary salon, where African Negroes, West Indians, and American Negroes used to get together."[2] While the black writers of the United States made a profound impression on Césaire, Senghor's statement should be qualified: Césaire himself had little contact with these salons "for reasons that are indicative of his own social origins and his future evolution. He considered them too bourgeois, too *mulatto*—a term that described quite perfectly the Martinican middle class at the time—and too Catholic."[3]

The Jamaican-born Claude McKay appears to be the Harlem Renaissance writer who gave Césaire the most to think about. McKay's novel *Banjo*, published in French in 1928, offered an explanation for the alienation of black intellectuals everywhere. McKay saw it in the loss of a folk tradition, with its concomitant folk wisdom, as well as in the deep inferiority complex of blacks, brought about by the need to imitate the "civilized" white, and to stifle in themselves anything that might appear strange and unique. For McKay, such negativity had a positive aspect: the very backwardness and unadaptability of the black race might be seen as preserving a vital resource, a close biological kinship to the primitive earth. Although Césaire's actual contacts with the black American writers belong mostly to this early period, their timing was important as the Americans' "primitivism" gave a contemporary focus to ideas he was getting through Frobenius in an even more massive dose.

· In *Tropiques* 2 (July 1941) Césaire wrote an introduction to a translated selection of poems by James Weldon Johnson, Jean Toomer, and Claude McKay, but his own poetry does not draw on their forms of expression. As a writer who had repressed his own Creole background and was at this time being influenced stylistically by the imaginative synthesis promised by French surrealism, he responded to the Harlem Renaissance writers mainly as a new collective black voice. They provided him with a gate through which he could glimpse a sense of interiority and wholeness. He summed up his feelings about the black Americans in the following way:[4] "From this poetry, which might seem like the sort Valéry called 'loose,' 'defenseless,' written only to the rhythm of a juvenile spontaneity, at the exact point of intersection between the ego and the world, a drop of blood oozes. A drop. But it is blood. . . . There is its value: to be open to man in his wholeness." And Césaire praised the new generation of black writers in these words: "the ordinary Negro, the everyday Negro, whose grotesque or exotic aspect an entire literature is bent upon finding, the black poet makes him a hero; he describes him seriously, with passion and the limited power of his art—by a miracle of love—succeeds, where more considerable means fail, in suggesting even those inner forces which command destiny." "The spectacle of crude puppets," Césaire concluded, "has been replaced by that of a new way of suffering, dying, enduring, in a word, of carrying the sure weight of human existence."

Césaire's remaining years as a student can be briefly summarized: in the summer of 1935 he visited the Adriatic coast of Yugoslavia with a friend, and while there, perhaps moved by the name of one of the islands—Martinska—began his celebrated Notebook. He actually did return to Martinique the following summer, but went back to Paris that fall, where he continued to work on the Notebook while completing a Diplôme d'Etudes Supérieures on the theme of the South in black American literature. By 1939, when he returned to Martinique for good, he had stopped short of becoming an agrégé, but he had published the first version of the Notebook in the Parisian review Volontés, and had assembled most of the ideological materials which would begin to be transformed in the poetry and essays he published in Tropiques.

Thought of as a Martinican cultural review and printed in editions of five hundred copies, Tropiques mixed European modernism with a Martinican form of negritude. Within months of the Césaires' return, the French possessions in the West Indies felt the impact of the European war. Until 1943 Martinique was governed from Vichy, and Fort-de-France swarmed with thousands of French sailors contained there by the United States Navy. It has been suggested that one of the explanations for the surreal language in Tropiques is that only by such means could Césaire and his group express themselves creatively and attack the Vichy regime, which controlled the island. The racism of the sailors undoubtedly contributed to radicalizing Césaire and preparing him for a political commitment to fight colonialism after the war, but it should be pointed out that his adherence to surrealism had taken place before he left France.

The early issues of Tropiques reflect the interest Césaire and his collaborators had in Nietzsche. Nietzsche's theory of the will, as well as his ideas on the cycle of culture, were particularly attractive to Césaire, as they reinforced surrealist attacks on the constraints of reason and affirmed the possibility of a heroic rebirth of negritude. At this time, Césaire, writing in the fall 1943 issue of Tropiques (p. 8), also admired the Nietzschean qualities in Paul Claudel: "Claudel, never so fulgurating as when he ceases to be Catholic to become earth, planet, matter, sound, and fury, super ego, superman, whether he exalts the will to power or opens the homicidal floodgates of a humor à la Jarry."[5] Such excitements echo the often demiurgic tone of Césaire's Notebook, for instance the strophe beginning with "I would rediscover the secret of great communications and great combustions. I would say storm. I would say river. I would say tornado."

During that period, Césaire meditated particularly on Nietzsche's Birth of Tragedy and on its central concept of the voluntary sacrifice of the Hero so that the collectivity may live. It is an interesting coincidence—if it is one at all—that he was himself shortly to give priority to politics over poetics. It is perhaps in this light that one should see his sudden election in 1945 as the mayor of Fort-de-France and his subsequent involvement, as a surrealist poet commited to black particularism, with a colonial branch of European communism.

Césaire's involvement in politics developed out of a seven-month visit to Haiti in 1944. Through the key figures of Toussaint L'Ouverture and Henri Christophe, and in spite of their tragic fates, Haiti symbolized for Césaire the possibility of a Caribbean political independence and cultural autonomy. While there, he lectured on Mallarmé and Rimbaud, and absorbed what would eventually result in two works dealing with Haiti's history: the book-length essay Toussaint Louverture: la révolution française et le problème colonial, and his play La Tragédie du roi Christophe. According to Hale, "Upon his return to Martinique at the end of 1944, friends active in the local section of the French

Communist party asked him to give a series of lectures on Haiti. . . . Soon after, Césaire was invited to run on the party ticket in the municipal elections. Although he shared Marxist principles with his friends, Césaire had not given serious thought to full-time political activity. Before the war, the Martinican Communists had been able to garner only a few hundred votes in municipal elections, and thus it was more as a service to his friends than as a serious commitment to politics that Césaire offered his candidacy for a seat on the municipal council (and by the party's placement of his name at the top of the list, for the position of mayor). But in an astonishing upset, the Césaire list won a majority of seats in the May 27, 1945, election, and the next day the poet was formally elected mayor by his fellow councilors. After election as a cantonal *conseiller général* (October 7, 1945) and as one of Martinique's *députés* to the Première Assemblée Nationale Constituante (October 21, 1945), Césaire was sent to Paris to participate in the formation of a new constitution of the Fourth Republic."[6]

A word on Césaire's relationship with Marxism is in order here. His joining the French Communist party during the war was primarily an act of patriotism, and in part a reaction against the racist nature of the Vichy government's administration of Martinique. There is no evidence of Marxist influence in Césaire's writing before he was elected to the French legislature. His second book, *Les armes miraculeuses (The Miraculous Weapons)*, published in 1946, is primarily concerned, theoretically speaking, with resolving an African world view with surrealism. In the same year he prepared the following statement for a party brochure: "I joined the Communist party because, in a world not yet cured of racism, where the fierce exploitation of colonial populations still persists, the Communist party embodies the will to work effectively for the coming of the only social and political order we can accept—because it will be founded on the right of all men to dignity without regard to origin, religion, or color."[7] In other words, his position was not far distant from that of other French intellectuals of the postwar period who allied themselves with the Communists because, as Sartre said, having the same enemies was more important than having the same friends.

Throughout the decade from 1946 to 1956, Césaire wrote most of the poetry to appear in his next three collections, which to varying degrees accommodate the real world of contemporary history and politics. Although at points the internal dialectic, synthesized from ethnography, surrealism, and negritude, is influenced by dialectical materialism, it never indicates a total commitment to Marxism.

While the poet-mayor was able to improve the quality of life among his black constituents during this decade, his successful struggle to change the political status of Martinique from a colony to a department backfired. Civil servants imported from France replaced local people in administrative positions, and black Martinicans realized again and again that they were still second-class French citizens. Increasingly Césaire realized that the orthodox Marxist analysis of a capitalist economy did not apply to Martinican conditions and, with Maoist China as a model, he argued for the creation of an African brand of socialism. At the same time, he was involved with the most hidebound Stalinist party in Western Europe. As Césaire came to see it, on a political level the Marxist dialectic was being used to subordinate Martinican culture to the dominant culture shared not only by the former colonizers but also by the French Marxists. Literarily speaking, he realized that his poetry was essentially surrealist in nature and that he could not conform to the party line on social realism.

Césaire's official break with the party (signaled by his *Letter to Maurice Thorez*) came in 1956 and coincided with the invasion of Hungary by the Soviet troops. It is difficult, however, to assign a specific date for his change of heart. All one can say is that some time between his *Commemoration of the Centennial of the Abolition of Slavery* (1948) and the notorious *Discourse on Colonialism* (1950) Césaire must have begun to experience second thoughts about Marxism. Some sections of the *Discourse* pay their dues to Marxist orthodoxy. Yet others suggest a tension between the requirements of politics and those of poetics, judging by the fact that the Marxist argument in them seems little more than the argument in "Poetry and Knowledge"[8] under a faint disguise.

In spite of criticism by Martinican Communists, Césaire was able to carry the majority of his supporters with him in the elections that followed, and in 1958 he became the leader of the independent socialist Martinican Progressive party (PPM), whose emblem is the balisier so ubiquitous in Césaire's poetry. In April of that year, the PPM started its own newspaper, *Le Progressiste*, which has become the main source of information on Césaire's activities to this day. Since 1958, Césaire, favoring a qualified autonomy for Martinique, has kept the PPM intact and has been returned to the French legislature in every subsequent election.

Césaire's literary output in the sixties was mainly confined to the stage. With *La Tragédie du roi Christophe* (1963), *Une Saison au Congo* (1966), and *Une Tempête* (1969), he became the leading black dramatist in the French language. All his plays deal with colonialism, liberation, and the problems of political power.

In politics, he and his followers continue to press for greater autonomy for Martinique. An ally of François Mitterand, Césaire had new cause for optimism after the Socialist landslide in 1981. Now for the first time since 1947, he finds himself in the majority. But he refuses to press for independence in the short run. He has repeatedly asserted in interviews that there must be a transitional period of self-rule during which fundamental economic, social, and psychological changes take place in Martinique.

Césaire sees culture as playing a key role in these changes. In the early 1970s, he launched the Service Municipal d'Action Culturelle in Fort-de-France. The SERMAC holds an annual cultural festival in the city, sponsors local theater groups and filmmakers, and invites companies from Africa and Afro-America to participate. The SERMAC represents, in a sense, a contemporary approach to a problem which Césaire first attacked with his early poetry in *Tropiques* during the 1940s.

II

Although Césaire was by no means the sole exponent of negritude, the word is now inseparable from his name, and largely responsible for his prominent position in the Third World. This neologism, made up (perhaps on the model of the South American *negrismo*) by latinizing the derogatory word for black (*nègre*) with an augmentative suffix, appeared in print, probably for the first time, in the *Notebook of a Return to the Native Land*:[9] "My negritude is not a stone, its deafness hurled against the clamour of the day / my negritude is not a leukoma of dead liquid over the earth's dead eye / my negritude is neither tower nor cathedral." What was negritude then? A subsequent passage of the *Notebook* answered the question: negritude "takes root in the ardent flesh of the soil / it breaks through the opaque prostration with its upright patience." In more prosaic terms, it signified a response to the century-old problem of the alienated position of the blacks in history. Once upon a time, the blacks inhabited their homeland: a whole continent. And then, there was the diaspora which all over the world left the blacks enslaved or colonized, with neither a present nor a future nor even a language of their own.

The case of the Antilleans was particularly complex since they had been colonized for three centuries and since—Creole being mostly an oral vernacular—they had no other way to express themselves in print than in French. This frustrating situation was perceived by some as making them the "bastards" of the father figure of Metropolitan France, which had a culture but no love, and of the mother figure of their native land, which had love but no culture. In 1931 the Haitian poet Léon Laleau had also described this predicament movingly, though in conventional verse, as "this despair without parallel to tame with words received from France / This heart received from Sénégal."[10] A relative cultural revival followed the 1915 American occupation of Haiti and gave birth to an efflorescence of local publications such as the works of Jean Price-Mars and the *Revue des Griots*. Yet, up to the Second World War, most of the black intellectual world was still espousing (at least in their writings) the cultural values and literary forms of the white world. Such exceptions as the *prises de conscience* represented by the Haitian magazine *Lucioles* around 1927 and by the radical Paris-based journal *Légitime Défense* around 1932 hardly altered the situation. What Damas was later to call "tracing paper" poetry was the rule.[11]

The negritude movement, therefore, set as its initial goal a renewed awareness of being black, the acceptance of one's destiny, history, and culture, as well as a sense of responsibility toward the past. In a later interview (1959) Senghor viewed it as the upholding of "the cultural patrimony, the values and, above all, the spirit of the Negro African civilization."[12] While the public statement of these goals was a novelty, however, the underlying concepts were not. As in other domains, Rimbaud had played a prophetic role in choosing Africa as his ultimate destination as early as 1880. Even though former slaves were still living in the shadow of their masters in twentieth-century Africa and the Caribbean, in Europe times were propitious for a rediscovery and rehabilitation of the African heritage.

In France in the 1920s a number of unconnected but seminal works showed this trend. René Maran published an almost scandalously realistic colonial novel, *Batouala* (Goncourt Prize in 1921), and Blaise Cendrars a collection of African legends (1921). Maurice Delafosse's volumes on the African blacks (1922–1927) praised their ability to administer themselves, which they had demonstrated in the past. The geographer G. Hardy's *Negro Art* (1927) continued the revival of interest in African art already present in Cubist painting. But the most important study for Césaire was undoubtedly anthropologist Leo Frobenius' *Histoire de la civilisation africaine*, translated from the German in 1936. Subsequently, anthropologists were to be suspicious of Frobenius' facts; but no one can deny the importance nor the magnitude of his vision. He conceived of an African essence—or soul—permeating all aspects of black culture and responsible for its striking aesthetic dimension. That culture he considered as the cradle of and a model for all others.

Such were but a few of the milestones along the road leading to the increasing decentralization of Western culture. We tend to think of this movement as characteristic of our era. It is nonetheless clear that the twentieth century's eagerness to accept other cultures and to judge them by their own (and non-Western) standards, goes back to the nineteenth-century travelers—anthropologists such as Alexander von Humboldt—and even as far back as Rousseau's *Second Discourse on the Inequality of Mankind*. One should therefore not be entirely surprised to see Césaire give Spengler and a legendary champion of white superiority like Gobineau their due.[13] The leaders of the negritude movement read Gobineau apparently more attentively than the public at large. It did not escape them that this infamous "Aryanizer" extolled the profound quasi-biological fusion of the black race with nature—a fusion which (in Gobineau's opinion) accounted for an artistic sense more spontaneous and more acute than that of the white race.

In the fifties negritude was to become as much of an arena as *engagement* had been in the 1940s. In retrospect, there were deep differences in the way various people conceived it—too many to do more here than just allude to some of the positions. Senghor was understood—perhaps wrongly—to consider black culture as the product of a black *nature*. If as a result of some covenant with nature, black Africans were a chosen race, they were bound to be both more secure about their roots and less alienated than deported blacks. Senghor's poetry and many contemporary African novels tend to prove this point. Césaire seems to have shared Senghor's view in the early part of his career—and he was later to be criticized for it by a younger generation of black intellectuals. In an interview with Jacqueline Leiner in 1978, however, he maintained that for him black culture had never had anything to do with biology and everything to do with a combination of geography and history: identity in suffering, not in genetic material, determined the bond among black people of different origins. If history had made victors of the blacks, there would not be what he called elsewhere "a greater solidarity among black people."[14]

But whether innate or acquired, the characteristics of black culture on which all interpreters of negritude agreed were antipodal to the Western values of rationalism, technology, Christianity, and individualism. They spelled not the control of nature by reason and science but a joyful participation in it; not its control by technology but a coexistence with other forms of life; not the Christianity of the missions but the celebration of very ancient pagan rites; not the praise of individual achievement but the fraternity and communal soul of the clan, the tribe, as well as the love of ancestors. "A culture is born not when Man grasps the world, but when he is grasped . . . by it."[15] Let us insert here that for Césaire (as for many other non-African blacks) the African heritage had been acquired through books and espoused spiritually—which made it perhaps an even more aggressive ideal.

The rallying motto of negritude had been conceived in the fervor of youthful militancy just before the Second World War. It was further promoted during the war and the occupation of France when Césaire and his entourage elaborated on these principles in the Martinique-based *Tropiques*. After the war, their success resulted in the foundation—by Alioune Diop and other well-known intellectuals—of a Parisian periodical and of a publishing house under the common name of *Présence Africaine*. The idea was also to find a theoretician in the High Priest of postwar French letters, Jean-Paul Sartre. His essay, "Orphée Noir" ("Black Orpheus"), which served as an introduction to Senghor's *Anthology of the New Black and Malagasy Poetry* (1948), gave negritude an existential and Hegelian imprimatur in a period when every aspect of intellectual life had to be viewed in those terms.

In the framework of Hegel's dialectics, Sartre saw the negritude movement as the moment of separation, of negativity, that is like the "antithesis" following the "thesis" of the colonial situation and preceding the "synthesis" in which not only blacks but all oppressed people would unite and triumph over their oppressors. As ultimately "the song of everyone of us and for everyone of us," negritude per se was therefore to be transcended at some point in the future when the "recognition of all by all" is achieved. Blacks would eventually have to put their blackness aside in favor of more universal ideals. "Born from evil," "pregnant with a future good," and entertaining the thought of its own mortality, the negritude ideal was itself a quasi-Dionysian passion in which dance and death were intimately mingled in the best Nietszchean fashion. It amounted to a sacrificial ritual by which the blacks took upon themselves the suffering of mankind as well as the sins of the white race. Since, unlike the white proletariat, blacks were not fully integrated into the materialistic, objective Western world, the expression of negritude should blend objective elements (the traditions of the black race) with subjective ones (the essence of the black soul). In summoning this return of the blacks to their original beings, their attempt to, at last, coincide with themselves, Sartre was describing the process of *naturation* which Césaire had equated with poetry in his previous "Poetry and Knowledge." Consequently, the black writer was confronted with the necessity to de-alienate the means of expression, that is, to systematically alter, even destroy, the language of the master race.

Sartre's definition of negritude was not the last one. It was, in fact, to become the touchstone of most subsequent definitions. Later exponents of the concept found Sartre too race conscious and not sufficiently class conscious. What they wanted was a classless society in which all races would be equal, and not a raceless society. Some (like Césaire himself more recently) felt that the concept of a black essence reeked either of determinism or of mysticism and that negritude would cease to exist in a world with more equitable economic conditions. The Marxists in particular (such as Adotevi) refused to distinguish colonialistic from capitalistic exploitation. Others thought the negative aspect of negritude encouraged the status quo: the validation of race, a useful notion at first, might become an artificial and restrictive framework in the future. Still others said that the very distinction between "black" and "white," between prelogical and logical mentality betrayed an Occidental point of view: a black should not have to wonder how to be black, just as in Wole Soyinska's famous quip, the tiger does not have to proclaim its tigritude. Others contended that negritude was but a slogan masking the reality of profound and in fact desirable differences among the black groups. At issue in this debate (a more complex one than we can possibly demonstrate here) were some fundamental questions. Should negritude be "serene" à la Senghor, or "agitated" à la Césaire? Was it a reality or a myth, a policy or a passion, past or future, black or multicolor, that is for all oppressed people?

From our perspective, there is no easy answer: negritude is a dynamic concept. How relevant it was and will remain in the future depends on the situation and history of each particular colonized group. Politically speaking, as a number of African nations acquired their autonomy in the fifties and sixties, negritude lost some of its spark. Culturally speaking the future is open. Possibly some black literature will be written in native vernaculars; or, on the contrary, it is conceivable that young nations might lose their inferiority complex to the point where using the literary tools of their former masters will no longer be an issue. It is true that negritude was at its most potent in countries colonized by the French, that is, in which there existed a rigorously structured and policed official language. Former colonies in which the official language is English seem less sensitive to the problem. Some countries, such as Cuba, have chosen to emphasize the hybrid aspect of the culture and to promote a *mestiza* literature. Finally, black literature might be lured by its own success into joining the mainstream of Western literature.

III

One may infer from recent statements[16] that, although by 1979 Césaire had given up the word "negritude" as an electrifying motto, his politics, the way he conceived the future of Martinique, were still imbued with its main principles. But even if negritude has lost its practical *raison d'être*, it has changed the contemporary world in the same way as psychoanalysis, cubism, surrealism, structuralism or, for that matter, the counterculture of the sixties and the American "Black Consciousness." Moreover, as a powerful agent of literary renewal, it will continue to affect our sensitivities long after its historical moment has passed.

Naturally, the negritude poets do not come out of one single mold. While Senghor's harmoniously flowing style and ceremonious nocturnal lyricism might remind one of Vigny, Claudel, or Saint-John Perse, Damas is concise, syncopated, ironical, and probably the most jazz-inspired of the major black poets. To the extent that he is the least European, he is sometimes considered as the "purest" in their ranks. In fact, some critics (Tougas and Jahn, for instance) deny that Césaire really breaks away from the French tradition since he remains conceptual, that is, Western. Yet it is in his poetry that the components of negritude found their most complex formal equivalents. For Césaire's avowed goal is to "marronner," that is, to run away from accepted French poetry, as the maroons ran away from their masters.[17] Thus the question of the puzzling coexistence in Césaire of a militant emancipator of his race and a thorny, erudite, often obscure poet becomes a moot point. The renewal of poetic techniques that result in his esoteric style are an integral part of the negritude strategy. Moreover, since both negritude and modernism share some of the same concerns, it is no surprise that Césaire ends with what seems a revised ("cannibalized," as Arnold says) version of modernism. The reader of modern poetry who might perceive the forthcoming remarks on Césaire's poetics as *déjà vu* should keep in mind that even when his goals coincided with those of his European antecedents, his *motivations* were different.

He voiced his own *art poétique* in "To Uphold Poetry" ("Maintenir la poésie"), in various other *Tropiques* pieces on poets (Lautréamont, Mallarmé, Valéry), and especially in "Poetry and Knowledge."[18] While scientific knowledge "numbers, measures, classifies, and kills," poetry provides the way to a "replenishing knowledge," Césaire wrote. In the same way Descartes used algebra to make the physical structure of the universe intelligible, the poet will use the word to summon up "everything that ever was, that is ever possible . . . all pasts, all futures in all fluxes, all radiations," in brief, "the cosmic totality" (p. 162). Such an all-encompassing concept of poetry was not new, but negritude gave it a new look: in the hands of black poets, antirationalism became a political value. Césaire meditates at length on this sentence in Breton's manifesto: "No fear of madness will ever force us to put at half-mast the flag of imagination." Moreover, for the "Wretched of the Earth" (to use Fanon's phrase) whom the modern world had bypassed, the image could be a "miraculous weapon." Through it, the world could be returned to its original simplicity and unity for the image had the power to resolve contradictions.

The image exposes the conflicts, obsessions, phobias, fixations of the self—and then goes farther. It descends in time: "I whistle yes I whistle very ancient things / as serpents do as do cavernous things" ("Lost Body"). It taps not only the ancestral vein but a universal one in which African, Greek, and Asian myths have their common source: "As for me I have nothing to fear I am from before Adam I do not come under the same lion / nor under the same tree I am from a different hot and a different cold" ("Visitation"). In the end it bypasses the "secondary scattering of life" to reach "the gnarled primitive unity of the world" where the antinomy between man and nature no longer exists. The absence of Christianity in this perspective is conspicuous. Whenever Césaire alludes to Christian myths, he handles them ironically, as, for instance, in "The Virgin Forest," or substitutes a pagan content for the Christian one as in "Visitation." Evidently, in Césaire's eyes, Christian myths were not as old, not as universal as others and, moreover, inseparable from the culture of the Western colonial powers. In retrospect, one can say (as Arnold does) that this was a mythic view of the past and that the collective soul of the black race, even more so of mankind, has a questionable psychological reality. Nevertheless, the fact that Césaire's works belong to the era of Jung and Freud as well as of modern cultural anthropology helps place this eccentric poet in the mainstream of modernism.

For him, poetry was nothing less than "insurrectional": "The truth is," he wrote, "that, for almost a century, poetry has been hell-bound . . . that our heritage is one of fevers, of seisms, and that poetry . . . must never cease to lay claim to it: with its raven-like voice, its voice of Cassandra, of Orpheus, of violent death."[19] It was urgent to return the world to its primordial chaos and order to disorder so that a truer, more just order might be born. In this respect Césaire was indeed a disciple of Sade and Laclos, the contemporary of Bataille, and of the same spiritual family as those writers whom Malraux, giving a different meaning to the color, gathered under the banner of "the black triangle."

Césaire praised Lautréamont as the inventor of a modern mythology. He himself had been much influenced by Greek tragedy as the most basic embodiment of the tragic principle, as well as by Nietzsche's *Birth of Tragedy*. His first African drama, *And the Dogs Were Silent*, took its form from Sophocles and Aeschylus. He meant his poetry to be a mythopoeia. Myth was to serve as "a dynamic plan, a catalyst for the aspiration of a people, and a prefiguration of the future, precisely because it is capable of mobilizing the emotional energy of the collectivity."[20] And his own poetry came to be the locus of many myths. The Earth-Mother is venerated in the form of Omphalus, the earth's navel ("Lost Body"), and as providing the phallus with an access to cosmic unity. The sun's horses stampede in the opening lines of "The Thoroughbreds." The phoenix appears often enough as a symbol of the rebirth of the Self and of the black race for critics (Kesteloot, Songolo) to refer to Césaire's "phoenicism." The poet labors as Hercules in "Lost Body," challenges the eagle devouring his liver like Prometheus ("Ferment"), sustains the Gorgon's assault in "Perseus Centuplicating Myself." But, as in the case of Christian myths, Césaire adapts the classical ones to the context of black history and culture. His Prometheus and his Perseus dwell less on their triumphs or their inventions than on their agony— perhaps even with the shrewdness of the weak, aware of the extent to which the torturers depend on their victims for their own ontological fulfillment.

Most myths imply transformation, especially the cosmogonic ones. Césaire's poetry conveys not only the substance of this cosmogony but its dynamics. For the images often ignite one another, set off a chain reaction, and climax in moments of total incandescence, silence or void especially in *The Miraculous Weapons* and *Solar Throat Slashed*: "Behold— / nameless wanderings / the suns the rains the galaxies, / fused in fraternal magma / pass by toward the safe necropolises of the sunset / and the earth . . . blew out / . . . the earth makes a bulge of silence for the sea / in the silence / behold the earth alone . . . / empty" ("The Thoroughbreds"). The latter poem is a particularly rich example of Césaire's personal mythology. A cosmic death and rebirth parallels that of the hero-narrator who accepts the dissolution of his self to be reborn as a plant-man totally connected with the cosmos. "The Thoroughbreds" offers a, so to speak, "passive" version of the hero's quest and sacrifice, an Orphic version since the poem ends with a recreation of the world by the word ("And I speak and my word is earth / and I speak / and / Joy / bursts in the new sun"). Critics have indeed pointed out several Christlike figures in Césaire's works, such as Toussaint Louverture awaiting a white death amidst the snows of the Jura Mountains (*Notebook*), the Rebel in *And the Dogs Were Silent*, or Patrice Lumumba in *A Season in the Congo*. But to find models for this structure he did not have to depend on either Greek or Judeo-Christian mythology. The mysteries of Ogun of the Yoruba culture or the dead-alive Zombi of Haitian voodoo stood for similar concepts. Likewise the Africans had their own version of Orpheus or of the biblical Word in the form of the *Nommo*, the magician's word empowered to create.

Passivity and resignation are not the only aspect of the hero. Many pieces demonstrate a truly Dionysian violence. The Bacchantes are at work in Césaire's poetry, making it a perpetual scene of dismemberment and mutilation: "Everything that was ever torn / has been torn in me / everything that was ever mutilated / has been mutilated in me" ("Lay of Errantry"). There are no fewer than nineteen poems in this volume of which the first line or the title conveys a violent and bloody assault. There is some disagreement in the critical response to these structures. For instance, while Kesteloot and Kotchy felt urged to make a graphic representation of the development of the poems showing that they oscillate between depression and elation, always ending on the upbeat, Arnold emphasizes the tragic consummation of the hero in a true Nietzschean tradition. He prefers to think of the rebirth as spiritual, the self having renounced itself and therefore any temporal presence in order to play the game of the cosmos. This latter reading is, no doubt, more to the taste of a period obsessed with entropy. It is also confirmed by Césaire's recent interview (*Le Monde*, December 6, 1981), in which he states that the will to power has never been a motivation for him. [21] Nevertheless, the poems frequently end on an opening—if not on a lifting, such as: "My ear against the ground, I heard Tomorrow / pass" ("The Thoroughbreds"), or "a melody nevertheless to be saved from Disaster" ("To Know Ourselves"), or "a child will half-open the door" ("In Truth"). A child of course, but also a child only; for it seems that following the violent convulsions of *Miraculous Weapons*, and intermingled with the exultant African celebrations in *Ferraments*, *Lost Body*, and *Solar Throat Slashed*, an elegiac voice makes itself heard, reflecting perhaps the gap between idealistic hopes and political realities and, like Orpheus, resigned to triumph by the word, not by the sword.

It must be pointed out here that Césaire's revolutionary position remains rhetorical. It is never clear, in fact, in his poetry at least, whether he expects the neocolonial situation of Martinique to change. As Arnold remarks, "the violence that frequently precedes the renewal of the self should not be confused with a socially revolutionary activity. It is the violence of repressive desublimation, to use Marcuse's felicitous term. The goal of this project is not social in the usual sense; it is meant to sustain the wounded self, which an unjust oppressive, social and racial system has alienated from itself."[22] The validity of a common African ethos rested on oppression. Césaire's Prometheus had to remain bound and be daily devoured as well as to wrest his survival by his wits. It is not therefore surprising that, other than for a handful of topical pieces, Césaire's poetic production decreased at the end of the fifties when numerous African states became independent new republics, and that he turned to a different media, the theater, through which the dialectics of emergent power and its consequences could better be explored.

Mythology also entails metamorphosis. Césaire's poetry exemplifies and expands Rimbaud's famous pronouncement in the *Lettre du voyant*: "I is someone else." Here again, Césaire had behind him an African folklore and culture that gave to this abstract philosophical Western concept a curiously vivid concreteness. For examples of metamorphoses, he could draw from a rich tradition of African and Caribbean folktales such as those collected by Lafcadio Hearn (to which he gives credit in a poem in *Ferraments*), or those one finds nowadays in the works of Birago Diop and Bernard Dadié. Moreover, the structure itself of some African languages encouraged him in this direction. His friend Senghor had pointed out that in some of these, comparisons could be made without using a comparative device; that words could change grammatical categories and were, in a way, relieved from any rigid function. For instance, in Wolof, there is no basic difference between a verb and a noun. "Thus," B. Cailler points out, "the deletion of the verb . . . goes truly in the direction of a return to an original unity,"[23] since the chasm between action and acting subject, that is between the I and the world, is bridged. Césaire conveys a state of complete participation in nature with startling lines such as these in "Lost Body": "I who Krakatoa / . . . who Zambezi or frantic or rhombos or cannibal . . . "

The type of metamorphosis most frequently suggested by Césaire's poetry is that of human into vegetal objects. It is once more in Frobenius that Césaire found—or at least understood—that the vital force of the black races (what Frobenius called *paideuma*) was biologically founded on a polarized perception of nature: Hamitic culture identified itself with animal symbolism, Ethiopian with vegetal forms of life. The special place Ethiopia will continue to occupy in the personal mythology of negritude writers is clear enough from poems like "Ethiopia" in *Noria* and from the title of Senghor's collection, *Ethiopiques* (1956). As an ancient kingdom, Ethiopia embodied the dignity lost to other African people. But, more important, the founders of negritude had recognized themselves in Frobenius' plant man. In *Tropiques* (no. 5, April 1942), Suzanne Césaire described the Martinican as without any desire of harnessing nature, lazy, docile, but also "trampled alive, dead, but growing back," and "free, silent and proud" like a plant.

A mere leafing through Césaire's poems shows the pervasiveness of plant imagery: "I grow like a plant / remorseless and unwarped . . . / pure and confident as a plant" ("The Thoroughbreds"). In "I Perseus," the metaphor is continuous and provides the backbone of the poem: in spite of the attacks of the beak on the bark, and of the slow destruction of termites, the poet finds nourishment and growth in the invulnerable sap. To a dispersed race the tree offered the advantage of being rooted in telluric solidity and security while reaching for the sky. It had both the openness to the cosmos that constituted the special gift of the blacks and the strength necessary for survival and regeneration. It partook of the Orphic quest and of the Apollonian triumph, or death and joyful life. Finally, in its horizontal dimension, the tree could also allude to the fraternity of the black world, of mankind for that matter. Perhaps its fusion of opposite but complementary principles solved man's existential dilemma. Césaire had written once (in "Poetry and Knowledge") that the weakness of many men was that they did not know how to become a tree, how to say "yes" like a tree. And that is why man did not flower. One can see that in contrast with the Western need of control and assertion (think of the pitiful role played by the vegetal objects in Sartre's imagery), Césaire's position was tinted with African wisdom; and the passive principle was as much a part of his ideal as the active one.

However, the leader in him continued undoubtedly to be spurred by the necessity for action. Such a tension may explain the recurrence of oxymoronic images which Sartre (in "Black Orpheus") traces back to André Breton's "exploding-fixed" metaphor. Breton saw in it the fusion of contradictory principles, a type of transcendence only poetry could offer. In Césaire they are often conspicuously placed at the close of stanzas or poems, as, for instance, the "firm conflagration" and the "immobile veerition" (see below pp. 77 and 85) of the *Notebook*, or the "bloody eagle disentangled jolt of dawn" of "Ferment." They also create in the reader a state of indecision and suspense symbolic of the period of transition in which black history finds itself.

The identification with plants is the most important but not the only metamorphic process. Animal dynamism (as in Lautréamont) counterbalances vegetal life. To give just one example, a poem like "The Thoroughbreds" runs the complete gamut of animal orders. On his way to the cosmic fusion and obliteration of the ego achieved in becoming a plant, the hero-narrator descends the echelons of animal species (from ancestral primates, to fish, to primitive sea creatures) in the same way Roquentin, the narrator of Sartre's *Nausea*, descends into the hell of pure existence, but without Roquentin's Western resistance to the relinquishing of his individuality. All in all, what we have here is a sort of generalized metamorphosis of universal scope. Rocks can turn into plants, then into flesh: "And roots of the mountain / raising the royal descent of the almond trees of hope / will blossom through the paths of flesh" ("Survival"), or coal mines revert to forests in lines from "New Year" (eliminated by Césaire from the version printed here). At the end of the quest, the poet leads us to "the sacred / whirling primordial streaming / at the second beginning of everything" ("The Thoroughbreds"). At his side, we watch "the shivering spawn of forms liberating themselves from facile bondages / and escaping from too premature combinings" ("Wifredo Lam").

As often with Césaire, what might have remained intellectual games for other writers rests on a concrete background. Next to "Remarks on Lautréamont" in *Tropiques* (no. 6−7) we find an article on mimesis, that is, the biological ability of some organisms—many of which were common in the Caribbean—to take the appearance of other animal or vegetal forms. In another domain, obvious rapprochements are to be made with totemism, of which Frobenius again had given an anthropological view, and with a number of religious rituals: the Eshu and Legba cults in Haitian voodoo and the African Yoruba beliefs which Wole Soyinka's *Myth and Literature and the African World* later made known in the Western world. But equally true, the motive of metamorphosis can be put in the more general framework of the quest for an identity or the desire to dissolve an unwanted one. Césaire shares this motive with contemporary writers other than ethnic ones. Did not Artaud leave us the famous "Here Lies": "I, Antonin Artaud, am my son, my father, my mother and myself."?[24] Does not Genet's insistence on his characters (in *The Blacks*) wearing masks and buskins and exaggerating their gestures partake of the same desire?

Pushed to its extreme, metamorphosis could take the form of cannibalism. In response to the facile exoticism of previous Caribbean poets, Suzanne Césaire's splendid manifesto in *Tropiques* 4, January 1942, had ended with the lapidary sentence, "Martinican poetry shall be cannibalistic or shall not be." When a recent critic (Arnold) shows Césaire as "cannibalizing" Western myths—that is giving them a countercultural twist—should we read this as a pun? Perhaps so, since Césaire himself claimed cannibalism as part of his de facto African heritage ("We claim kinship / with dementia praecox with the flaming madness / of persistent cannibalism," he wrote in the *Notebook*). It was a matter of pride instilled with the ontological necessity to assert oneself. Genet describes the same motivation in *The Blacks*: "Let Negroes negrify themselves. Let them persist to the point of madness in what they're condemned to be, in their ebony, in their odor . . . in their cannibal tastes."[25] Césaire is prompt to point out that the white man can be just as cannibalistic and with much worse reasons. The narrator of the *Notebook* fantasizes that an English lady is being served a Hottentot skull in a soup tureen. In the midst of bloody political repression in Madagascar, the Ivory Coast, Indochina, and the French West Indies, Césaire castigated in *Discourse on Colonialism* (1967) "the scenes of anthropophagic hysteria" he had witnessed in the French Assembly, concluding with this apostrophe: "Shucks, my dear colleagues, I take my hat off to you (my cannibal's hat, it goes without saying)."[26]

It would be of course grotesque to say that in Césaire's mind the word is used concretely; but to relegate it to a mere rhetorical use also falls short of the truth. It may be the most comprehensive label for the obsession of this otherwise most dignified poet with the inside of the body, with devouring, swallowing, licking, spitting, viscera, and (occasionally) excrement. See, for instance, "The Virgin

Forest," or the opening of "Magic," of "Debris," the title "Viscera of the Poem," the last few lines of "The Tornado." It is certainly part of the mythology of blood, of fertility, menses, painful birth, violent death, and sacrifice. In this regard, it may be that, as in the case of Rabelais, the genital belly associated with cosmogonic myths is not always easy to distinguish from the digestive one. Going one step farther, cannibalism carries to its fullest degree the idea of participation; it symbolically eradicates the distinction between the I and the Other, between human and nonhuman, between what is (anthropologically) edible and what is not and, finally, between the subject and the object. It goes insolently against the grain of Western insistence on discrete entities and categories. An economic interpretation has even been suggested, at least for similar patterns in Haitian poetry, that in underdeveloped countries everything is validated by becoming food. Ultimately, in a political frame of reference, cannibalism may summarize the devouring of the colonized country by the colonizing power—or, vice versa, the latent desire of the oppressed to do away with the oppressor, the wishful dreaming of the weak (the scolopendras of "The Miraculous Weapons") projecting themselves as warriors and predators.

All this does not make for an easy poetry. Negritude writers are aware of their dilemma: as spokesmen and educators of their people and committed to bettering their lot, should they not be intelligible to everyone? Some think so. Others consider that finding their inspiration in the people and being called to express their destiny are not synonymous with lowering their aesthetic standards. Their duty as black intellectuals is to reach the outside world by the most effective means. Césaire is among those. Moreover, he claims (in the Leiner interview) that simple people understand his poetry as well or better than intellectuals. By this he means that there is another way to perceive it than conceptually, such as through its rhythm. So here again, the commitment to the black world results in formal characteristics.

One of Césaire's seven *Propositions poétiques* (in "Poetry and Knowledge") states that "the music of poetry . . . comes from a greater distance than sound. To seek to musicalize poetry is the crime against poetic music, which can only be the striking of the mental wave against the rock of the world" (p. 170). Indeed, to the fluidity of traditional poetry Césaire opposes the exotic rhythms of African tom-toms, a word he uses in the title of three poems. His percussive effects are definitely influenced by African dances and voodoo rituals. But they also affect us somewhat like a *mantra* technique designed to weaken the resistance of the intellect. The accelerated repetition of some words or phrases often permit an entry into the poem other than the rational one.

Yet, although most of his critics touch on the subject, they tend to become evasive when enjoined to analyze the rhythm. Even Arnold's excellent phonemic analysis of "Lost Body" in terms of immediate physical effects of this poem is less successful when it comes up to rhythm per se.[27] The fact is that, no matter how much Césaire meant to rape the French language, it was not in his power to give it a tonic stress or vowel lengths that would accurately imitate a tom-tom. If the much glossed over seven lines of "Lost Body" give a simulacrum of explosive and barbaric violence, it is not so much by their rhythm itself as by a succession of syntactic ruptures and incongruities. But it would be equally wrong not to recognize the impact of this poem and of many others as immediate and physical. Césaire's skill in manipulating the physical elements of language results in what Arnold calls "a hybrid prosody," that is, one stretching the limits traditionally considered as those of French prosody. This is what Césaire meant by his early promise of creating a "rupestral design in the stuff of sounds." Thus the language that has become his trademark displays the same recombination of elements characteristic of his cosmic vision.

For instance, in "Batouque," the repetition of the title word reproduces the brief punctuation of hands clapping and draws attention to the next musical phrase or dance figure. The acceleration of the repetition parallels that of the dance. Elsewhere, the repetitive structure of short lines as "standing in the rigging / standing at the tiller," building up to "standing / and / free," or the "Dove / rise / rise / rise /" (*Notebook*) creates climactic effects. In "Miraculous Weapons" the recurrent three syllables of "scolopendre" with its initial consonantal stress seem to crush the black race flat against the ground, deriding it for its lack of dignity. The thrice-repeated "we will strike" at the opening of "Perdition" sounds like the stamping in a warriors' dance. The alternating of hard and soft explosive consonants in the French of "Tom-tom II" ("à petits pas de . . . ") conveys cautious progress; the accumulation of sibilants in the opening lines of "The Thoroughbreds" evokes a pressure system about to explode. Often, Césaire establishes a strong beat with the mere repetition of a single word ("Kolikombo" in "High Noon"), or with onomatopoeia ("voum rooh oh!" in the *Notebook*, "bombaïa" in "The Verb 'Marronner' "). Nevertheless, some of his most powerful effects are also the most subtle and depend on syntax rather than sounds. What he does amounts to returning the syntax to what should be its privileged function, that of espousing human breathing and, in the long run, human feelings. The strategic disposition of "nous savoir" ("To know ourselves") creates an introspective mood as well as suspense on the threshold of some astonished reckoning; that of "who then" ("Who then") gives urgency to the question. To turn a complicated and heavily latinized French syntax into the vehicle of powerful emotions, that is true hybridization, that *is* true *savoir faire*!

IV

No wonder, then, that some scholars (Tougas, for one) deny Césaire's Africanism and insist he is not different in his inventiveness from other poets of the French tradition. Certainly, negritude does not tell the whole story. Who would contend that this alumnus of the prestigious Ecole Normale Supérieure, whose father read Hugo aloud in the evenings, had not totally assimilated this tradition? In the Leiner interview, Césaire recognized that he had the same ancestors as the surrealists: Rimbaud and Mallarmé, the Symbolists, Claudel and Lautréamont. Elsewhere he claimed Leconte de Lisle and Verhaeren as predecessors. For that matter, he is also indebted (as we have suggested above) to some of the components of the great intellectual vortex one calls modernism, such as Marxism, psychoanalysis, and existentialism. Consequently, for a complete study of Césaire's sources, we have to refer the reader to the comprehensive works acknowledged at the beginning of this essay. All we hope to do here is suggest with a few examples how Césaire connects with the mainstream of French poetry.

To all of it, starting with no less than Hugo, Césaire owes his concept of the poet as Seer and Spokesman. With many of the masters of modernism, he has transcended a painful personal situation through the dignity of the written word. And the commitment against logic also goes back a long way. The praise of folly is an ancient theme that has coexisted with rationalism during the centuries of Western humanism, from Horace to Erasmus, Rabelais to Romanticism, and from Shakespeare to M. Foucault. All the same, in "Poetry and Knowledge" (p. 159), Césaire takes the year 1850 as the cornerstone of modernism: "France was dying of prose" when all of a sudden, "with all weapons and equipment [it] went over to the enemy" (that is, the forces of a beneficial madness). Which ones of these "miraculous weapons" and what articles of the baggage found their way into Césaire's poetry?

Any answer to the question should start with the founding father of modern poetry, Baudelaire. Césaire shares with him a vision of the universe as a network of interlocking signs, except that (as Arnold points out), Césaire's *correspondances* do not allude to some vertical Platonistic hierarchy. On the contrary, their profusion implies an anarchistic equivalent in which black countervalues keep in check the traditional Western ones. Both Césaire and Baudelaire are concerned with social and economic outcasts (Césaire quoted Baudelaire's "The Ragmen's Wine" in his *Discourse on Colonialism*). And both have a special talent: that of extracting from the most ordinary language its maximum poetic charge by creating around the words a zone of silence in which they seem to take on a renewed and startling value. The first stanza of "The Griffin" unfolds with the same ceremonial simplicity as some of Baudelaire's famous sonnets, for instance "Spleen" ("J' ai plus de souvenirs que si j'avais mille ans . . . "): "Je suis un souvenir qui n'atteint pas le seuil / et erre dans les limbes où le reflet d'absinthe / quand le coeur de la nuit souffle par ses évents / bouge l'étoile tombée où nous nous contemplons" ("I am a memory that does not reach the threshold / and wanders in the limbo where the glint of absinthe / when the heart of night breathes through its blowholes / moves the fallen star in which we contemplate ourselves"). If this stanza is also reminiscent of Nerval (the first line of "El Desdichado"), the last line of the first stanza of "Redemption" which echoes (parodies, perhaps) the famous last line of "Harmonie du Soir" could (*mutatis mutandis*) pass as Baudelaire's: "Le bruit fort gravite pourri d'une cargaison / désastre véreux et clair de soldanelle / le bruit fort gravite méninge de diamants / ton visage glisse nu en ma fureur laiteuse" ("The loud noise gravitates rotten with cargo / wormy and bright wreckage of a soldanel / the loud noise gravitates a meninx of diamonds / your face glides naked into my milky frenzy"). Since Césaire's "Baudelairianism" seems to occur when he uses Alexandrine (or other regular) meters, it is of course difficult to preserve its flavor in translation.

The influence of Lautréamont is more obvious and more prevalent. In *Tropiques* (no. 6–7, February 1943, pp. 10–15), Césaire, punning perhaps, referred to Lautréamont as the "fulgurating Prince of Caesarian sections" and celebrated him as the first to have understood that poetry begins with excess, with a lack of measure, "with forbidden quests, amidst the great blind tom-tom, in the unbreathable absolute void, [and goes] as far as the incomprehensible rain of stars." Later, in the *Discourse on colonialism*, Césaire will praise Lautréamont's boldness in denouncing capitalism, this "anthropophagic brain-snatching 'creator' . . . perched on a throne made of human excrement and gold!" It is, indeed, in the text of Isidore Ducasse that he found his first model of an organic and cosmic violence, of vehemently repetitive structures ("Vieil Océan" in the first Canto of *Maldoror*). But Lautréamont's marine imagery finds a more realistic arena in Césaire's Caribbean landscape. The motive of the whirlwind which is symbolically descriptive in Lautréamont corresponds to Césaire's real Caribbean "strom." The explosive force in *Miraculous Weapons* is that of volcanos—not merely of adolescent rebellion.

More important, it is to Lautréamont (as well as to the surrealists and, according to Arnold, Freud) that Césaire owes his concept of "humour noir," or black humor. Humor could be a strategy denying, on one hand, the unacceptable reality that was the lot of the blacks, and on the other hand, the patriarchal values of seriousness, purpose, and reverence. "He was the first," Césaire wrote of Isidore Ducasse, "to have understood the shattering demiurgic value of humor" (*Tropiques* no. 6–7, p. 15). And elsewhere, "It is humor, first and foremost, that assures Lautréamont—in opposition to Pascal, La Rochefoucauld, and so many other moralists—that had Cleopatra's nose been shorter the face of the world would not have been changed" ("Poetry and Knowledge," p. 165). Humor made it possible to say that "2 and 2 are 5" (*Notebook*) right under the doctors' noses and without penalty—but then, one had paid the penalty for centuries! A reading that does not take this dimension in account would betray Césaire's intentions.

His irony lashes everyone: the colonizers for their pompous monument to Joséphine de Beauharnais (*Notebook*); the blacks for their servility ("pay no attention to my black skin: the sun did it," again in the *Notebook*); himself in "NonVicious Circle" and in "Trite." Sometimes, his irreverence amounts to a thumb-to-the-nose gesture: in an anticlimactic moment of "Batouque," a ship lets fly "a volley of mice / of telegrams of cowries of houris," while a Wolof dances on points at the top of its mast. Quite often the translator encounters devilish and usually untranslatable puns: "tirer à blanc" (in "Noon Knives") puns on blank (bullets) and white (people); "soleil, aux gorges" (in "Batouque") enjoins the sun to go for the jugular . . . or into the canyons; "nos gueules claquantes" (in "The

Scapegoat") combines "têtes à claques" (slappable, that is exasperating, mugs), croaking mugs (the French "claquer" being slang for "to die"), and probably chattering teeth (because the French "il claque des dents" means "his teeth are chattering"). But most of the time, humor is simply part of a deliberate exaggeration and of an unrestrained imagination. The poem "Demons" describes minutely some infernal, absurd, and purposeless machine-monster. Not only does it resemble Lautréamont's monsters but its gigantic laughter, meant to frighten the children as well as the bourgeois, is right out of Rabelais.

When Césaire was asked to name his most important initiator, he settled on Rimbaud, whom he read during his youth in Fort-de-France. Both poets follow a spiritual path that includes a descent into hell, an epiphany, and a journey to Africa. Only here, as in the case of Lautréamont, everything that was symbolic for the European poet becomes concrete in Césaire's world. Thus in A *Season in Hell*, Rimbaud views himself as an outcast ("I am a beast, a nigger").[28] No wonder Césaire identified particularly with the Prodigy and Prodigal Son of nineteenth-century French letters. While the word "nigger" had a different meaning for each of them, it connoted for both a rejection of self-satisfied Western culture, particularly in its Christian aspects. Both entitled a poem "Barbare." Both undertook a quest, Césaire's season in hell teeming with tropical and nautical metaphors reminiscent of "Le Bateau ivre": "Je bourlingue" (a Rimbaldian verb if there ever was one) "gorge tendue à travers les mystérieux rouissements les atolls enroulés" ("I toss about / throat stretched amidst the mysterious rettings the coiled atolls") in "High Noon"; or "Mais déjà la veille s'impatientait vers l'astre et la poterne et nous fuyions / sur une mer cambrée incroyablement plantée de poupes de naufrages" ("but already the vigil was straining toward the star and the postern and we were racing / across an arched sea incredibly planted with shipwrecked sterns") in "Visitation." For Césaire, Rimbaud was a test and an example of the total commitment to the "calculated disordering of all senses" and to the anarchy of the form that, for instance, the French Marxists (and Depestre in their wake) were unwilling to make. Rimbaud's *Illuminations* and Césaire's *Miraculous Weapons* convey violence by the same mixture of interjections and parataxis. In both we find the same ongoing cosmogony, and ongoing alchemy, not only of the word but of all elements, both poets having accepted their total consummation to be, like the phoenix, reborn from their ashes.

Strangely enough, Césaire also acknowledges a debt to a poet seemingly antipodal to Lautréamont and Rimbaud: Mallarmé. In *Tropiques* (no. 5), he senses the author of *Hérodiade* as a fellow traveler in a "gigantic intellectual adventure" that led away from the conventional forms of poetry. For Mallarmé, they would have implied a reality which the poet perceived as unworthy of his art. For Césaire, the problem was to escape the pallid conventionality of previous black poetry, on which Suzanne Césaire bravely declared war in a 1942 issue of *Tropiques* (no. 4): "Bamboo, we decree the death of *froufrou* literature. And to hell with hibiscus, the frangipane, and bougainvillea" (p. 50). Not only is it a fact that Césaire cultivates the *mot rare* no less than Mallarmé but a number of his stylistic devices that at first reading might be traced back to a surrealistic obscurity turn out under scrutiny to be the same learned hypallages and tight syntax characteristic of Mallarmé's sonnets. Arnold remarks that Césaire is especially Mallarmean in poems with Creole topics, as if only an extreme sophistication of form could validate the particularly native content—a somewhat paradoxical mechanism which the negritude world would hardly endorse as its own.

These are mere glimpses; there is no room here to do justice to all French poets who may have contributed to the genesis of Césaire's poetry. Without even mentioning possible and probable links with major foreign poets such as Rilke, Garcia Lorca, Neruda, and Vallejo, in France alone one would have to go back to Apollinaire (from whom Césaire borrowed some typographical experiments as well as the title of *Soleil cou coupé*), to Claudel, to St. John Perse (who inspired him with one of his most beautiful *tombeaux*). And one would have to scan the entire body of French poetry as well. Who knows if Hugo's "A Villequiers" is not in transparency behind "Crusades of Silence"? Villon's ballades faintly echo in the title and many lines of "Lay of Errantry," of which the litany-like tone is somewhat lost in translation: "Corps féminin île retournée / corps féminin bien nolisé / corps féminin écume-né / corps féminin île retrouvée" ("Woman's body island on its back / woman's body full freighted / woman's body foam-born / woman's body recovered island"). And what about these other lines that seem straight out of the inscription on the gate of Thélème: "Nous sommes âmes de bon parage / corps nocturnes vifs de lignage" ("we are souls of noble birth / nocturnal bodies lively with lineage")?

But a special place should be made for the connections of Césaire with surrealism, Breton, and Artaud.

Césaire's relationship to surrealism is complex. While the poet has identified himself as a surrealist but not as a French surrealist, his literary connection with the movement is certainly André Breton, whom Césaire first met in Fort-de-France, in 1941, during the Vichy government when Breton was in exile and on his way to America. Reflecting on the effect of this meeting, and how it related to *Tropiques*, Césaire said in 1978: "Breton brought us *boldness*; he helped us to take a straightforward position: he shortened our search and our hesitation. I became aware that most of the problems I was pondering had been resolved by Breton and surrealism. . . . I will say that the meeting with Breton confirmed the truth of what I had discovered on my own. That enabled us to make up time; to go much faster, much farther. . . . The meeting was *extraordinary*."[29]

To understand Césaire's unique allegiances and differences with the French surrealists, it is important to realize that surrealism was not merely an isolated French literary movement of the mid to late twenties whose basic premises were confined to a return to childhood, idealization of madness, Freudian free associations, anticlericalism, eroticism, and the occult. As part of a reorganization of identity in the twentieth century, surrealism extended the perimeters of consciousness in a way that not only reaches back to Romantic and Symbolist sources but dissolves the boundaries of time altogether. Meditating on this desire for wholeness in being, the American contemporary poet Robert Duncan writes: "The intense yearning, the desire for something else . . . rises . . . in our identification with the universe. To compose such a symposium of the whole, such a totality, all the old excluded order must be included. The female, the proletariat, the foreign, the animal and vegetative, the unconscious and the unknown, the criminal and failure—all that has been outcast and vagabond must return to be admitted in the creation of what we consider we are."[30]

One can see immediately from the preceding description how parallel the goals of negritude and those of surrealism were. Yet, this rapprochement needs to be qualified because the contexts to which European surrealists and Césaire were responding were very dissimilar. In the first instance, it consisted of a long entrenched bourgeoisie and a pervasive Catholicism. In that instance, culture, people, and land were part of the same entity. In Césaire's case, the culture and the religion he rejected had been imposed from the outside. Consequently, on the one hand, he never showed toward his countrymen and their land the deliberate antipatriotic desecration nor the cosmopolitism that is the trademark of the French surrealists. Césaire, therefore, remained profoundly in love with the natural world and the simple people that surrounded him. On the other hand, as Leiris pointed out, it was easier for the Martinican to depart from what Mallarmé called "the words of the tribe," that is, ordinary language. Finally, his revolt against injustice and oppression was much more concrete and specific than that of the French surrealist group, composed mostly of bourgeois intellectuals whose causes were theoretical.

An exception has to be made for Artaud whose attempts to step outside of Western civilization are clear from his poetry and his correspondence, especially from 1945 to his death in 1948.[31] Unlike Artaud, Césaire did not ride off on a burro to the land of the Tarahumara, in a state of laudanum withdrawal, to eat peyote with Northern Mexican Indians. And he never became mad. Nevertheless both poets set themselves apart from other surrealists by the awesome wholeness of their respective experiences and by their common willingness to tamper with French syntax in a way that makes Breton and Eluard sound like Mme de La Fayette.

As to the specific surrealistic technique of automatic writing, Césaire experimented with it, especially during the years when surrealism was the major influence on him (1940 to 1950). The eighth and ninth issues of *Tropiques* (1943) include two automatically written poems by Charles Duits and S. Jean-Alexis' "Notes on chance." But, on the whole, Césaire's poems remain too thematic to be labeled automatic: their associative metaphors (*métaphores filées*) usually connect with an intertext, thus corroborating M. Riffaterre's argument against the very existence of automatic writing. In revising the various editions of his works, Césaire either eliminated altogether his most "automatic" poems (such as "The Sun's Knife Stab in the Back of Surprised Cities" deleted from *Solar Throat Slashed*) or cut them into several separate poems (as in the case of "The Virgin Forest," "Another Season," and "Day And Night"), thus conferring on each one some inner consistency.[32]

V

When all is said and done, an introduction should answer the question: why read Césaire? Why read poems that require long exegeses, which stern readers have in the past deemed, at best, a brilliant intellectual game, at worst, arrogantly obscure, and riddled with typographical, grammatical, or semiotic idiosyncracies? We would like to reply that these flaws are not, in the case of Césaire, artificial and derivative tricks but simply occasional alterations inherent in sustained profundity and abundance. In the long run, only being "inside" a poem can truly expound Césaire's poetry. It is impossible, of course, to reconstitute a paradigm of what can only be an individual and multiform experience. But, were we pressed to do it, we would say that the first element characteristic of Césaire's poetic voice is its solemnity. Consider, for instance, the last lines of "Bitter Season" ("Then wind bitter and sole judge of white days / . . . you shall weigh me guardian of the word nailed by the decree") or of "But There is This Hurt" ("About this blood of mine you will say / . . . that more just before God than their correct mouths / my lie / before his distraught face soared"). The prophetic voice here commands attention with an authority unmatched by any other living French poet.

A second characteristic might be an exquisitely subtle blend of ferocity and tenderness. It is plain that Césaire is a master at turning the screw: a poem like "Fangs" depicts suffering as "map of blood map of the blood / bled raw sweated raw skinned raw / . . . blood which rises in the tree of flesh / by catches by crimes / No remittance / —straight up along the stones / straight up along the bones—for / copper weight shackle weight heart weight / venoms caravaners of the bite / at the tepid edge of fangs." Each line probes the wound further, increases the pain in short ineluctable jerks articulated by parallel constructions. But Césaire is not always so single-minded. The last section of "Elegy" (which is also a description of suffering) seems to us more typical because of the complexity of the structure: "then it is no use for me to press my heart against yours / nor to lose myself in the foliage of your arms / the herd finds it / and very solemnly / in a manner always new / licks it / amorously / until the first blood savagely appears / on the abrupt open claws of / DISASTER." The first two lines with the alliterations of *f, l, m* (which happen to be the consonants of "female") evoke the comfort of a loving embrace. The next five lines, short and of more or less equal length, recall the structure of "Fangs": the herd of old pains (previously described as a foraging animal), reaches up to the narrator's heart. It licks it *amorously*, however, thus connecting pain with the love theme at the beginning of the stanza. In the next line, cruelty prevails again with the apparition of the blood, while the last two lines suggest a surrendering— whether to love or destruction is hard to tell. One finds a similar ambiguity in the final lines addressed to "Your Hair": "mane bundle of lianas violent hope of the shipwrecked / sleep softly by the meticulous trunk of my embrace my / woman / my citadel." The effect here is that of a curiously springy texture created by the alternation of hard "male" consonants (bundle, hope, shipwreck, meticulous, trunk, citadel) and soft "female" ones (mane, lianas, sleep, softly, embrace, woman) the two consonantic chains simulating the actual braiding together of a soft and a hard body.

Finally, another characteristic is Césaire's ability to surprise. We are delighted by this "truly wild disappearance / tropical as an apparition of a nocturnal wolf at high noon" which abruptly succeeds the quasi-epic tone of "Visitation"; a "pretty nymph sheds her leaves amidst the manzanilla milk and the accolades of fraternal leeches" at the end of the otherwise grim "Day and Night"; or (in the middle of "Patience of Signs"), a worm "tolling its new flesh," beats almost proudly in the apocalyptic landscape of fire shards, bones, and dried-up fires. Césaire has the ultimate cleverness to appear surprised himself by his surprises, thus making them more credible. It is as if, in spite of him and almost behind his back, the world in its boundless luxuriance performed magical tricks for the common pleasure of writer and reader. Perhaps the poem "Son of Thunder" must be understood to mean just this: "she speaks to me a language so soft that at first I do not / understand but eventually I guess she is assuring me / that spring has come countercurrent / that all thirst is quenched that autumn is kindly disposed to us / that the stars in the street have blossomed at high noon and / dangle their fruit very low." Without this intertwining of pleasurable elements with the somber and violent themes, Césaire's poetry would perhaps in our era occupy a niche as distinguished but as eccentric as that occupied by D'Aubigné's *Les Tragiques* in the sixteenth century.

We have chosen these three characteristics because together they seem to speak to the contemporary psyche better than would a homogeneous voice: the prophetic to our need for certainty and authority; the mixture of cruelty and tenderness to our need of being alternatively object and subject; the surprise to the child in us. We prefer to think of ourselves as unresolved. We also prefer to think of ourselves as fabricators of meanings, and the "courage of the imagination"[33] Césaire requires of his readers amply fulfills the *bricoleurs* in them.

Those still unconvinced by the aesthetic case must not overlook the equally compelling historical and moral one. In the *Tragedy of King Christophe* Césaire has the main character say that one has to demand more from the blacks than from any other race: more work, more faith, more enthusiasm, more persistence. As one looks back over Césaire's amazing career, it appears that he has lived up to his hero's ideals and even added one to the list: vision. On the black child from the slums of Basse-Pointe an almost messianic role was bestowed. For he was to become a bridge between the twain that, in principle, should never meet, Europe and Africa. Thus he symbolizes and sums up what is probably the twentieth century's most important phenomenon: the powerful surge next to the old and the new world, of a third world both very new and very old. Rather than aiming at the lowest common denominator between the two cultures, Césaire sought to fulfill his Africanism with "the zeal of an apocalyptic wasp," and the adjective here conveys adequately the extreme quality of this choice. As he pointed out again in his recent interview (*Le Monde*, December, 1981), however, it was by borrowing European techniques that he succeeded in expressing his Africanism in its purest form.

Césaire seems to have been constantly driven by the vision that the end result of this Africanization would be an elemental man in whom all mankind would recognize itself. Thus he claimed to have demonstrated Hegel's idea that the universal is not the negation of the particular, that it is by going deeper into the particular that one reaches the universal. In making the universal man black (and vice versa) Césaire was paradoxically putting the finishing touch to an image of man toward which Europe itself had been groping in the wake of Rousseau, Diderot, and the Enlightenment and which continued to develop through nineteenth- and twentieth-century anthropology. In expanding Man's image, he gave the white world, which had educated him, a hundredfold more than what he had received from it. And, as a bonus, he gave a more genuine meaning to the traditional claim of the French language to be a universal one.

The transcendence of reality through the poetic word has become a cliché of the critique on modernism. In the case of Césaire the validity of this idea tends to obliterate the less intellectual but not any less admirable truth that such a transcendence implied no small amount of forgiveness. That Césaire the African, the descendant of the Cannibals, could give the Christian world a solemn lesson in one of its major articles of ethics is witnessed by his poetry. The fist which, he states (in "Memorial to Louis Delgrès"), always obsessed him, the incendiary fist from which a whole forest burns angrily in "High Noon," the poinsettia's "young green hand stiffening out of its massacre gloves" (from "Trite") surfaces in the "Salute to the Third World" as "a hand free of the cestus," bruised, wounded, yes, but open, "extended to / all hands . . . / to all the wounded hands / in the world." And the last poem of the *Complete Works* ("A Freedom in Passage") leaves to the birds the task of pollinating the future and correcting "the Erynnies' blunders and the inflexible wine of moray eels." That wine, sacrificial wine if there ever was one, is, let us not forget, the blood of slaves who were thrown (or in despair threw themselves) overboard from the slave ships. Thus Césaire's last word clearly intends to wash this blood in the ocean of fraternity.

Negritude may well be, as we suggested before, politically outdated. Césaire himself (in the haunting and hieratical "Lay of Errantry") hints that Africa's glory may be only an ancient tale in a now closed wizard's book. But perhaps it is precisely there, in its visionary status, that lies the real beginning of negritude. For the Africa of oil wells, supertankers, commodity markets, gigantic dams, and labor problems may need its guiding light even more than it needs tractors, guns, and capital, if it is not to become just another alienated industrial world. Negritude has the potential to remain, according to Camus' prophetic paradox, the end that, in turn, shall be justified only to the extent that the means are justifiable.

Césaire's career as a political figure or as a poet is far from completed. He is still at the helm of his native island and in the interview in *Le Monde* mentioned above he announces the forthcoming publication of another collection of poems, "Moi, laminaire." He might surprise us in both these domains. But we venture to say that in neither will it be by revolutionary stances. To him, revolution and violence were only a phase. The readjustment of his political goals so as to focus on the development of Martinique and on local issues and the increasingly elegiac tone of his poetry are symmetrically significant of his present position. He admits that politics are for him a necessary authentication of his ideas but that his true vocation is elsewhere than in material power. For he was all along, after a much less ephemeral kind of power, one whose weapons are miraculous. He described himself in an early intuition of his destiny: "the poet is that very ancient yet new being, at once very complex and very simple who at the limit of dream and reality, of day and night, between absence and presence, searches for and receives in the sudden triggering of inner cataclysms the password of connivance and power."[34]

VI / THE COLLECTIONS

The text on which these notes are based is Volume I of *Oeuvres Complètes* (*OC*, see the note to the Acknowledgments). In the case of several of the collections, Césaire made extensive revisions as new editions appeared (twenty-nine of the original seventy-two poems in *Soleil cou coupé* are omitted in the *OC*).

While referring the reader interested in more detail to Hale's bibliography, *Les Ecrits d'Aimé Césaire* [see n. 1], we would like to give minimal bibliographical notes and to point out the main characteristics of each of the six collections that comprise this volume.

NOTEBOOK OF A RETURN TO THE NATIVE LAND (CAHIER D'UN RETOUR AU PAYS NATAL)

First version in the Paris periodical *Volontés*, number 20, August 1939.

First publication in book form (New York: Brentano's, 1947) under the title *Cahier d'un retour au pays natal: Memorandum on my Martinique*, prefaced by A. Breton, translated by L. Abel and Y. Goll, bilingual.

First French edition in book form (Paris: Bordas, 1947, prefaced by Breton).

"Edition définitive" (Paris: Présence Africaine, 1956, 1960, 1971, this last one a bilingual edition, translated by E. Snyder).

Outside of France and the U.S. there exist editions in Great Britain (Penguin Books), Germany, Italy, Mexico, and Cuba.

OC, 1976.

With its 1055 lines the *Notebook* is more of an extended lyric poem than an epic; it opens, after the initial burst (which contains virtually all Césaire's themes), with a brooding, static overview of the psychic and geographical topology of Martinique, generally in strophes that evoke Lautréamont's *Maldoror*. A second movement begins with the speakers's urge to go away; suddenly the supine present is sucked into a whirlpool of abuses and horrors suffered by blacks throughout their colonized and present history. The nonnarrative, exploding juxtapositions in this movement immediately reveal Césaire's interest in surrealism, though as Arnold points out, thematic development is always in sight. The second movement reaches its nadir in the passage where the speaker discovers himself mocking an utterly degraded black on a streetcar. The final, rushing third movement is ignited by the line: "But what strange pride suddenly illuminates me?" In a series of dialectical plays between the emergence of a future hero giving new life to the world and images from the slaves' "middle passage" of the past, the "sprawled flat" passivity of the first movement is transformed into a standing insurrection that finally wheels up into the stars. The incredible burden of the poem is that of a parthenogenesis in which Césaire must conceive and give birth to himself while exorcising his introjected and collective white image of the black.

THE MIRACULOUS WEAPONS (LES ARMES MIRACULEUSES)

Paris: Gallimard 1946, 1961 (without modifications), and 1970 (with numerous changes).

Translated editions in Italy (1962) and Germany (1968, incomplete). *And the Dogs Were Silent (Et les chiens se taisaient)*, a "lyrical oratorio" that constitutes the last section of *Armes*, was published separately in 1956 (Paris: Présence Africaine; Emsdetten: Germany). In the *OC* it is collected with his dramatic works. Therefore we do not include it in this volume.

OC, 1976.

Although the volume represents the climax of the surrealist influence on Césaire, one finds in it possible topical allusions to the oppression of the French territories under the German occupation. For instance, at the end of the title poem, we are told of a bewildered great king and of cities deprived of water and sleep. *The Miraculous Weapons* was received by the French public with various degrees of praise (André Breton) or reservation (the Communist critic Garaudy), depending on individual commitments to politics or avant-garde literature. In this volume of (now thirty-one) poems and prose poems, the historical armature of the *Notebook* is dissolved in a swamp teeming with mythological particles. The vision of a fatigued, raped earth alternates with that of surging, primal earth; negritude and surrealism become a poetic trampoline which resists penetration at the same time it affords an exhilarating "ride." At times the writing in *The Miraculous Weapons* appears to be automatic. Actually, while the poems often proceed associatively, the range of associative possibility is restricted to some thirty or forty key words often antiphonally used (for instance night, day, dawn, evening, sun, water, volcano, swamp, blood, revolt, plundering, death, madness, logics) which, like elements in a molten substance, rise to the surface and descend. The progression of the poems adumbrates some heroic itinerary from the "gunnery warning" at the beginning to the symbolic death and renewal of "The Thoroughbreds," on to perdition, survival, the beyond, conquest, epiphanies, and prophecies—all themes that are orchestrated in a dramatic format in the coda, *And the Dogs Were Silent*. The frequent occurrence of "exploding-fixed" metaphors à la Breton suggests a non-resolved tension caused perhaps, on the topical level, by the double oppression of colonialism and of the German occupation and, at the level of discourse, by the struggle between thematic and associative techniques of writing.

SOLAR THROAT SLASHED (SOLEIL COU COUPÉ)

First edition: K. editeur, collection "Le quadrangle," 1948. Reedited under the same title, along with *Corps perdu* as part of *Cadastre* (Paris: Seuil, 1961).

Reproduced (along with *Antilles à main armée* by Charles Calixte) by Kraus reprint (Liechten-stein, 1970).

OC 1976, where, along with *Corps perdu*, it appears after the later published *Ferrements*, according to the date of the Seuil edition. Our translation reestablishes the real chronology.

Once this collection was severely edited (with many remaining poems modified and shortened), it became clear that Césaire had lessened its surrealist impact and reoriented the poems toward a more direct ideological statement. *Solar Throat Slashed* is, however, as it stands, a very diverse volume. Some of the most impressive ideological pieces, such as "Mississippi," "To Africa," and "At the Locks of the Void," combine mythological and historical materials without committing the poems to either genre. The title of the collection is taken from the last line of Apollinaire's "Zone," and, according to Gregson Davis, "when transposed from the Parisian dawn to a subtropical ambiance, functions both as sign in an intertextual code (to use Roland Barthes' term), and as a vivid symbol for the assassination of a people."[35]

The collection is dominated by the solar theme in its physical as well as mythological and metaphorical implications. Some interpreters (Hale) emphasize the cautious optimism of the poems inspired by the situation of the blacks in the world. They would reflect the years (1945–1947) during which Césaire was at his most efficient and successful as a legislator in the French Assembly. Others (Arnold) maintain that the solar principle in these poems is far removed from a macho assertion and that the tragic sacrificial theme dominates the scene. American blacks make their first appearance in Césaire's poetry here. The language is less roily than before, more contoured and staccato, and at times takes on an austerity that prefigures the elegiac tone which is occasionally found in *Lost Body* and which becomes predominant in *Ferrements*.

LOST BODY (CORPS PERDU)

First edition: Editions Fragrance, 1950 (illustrated with thirty-two engravings by Picasso).

Reedited (along with *Soleil cou coupé*) under the same title as part of *Cadastre* (Seuil, 1961).

OC, 1976.

Lost Body is the least known and the least commented upon of Césaire's major works. Yet the ten poems that constitute it seem to have been written as an ensemble and present more unity than other collections.

Critics agree that *Lost Body* reflects a transition in Césaire's career. Hale reads it as a, so to speak, second return to the native land, the poet leaving behind a Europe which has rejected him and an Africa whose relevance is momentarily being questioned. According to Arnold, the collection shows us Césaire pulled apart by the opposite demands of modernism and of negritude, the one dictating an inner discourse, the other a public, open voice. The "Lay of Errantry" with its dismemberment theme especially reveals this conflict, Arnold suggests. Other poems in the collections document this interpretation. For instance, the opening piece, "Word," contrasts the magical efficacy of the poetic word with the recalcitrance of the historical substance of the word "nigger." In the title poem, "Lost Body," the reference to Hercules serving Omphale might signify a regression into the telluric female principle preceding the phallic rebirth of the final lines ("and with the arrogant jet of my wounded and solemn bole / I shall command the islands to be"), or it might also allude to the harnessing of the poetic voice in the service of Mother Africa. This movement is somewhat confirmed by the fact that in revising the text, Césaire emphasized the African elements at the expense of purely mythological ones.

All in all, the collection conveys a crisis that accounts for the nostalgic and plaintive stanzas of the "Lay of Errantry" at times strangely reminiscent of Villon and Du Bellay.

FERRAMENTS (FERREMENTS)

First edition: (Paris: Seuil, 1960. Eight poems previously published in *Présence Africaine* between 1955 and 1959).

Prix René Laporte in 1960.

OC, in 1976 (with minor changes).

Césaire's rare and ingenious title for his last separately published collection of poems is defined in *Webster's 1950 International Dictionary* as: "A piece of ironwork; pl. shackles, irons; irons tools, fittings etc. Obs." By choosing this word, instead of the common word for shackles ("fers"), Césaire was able to build constructive connotations into the iron that in black experience has been predominantly associated with torture and bondage. Even the obsoleteness of the word serves him because, while slave ships no longer exist, blacks are still "shackled" in many parts of the world. Finally, the word puns on the idea of a "ferment" brewing a hopeful future.

Arnold has identified three intermingled voices in *Ferraments*. One is inspired by various phases of the fight for black independence whether in Africa, the Caribbean, or the United States ("In memory of a Black Union Leader"). It sings, so to speak, of unshackling. The "African" poems, in particular, celebrate decolonization in a tone that carries praise almost into political speechmaking. Among them, "The Time of Freedom" was elicited by the tragic bloodshed of the Yamoussoukro and Dembroko revolts in Ivory Coast in February 1950 and coincide with Césaire's unceasing anticolonialistic campaign in the French National Assembly. "Hail to Guinea" was conceived as an homage to the only French African country which, under the leadership of Sékou Touré, voted for total independence from France in the 1958 referendum. "A Salute to the Third World," dedicated to Léopold Sedar Senghor, and "Africa" are in a similar spirit.

Another voice represented in at least thirty of the poems, one that relates to the first and justifies the title, consists of a fantastic evocation of black bondage throughout history. It is as if each line in these poems is the "Flying Dutchman" of a slave ship, each word the ghost of branded flesh. We are told a relentless tale of abducting, sacking, dumping, of vomiting broken teeth, of ants polishing skeletons, of chunks of raw flesh, of spitting in the face, of trophy heads, of crucifixion. The accumulation suggests in itself that the torture is almost as much self- as other-induced, as if, in a quasi-Manichaean way, Césaire was attempting to drain the world of black suffering through mere exhaustiveness. Needless to say, as moving as they are, these poems hardly sustain their author's claim that their "hermetic aspect has been significantly diminished."[36] They were not particularly relevant to the situation of the black world in 1960.

It is perhaps to Césaire's intuition of this fact, as well as to the relative abortion of the Martinican liberation, that we owe the third voice of *Ferraments*, the elegiac one. It appears in "Statue of Lafcadio Hearn," "The Tomb of Paul Eluard," "Memorial for Louis Delgrès," "In Memory of a Black Union Leader," "On the State of the Union," and "In Truth." Four of these poems are, in the vein of the classical elegy, lamentations for a dead hero. "Out of Alien Days" is a melancholic interrogation of the future of the Martinican people—on their limitations perhaps. "Always speaking beautifully as we die," Césaire reflects, not without irony, on himself and his countrymen ("On the Islands of All

Compass Points"). And even love becomes but a bittersweet mirror image of that other slavery ("Ferraments"). One can see by the preceding examples that the main element in this elegiac voice is the distance from the scene it evokes.

NORIA (NORIA)

First publication in *OC*, 1976.

Some of these seventeen poems were previously published. "Letter from Bahia-of-All-Souls" was included in W. Spies's *Pour Daniel-Henry Kahnweiler* (Stuttgart, 1965), in L. Kesteloot and B. Kotchy's *Aimé Césaire, l'homme et l'oeuvre* (Paris: Présence Africaine, 1973), and in *A Tarde* (Salvador-Bahia, May 1, 1976), translated into Portuguese. "Ethiopia" appeared twice in *Présence Africaine*: in no. 47 (1963), and in a special issue (on the summit conference of independent African states which took place in Ethiopia), in 1964 under the title "Addis-Abeba 1963." Moreover, "The Verb 'Marronner' " was previously published in slightly different versions: as "Réponse à Depestre poète haïtien (Eléments d'un art poétique)" in *Présence Africaine*, no. 1−2 (1955), and as "Lettre brésilienne" in L. Kesteloot and B. Kotchy's *Aimé Césaire* (pp. 109−111).

Noria is a heterogenous collection difficult to characterize as an ensemble. A few poems such as "Wifredo Lam," "In Order to Speak," "This Appeal Prohibited Blood," "To be Deducted," "Annonciades," and "Zaffer Sun" belong, loosely speaking, to a surrealistic vein. "Annonciades" in particular is a fairly typical example of surrealistic humor.

Some other poems are occasional. The "Letter from Bahia" is a record of Césaire's impressions of a voyage he made in Brazil in 1963 and celebrates exuberantly the fraternal Brazilian culture. "The Verb 'Marronner' " reflects the polemics that took place between Césaire and the Haïtian poet Depestre. Beyond Depestre, Césaire was aiming at Aragon, leader and spokesman of the orthodox communist writers in the mid-fifties. Against the Marxist *art poétique* which required clarity, nonindividualism, and ideology, Césaire held out for a personal and esoteric style. Depestre, a Haitian poet to whom the poem is addressed, was a friend; therefore the somewhat gentle—albeit ironical—tone of the scolding. Aragon's name which appeared (in a derogatory context) in the previous version was deleted from the *OC*.

The "Voodoo Ceremonial for St.-John Perse" is rather ambiguous. Césaire seems to be irritated by Perse's "otherness" (he calls him "the Stranger") and preciosity, but to admire the lofty and profound quality of his poetry.

Finally some of the poems could be considered as lyrical and elegiac. For instance, in the poem "Ethiopia," Césaire indulges in the evocation of Ethiopia's ancient and mythical past as well as in a discreet self-apology (fourth and fifth stanzas). This suggests that he was still affected at that time by the awareness of an increasing chasm between his poetics and his ideals, and the goals and means of fast (and at times ruthlessly) growing young African states. Ethiopia appears to play the role of an anchor in the overwhelming storm of contemporary history. The note of self-apology continues to sound in "I Guided the Long Transhumance of the Herd," "Lagoonal Calendar," "Banal," and "Ibis-Anubis." The "I" in these poems no longer is a stylized one, part of the mythopoesis as in previous collections, but a more concrete, human, and real one, reflecting on a full and difficult career.

VII / TRANSLATORS' NOTES

It is not our intention here to be theoretical. Anyone interested in the general linguistic implications of translating should refer to the many excellent books on the subject, such as W. Arrow-smith and R. Shattuck, eds., *The Craft and Context of Translation* (New York: Doubleday Anchor Books, 1964) or W. Benjamin's "The Task of the Translator," in *Illuminations* (New York: Harcourt Brace, 1968). But a few words are in order on the specific problems encountered in translating Césaire. Some are inherent to his syntax and word order; others to his vocabulary and images.

As we mentioned earlier, Césaire's syntax is disjointed partly in an erudite Mallarmean way, partly as the result of his often unbound lyricism. A typical stanza duplicates the structure of fireworks, each clause introducing a dependent clause, the sequence building up to the last clause which usually brings a climactic opening or an ironical juxtaposition. It is therefore extremely important not to be misled by the apparent digressions, to keep track of parallel subordinating or coordinating devices, and to make use of the very few cola provided by the author. Let us take the last ten lines of "The Wheel" as an example: "but you minutes won't you wind on your spindle for living / the lapped up blood / the art of suffering sharpened to tree stumps by the knives of winter / the doe drunk from not drinking / which on the unexpected well rim presents me with your / face of a dismasted schooner / your face / like a village asleep at the bottom of a lake / which is reborn to daylight from the grass and the year / germinates." In reading this passage, one must register several things to be wound on the spindle, of which the last one (the doe) presents the poet with his lover's face, which is compared with two things (the schooner and the village), the second of which is in turn depicted as first asleep, then awake; one must also not let the intervening clauses distract from connecting the subject "your face" to the verb "germinates." Another example of exasperating Césairean syntax is the final stanza of "My Profound Day's Clear Passage": "Surely there is me as a great serpent of the bogs which / the sun's trident aping itself nails and which nameless / frightened bifid at the very edge of a ruptured night crawls / fragilely avid avid for a tenuous milk." Leaving aside the oddity of this image, the startling fact here is the sequence formed by the main French verb "se singe" and its dependent infinitive "clouer," given that a reflexive verb does not take a direct object other than its reflexive pronoun. In the attempt to make sense out of the text, the translator is forced to stretch the normal syntax beyond any standard of acceptability. But he seems to have no choice in the matter. A close scrutiny of genders and numbers is usually profitable. For instance, in the last two lines of "Who Then, Who Then," the masculine gender of "attentif" (intent) is a clue to the identity of the subject in the preceding line ("qui") and bars the possibility of this subject being a relative pronoun representing the "full grown girl" ("grande fille"). Thus, one is led to read "qui" as an interrogative—but not without toil.

It is clear by the above examples that Césaire's syntax is often patterned after the Latin but without offering Latin's convenience of word endings. With their help the modern Theseus, which the translator becomes, would have less trouble finding his way out of such a syntactical labyrinth as, for instance, the opening lines of "Your Hair." In this poem, the mistress' hair is compared by means of the slightly archaic "dirait-on pas" ("wouldn't you have taken it for") to a beautiful tree, then to "the invincible and spacious cockcrowing," itself ready to depart for some witch's sabbath. The modifier of the tree ("Bombarded by lateritic blood") and that of the cockcrowing ("already in invincible departure") precede the things they respectively modify, each time suspending the meaning to the next line. Not only are the images strange enough in themselves (a mistress' hair *might* be comparable to a tree, but hardly to a bird's cry) but deciphering the French poem becomes a perilous obstacle course: the translator must simultaneously be aware of the inversions already mentioned, take the repetition of "invincible" as an invitation to link the third and fourth lines, make note of the strong verbal value of the noun "départ," and move the adverb "déjà" where it should be, that is before the preposition "en."

This example, by no means chosen among the most difficult, illustrates the schizophrenic exercise one goes through when translating Césaire. It requires a combination of yielding to the movement of the text and keeping a strict watch over its structure—a process approximating a *coitus interruptus*. Moreover, one is not always able to decide when the hyperbaton (reversal of normal word order) is meaningful and when it is not. When Césaire writes (in *Notebook*) that he summons "this egotism beautiful and bold" (cet égoisme beau et qui s'aventure"), the odd placing of "beau" and the fact it is balanced with a relative clause clearly signify special emphasis. In contrast, "constant a season" (in "Africa") and "clarteux l'élan épineux des belladones" (in the French version of "Poem for the Dawn") might boil down to a slightly precious or erudite grammatical tic on the part of a high school teacher so familiar with Latin that his Fort-de-France students used to pass the awesome *bachot* with flying colors. Only a delicate assessment can tell when these anomalies are worth keeping in English. Ignoring all of them might not impoverish the text as much as it might change its tone. The frequent occurrence of ablative absolutes patterned on the Latin is another of Césaire's latinized traits. "Chair qui soi prise de soi-même vendange" (in "Présence"), or "oubliée la morgue des orages" (in "The Thoroughbreds"), or "nous contus" (in "Salut au Tiers Monde") are samples of this structure.

The problems raised by the syntax, however, are far from equaling the lexicological ones. Let's not even mention the frequent use of homophony and echo effects which one should view as an interesting challenge. Let us pass quickly over the very large number of rare and technical words (there exist quantitative and qualitative analyses of them), which keep the translator bent over various encyclopedias, dictionaries of several languages (including African and Creole), botanical indexes, atlases, and history texts. If he is fortunate enough to identify the object, then he has to decide to what extent the esoteric tone of the poetry should be respected in the English. Dispatching the reader to the reference shelf at every turn in order for him to find out that the object of his chase is nothing more than a morning glory (convolvulus) or a Paraguayan peccary ("patyura") hardly encourages a sustained reading. Here, again, a delicate balance must be maintained between a rigorously puristic stand and a systematic vulgarization. The case of plant names is especially complex, as one must be wary to betray neither Césaire's use of vegetable forms as a symbol of black culture nor his concrete interest in Caribbean flora demonstrated in *Tropiques*. We have refrained from footnoting the words that can be found in current international English dictionaries.

But dealing with such exotic or technical objects as the Khamsin, chalaza, paraschites, souklyans, the cyathus, of flegrian birds is not as baffling as dealing with what Césaire does to ordinary words. Looming constantly on the translator's horizon are treacherous homonyms. Fortunately, there is enough scholarship on Césaire's imagery by now to help choose between the two meanings of "anse" (handle and cove), of "fût" (barrel and bole), or "bouche" (noun or verb). Keeping in mind the overall symbolic structure helps reduce the polysemy. For instance, in view of Césaire's obsession with the genital/fertility theme, we were bold enough to translate "les petites têtes du futur" etymologically as "the testicles of the future," and "la bourse du volcan" as "the volcanic scrotum." Some scholars will challenge these choices in the same way we have challenged those of previous translators.

Neologisms constitute another pitfall. Some are relatively easy to handle because their components are obvious. "Négritude," "nigromance," "strom," "mokatine" are immediately clear by association with "infinitude," "nécromancie," "maelstrom," and "nougâtine" (a rich French almond candy). But coining equivalents for "rhizulent," "effarade," and "désencastration" (which we translated respectively as "rhizulate," "frightation," and "disencasement," in this last case giving up on the hint of castration), requires a solid sense of semantics. Still, only Césaire himself was in a position to reveal (in a private communication) that "verrition" which preceding translators and scholars had interpreted as "flick" and "swirl" had been coined on a Latin verb "verri," meaning "to sweep," "to scrape a surface," and ultimately "to scan." Our rendition ("veerition") attempts to preserve the turning motion (set against its oxymoronic modifier) as well as the Latin sound of the original—thus restituting the long-lost meaning of an important passage (the last few lines of the *Notebook*).

From the point of view of the translator, Césaire is at his most devilish when he paraphrases and puns on idiomatic phrases with a fully surrealistic irreverence toward linguistic orthodoxy. He had admired Breton for turning upside down the old saying that "the thief creates the opportunity," since, even more frequently, Breton said, "the opportunity created the thief." He himself liberally used such twists, too liberally, some feel. For instance, in "To Africa," he speaks about "orgues végétales où / le vent épineux jouait des flûtes et des odeurs tranchantes." While the connection of the flutes with a pipe organ is obvious enough, the familiar meaning of "jouer des flûtes," which is "to run, to show a clean pair of heels" keeps fleeting through the translator's mind. Our translation ("vegetal organ pipes / in which the thorny wind took off amidst flutes and trenchant odors") is an attempt, successful or not, to maintain the double connotation of sound and movement. Likewise in "Perdition," translating the phrase "avalant la bride des tornades mûres" literally will not do justice to the French because it does not convey the not-so-faint echoing of "courir à bride avalée" (to run full tilt). Thus many a line in our English text might puzzle the reader whose French is sufficient to understand the most immediate meaning on the facing page but not the full substance of the sociolect. If this is preciosity in the eyes of some critics, it is not our doing, and those critics will be happier when we have altogether failed to approximate French puns. As for the translator, he often is a dead duck caught between saying less or saying as much which, mysteriously enough, tends to come out as too much. Traduttore traditore, yes. But by excess or by default? That is the question. Yet, we consider such lines as "take the wind out of the birds' wings" (for "couper le sifflet aux oiseaux," in "Millibars of the Storm"), "resheaths the dagger of your neverborn swagger" (for "rengaine ta dégaine jamais née" in "Tangible Disaster"), and many others as experimental. It would be timorous, however, not to try conveying the magnificent "il vit à pierre fendre" ("it is so alive the stones are freezing") of "Another Season."

Of course, beyond the inadequacy of the mediators, that of the language sometimes enters the picture. Unfortunately in Césaire's case, this is true in regard to several words that are part of his regular imagery. A word with an immense sensual and intertextual presence like the French "chevelure" does not have an English equivalent. In the text we have translated it by the rather pedestrian "head of hair," and, as a title, by "your hair," which is suggested by the context. Equally frustrating is the frequently used "sexe." The corresponding English word focusing on the masculine/feminine polarity is obviously unsatisfactory. "Phallus" and "vulva" are sometimes possible substitutes. Nevertheless, the English language does not offer any term as frank, yet as dignified as the French "sexe" to designate the female organ.

Finally, the problems involved in translating the word "nègre" form a whole chapter of scholarship, one Arnold entitles "the Dialectics of Blackness." Reduced to its sketchiest form, the lexical background is as follows: before the Second World War the French had three words to designate individuals or things belonging to the black race. The most euphemistic was "Noir" (noun or adjective). The most derogatory was "négro." In between, on a sort of neutral and objective ground, was the word "nègre," used both as a noun or as an adjective (as in "l'art nègre"). Delafosse had been among the first to give a scientific dignity to this word through his book, *Les Nègres* (1927). For the general public, "noir" and "nègre" may well have been interchangeable, but the very civilized and very complexed Antilleans considered themselves as "Noirs," the "nègres" being on that distant continent, Africa. And it is in this light that one must read Césaire's use of the word "nègre" and its derivatives "négritude," "négrillon" and "négraille": he was making up a family of words based on what he considered as the most insulting way to refer to a black. The paradox, of course, was that this implicit reckoning with the blacks' ignominy, this process of self-irony and self-denigration, was the necessary step on the path to a new self-image and spiritual rebirth. From the point of view of the translator, it is therefore important to translate "nègre" as "nigger" and its derivatives as derivatives or compounds of "nègre" and "nigger" (negritude, nigger scum, little nigger, etc.).

Regarding the punctuation, we have respected the remarkable absence of it as an important characteristic of Césaire's style, inserting commas and dashes with extreme discretion and only in cases when, because of the English lack of inflections, the reader would have been at a complete loss to make sense without these crutches.

In an illuminating article on translating Césaire, Gregson Davis wrote that the ideal interpreter (or translator) would be one with a profound knowledge of Caribbean history and culture, and of European literary history, ancient and modern. "Perhaps," he concludes, "a new and more accurate translation is an idea whose time has come for Caribbean studies."[37] Our work is a response to his challenge, not a promise to live up to his lofty ideal. We have no self-delusions of perfection. No one can be more aware of the limitations inherent in translation, of its Pyrrhic victories and of its many defeats as those who have lived in intimate contact with a text for almost six years. And, for that matter, would not perfection strike a slightly sad note in the case of a poet as complex as Césaire? Would it not mean that his poetry has ceased to generate meanings? The most we can claim is that we benefited from others' mistakes; and we hope that future translators and interpreters will in turn learn from ours as well as from our successes.

A. S.
C. E.

NOTES

I. ACKNOWLEDGMENTS

*The most complete analytical bibliography of Césaire's works (including quotations from his political speeches and news items) is Thomas A. Hales's *Les Ecrits d'Aimé Césaire. Bibliographie commentée* (Montréal: Les Presses de l'Université de Montréal, 1978, a special issue of *Etudes Françaises*, 14/3−4). For works on Césaire, see the bibliography section of *Cahiers Césairiens* (Pennsylvania State University, 1974−). The other major sources underlying this essay are: L. Kesteloot, *Les Ecrivains noirs de langue française* (Bruxelles: Ed. de l'Institut de Sociologie de l'Université Libre, 1963), translated as *Black Writers in French* by E. C. Kennedy (Philadelphia: Temple University Press, 1974); L. Kesteloot and B. Kotchy, *A. C., l'homme et l'oeuvre* (Paris: Présence Africaine, 1973); B. Cailler, *Proposition poétique: une lecture de l'oeuvre d'A. C.* (Sherbrooke, Quebec: Naaman, 1976); M. aM. N'gal, *A. C.: Un homme à la recherche d'une patrie* (Dakar: Les Nouvelles Ed. Africaines, 1975); J. Leiner, ed., *Tropiques* (ed. facsimile), 2 vols. (Paris: J. M. Place, 1978); A. J. Arnold, *Modernism and Negritude: The Poetry and Poetics of Aimé Césaire* (Cambridge, Mass., London: Harvard University Press, 1981). Unless otherwise specified the translations are ours and our comments on the poetry are based on the text of Vol. I of the revised—and presumably definitive—edition of the *Oeuvres complètes*, ed. Jean-Paul Césaire, one of the author's sons, 3 vols. (Fort-de-France: Editions Désormeaux, 1976), (hereafter cited as OC).

II. INTRODUCTION

1. This well-known essay serves as an Introduction to Vol. I of OC. See its translation by Arnold in *Sulfur* no. 5 (California Institute of Technology, 1982), pp. 17−32.

2. Letter of February 1960, trans. in Kesteloot, *Black Writers in French*, pp. 56−57.

3. See Arnold, *Modernism and Negritude*, p. 11.

4. All quotations in this paragraph are from *Tropiques* no. 2, pp. 41−42.

5. Trans. Arnold (*Modernism and Negritude*), pp. 53−54.

6. Hale, "A. C. A Bio-bibliography" in *Africana Journal* V, I (1974), 6.

7. From *Why I am a Communist*, a pamphlet published by the French Communist party in 1946. Quoted by Hale, *Les Ecrits d'A. C.*, p. 262 and trans. in Arnold, *Modernism and Negritude*, p. 174.

8. See n. 18.

9. Biographers disagree as to whether the word appeared previously in an essay by Césaire in *L'Etudiant noir*. Hale sees no evidence of it (private communication).

10. "Trahison," in *Musique nègre* (Port-au-Prince: Collection Indigène, 1931).

11. See L. Damas, *Poètes d'expression française* (Paris: Seuil, 1947), p. 9.

12. Interview with Senghor (June 1959) quoted in Kesteloot, *Black Writers*, p. 102.

13. Interview with M. aM. N'gal (1967) quoted in N'gal, *A. C.*, p. 186.

14. Interview with L. Kesteloot (June 1959) in Kesteloot, *A. C.*, (Paris: Seghers, 1962), p. 93.

15. J. Leiner, "Entretien avec A. C.," in *Tropiques* I, xvii.

16. See Arnold, *Modernism and Negritude*, pp. 280–281.

17. See n. to p. 51 in the notes to the translation.

18. This central essay was read by Césaire on September 28, 1944, to a Haitian audience, published in *Cahiers d'Haiti* in December 1944, and a revised version reprinted in *Tropiques* no. 12 (January 1945). All quotations from this text are from an English version translated by Arnold which appeared in *Sulfur* no. 5 (1982).

19. "Maintenir la Poésie," in *Tropiques* no. 8–9 (October 1943), p. 8.

20. Arnold, *Modernism and Negritude*, p. 281.

21. Césaire expressed this idea in various other forms and contexts, for instance in his interpretation of Shakespeare's *Tempest* (see "Le Noir, cet inconnu" in *Les Nouvelles Littéraires*, July 17, 1969, p. 12) and in the 1973 interview with M. Benamou ("Entretien avec A. C. à Fort-de-France, le 14 février 1973" in *Cahiers Césairiens*, no. 1, pp. 4–8) in which he already acknowledged his desire to return full-time to poetry.

22. Arnold, *Modernism and Negritude*, p. 260.

23. Cailler, *Proposition poétique*, p. 100.

24. "Here Lies," in *Selected Writings*, ed. with an intro. by S. Sontag (New York: Farrar, Straus and Giroux, 1976), p. 540.

25. *The Blacks: A Clown Show* (New York: Grove Press, 1960), p. 52.

26. *OC*, III, 372.

27. See *Modernism and Negritude,* pp. 235–239.

28. "Mauvais sang," in *Une saison en enfer, Oeuvres complètes* (Pléïade ed., 1963), p. 223.

29. J. Leiner, "Entretien avec A. C.," in *Tropiques* I, vi.

30. "Rites of Participation," in *Caterpillar,* no. 1 (New York, 1967), p. 7.

31. See *Le rite du peyotl chez les Tarahumaras, Du voyage au pays des Tarahumaras, Tutuguri* in vol. IX of *Oeuvres Complètes* (Paris: Gallimard, 1971); also Artaud, *The Peyote Dance,* trans. by H. Weaver (New York: Farrar, Straus and Giroux, 1976).

32. Césaire voices skepticism about the automatic writing attributed to him in the interview with M. Benamou (see n. 21).

33. Wallace Fowlie's phrase, borrowed by Roger Shattuck in *Selected Writings of Guillaume Apollinaire* (New York: New Directions Books, 1971), pp. 32–33.

34. "Poetry and Knowledge" (see n. 18 above).

35. "Towards a 'Non-Vicious Circle': The Lyric of Aimé Césaire in English," in *Stanford French Review* I, (1977), 135–146.

36. From an interview with J. Sieger (1960), quoted in Arnold, *Modernism and Negritude,* p. 263.

37. "Towards a 'Non-Vicious Circle' " (see n. 35), pp. 145–146.

CAHIER D'UN RETOUR AU PAYS NATAL

*

NOTEBOOK OF A RETURN TO THE NATIVE LAND

Wifredo Lam, untitled watercolor, 13½ × 15½"

Cahier d'un retour au pays natal

Au bout du petit matin . . .

Va-t'en, lui disais-je, gueule de flic, gueule de vache, va-t'en, je déteste les larbins de l'ordre et les hannetons de l'espérance. Va-t'en, mauvais gri-gri, punaise de moinillon. Puis je me tournais vers des paradis pour lui et les siens perdus, plus calme que la face d'une femme qui ment, et là, bercé par les effluves d'une pensée jamais lasse je nourrissais le vent, je délaçais les monstres et j'entendais monter, de l'autre côté du désastre, un fleuve de tourterelles et de trèfles de la savane que je porte toujours dans mes profondeurs à hauteur inverse du vingtième étage des maisons les plus insolentes et par précaution contre la force putréfiante des ambiances crépusculaires, arpentée nuit et jour d'un sacré soleil vénérien.

Au bout du petit matin bourgeonnant d'anses frêles, les Antilles qui ont faim, les Antilles grêlées de petite vérole, les Antilles dynamitées d'alcool, échouées dans la boue de cette baie, dans la poussière de cette ville sinistrement échouées.

Au bout du petit matin, l'extrême, trompeuse désolée eschare sur la blessure des eaux; les martyrs qui ne témoignent pas; les fleurs du sang qui se fanent et s'éparpillent dans le vent inutile comme des cris de perroquets babillards; une vieille vie menteusement souriante, ses lèvres ouvertes d'angoisses désaffectées; une vieille misère pourrissant sous le soleil, silencieusement; un vieux silence crevant de pustules tièdes, l'affreuse inanité de notre raison d'être.

Au bout du petit matin, sur cette plus fragile épaisseur de terre que dépasse de façon humiliante son grandiose avenir—les volcans éclateront, l'eau nue emportera les taches mûres du soleil et il ne restera plus qu'un bouillonnement tiède picoré d'oiseaux marins—la plage des songes et l'insensé réveil.

Au bout du petit matin, cette ville plate-étalée trébuchée de son bon sens, inerte, essoufflée sous son fardeau géométrique de croix éternellement recommençante, indocile à son sort, muette, contrariée de toutes façons, incapable de croître selon le suc de cette terre, embarrassée, rognée, réduite, en rupture de faune et de flore.

Au bout du petit matin, cette ville plate-étalée . . .

Et dans cette ville inerte, cette foule criarde si étonnamment passée à côté de son cri comme cette ville à côté de son mouvement, de son sens, sans inquiétude, à côté de son vrai cri, le seul qu'on eût voulu l'entendre crier parce qu'on le sent sien lui seul; parce qu'on le sent habiter en elle dans quelque refuge profond d'ombre et d'orgueil dans cette ville inerte, cette foule à côté de son cri de faim, de misère, de révolte, de haine, cette foule si étrangement bavarde et muette.

Dans cette ville inerte, cette étrange foule qui ne s'entasse pas, ne se mêle pas: habile à découvrir le point de désencastration, de fuite, d'esquive. Cette foule qui ne sait pas faire foule cette foule, on s'en rend compte, si parfaitement seule sous ce soleil, à la façon dont une femme, toute on eût cru à sa

Notebook of a Return to the Native Land

At the end of the wee hours . . .

Beat it, I said to him, you cop, you lousy pig, beat it, I detest the flunkies of order and the cockchafers of hope. Beat it, evil grigri, you bedbug of a petty monk. Then I turned toward paradises lost for him and his kin, calmer than the face of a woman telling lies, and there, rocked by the flux of a never exhausted thought I nourished the wind, I unlaced the monsters and heard rise, from the other side of disaster, a river of turtledoves and savanna clover which I carry forever in my depths height-deep as the twentieth floor of the most arrogant houses and as a guard against the putrefying force of crepuscular surroundings, surveyed night and day by a cursed venereal sun.

At the end of the wee hours burgeoning with frail coves, the hungry Antilles, the Antilles pitted with smallpox, the Antilles dynamited by alcohol, stranded in the mud of this bay, in the dust of this town sinisterly stranded.

At the end of the wee hours, the extreme, deceptive desolate bedsore on the wound of the waters; the martyrs who do not bear witness; the flowers of blood that fade and scatter in the empty wind like the screeches of babbling parrots; an aged life mendaciously smiling, its lips opened by vacated agonies; an aged poverty rotting under the sun, silently; an aged silence bursting with tepid pustules, the awful futility of our raison d'être.

At the end of the wee hours, on this very fragile earth thickness exceeded in a humiliating way by its grandiose future—the volcanoes will explode, the naked water will bear away the ripe sun stains and nothing will be left but a tepid bubbling pecked at by sea birds—the beach of dreams and the insane awakenings.

At the end of the wee hours, this town sprawled-flat toppled from its common sense, inert, winded under its geometric weight of an eternally renewed cross, indocile to its fate, mute, vexed no matter what, incapable of growing with the juice of this earth, self-conscious, clipped, reduced, in breach of fauna and flora.

At the end of the wee hours, this town sprawled-flat . . .

And in this inert town, this squalling throng so astonishingly detoured from its cry as this town has been from its movement, from its meaning, not even worried, detoured from its true cry, the only cry you would have wanted to hear because you feel it alone belongs to this town; because you feel it lives in it in some deep refuge and pride in this inert town, this throng detoured from its cry of hunger, of poverty, of revolt, of hatred, this throng so strangely chattering and mute.

In this inert town, this strange throng which does not pack, does not mix: clever at discovering the point of disencasement, of flight, of dodging. This throng which does not know how to throng, this throng, clearly so perfectly alone under this sun, like a woman one thought completely occupied with her lyric cadence, who abruptly challenges a hypothetical rain and enjoins it not to

cadence lyrique, interpelle brusquement une pluie hypothétique et lui intime l'ordre de ne pas tomber; ou à un signe rapide de croix sans mobile visible; ou à l'animalité subitement grave d'une paysanne, urinant debout, les jambes écartées, roides.

Dans cette ville inerte, cette foule désolée sous le soleil, ne participant à rien de ce qui s'exprime, s'affirme, se libère au grand jour de cette terre sienne. Ni à l'impératrice Joséphine des Français rêvant très haut au-dessus de la négraille. Ni au libérateur figé dans sa libération de pierre blanchie. Ni au conquistador. Ni à ce mépris, ni à cette liberté, ni à cette audace.

Au bout du petit matin, cette ville inerte et ses au-delà de lèpres, de consomption, de famines, de peurs tapies dans les ravins, de peurs juchées dans les arbres, de peurs creusées dans le sol, de peur en dérive dans le ciel, de peurs amoncelées et ses fumerolles d'angoisse.

Au bout du petit matin, le morne oublié, oublieux de sauter.

Au bout du petit matin, le morne au sabot inquiet et docile—son sang impaludé met en déroute le soleil de ses pouls surchauffés.

Au bout du petit matin, l'incendie contenu du morne, comme un sanglot que l'on a bâillonné au bord de son éclatement sanguinaire, en quête d'une ignition qui se dérobe et se méconnaît.

Au bout du petit matin, le morne accroupi devant la boulimie aux aguets de foudres et de moulins, lentement vomissant ses fatigues d'hommes, le morne seul et son sang répandu, le morne et ses pansements d'ombre, le morne et ses rigoles de peur, le morne et ses grandes mains de vent.

Au bout du petit matin, le morne famélique et nul ne sait mieux que ce morne bâtard pourquoi le suicidé s'est étouffé avec complicité de son hypoglosse en retournant sa langue pour l'avaler; pourquoi une femme semble faire la planche à la rivière Capot (son corps lumineusement obscur s'organise docilement au commandement du nombril) mais elle n'est qu'un paquet d'eau sonore.

Et ni l'instituteur dans sa classe, ni le prêtre au catéchisme ne pourront tirer un mot de ce négrillon somnolent, malgré leur manière si énergique à tous deux de tambouriner son crâne tondu, car c'est dans les marais de la faim que s'est enlisée sa voix d'inanition (un-mot-un-seul-mot et je-vous-en-tiens-quitte de-la-reine-Blanche-de-Castille, un-mot-un-seul-mot, voyez-vous-ce-petit-sauvage-qui-ne-sait-pas-un-mot-des-dix-commandements-de-Dieu).
car sa voix s'oublie dans les marais de la faim,
et il n'y a rien, rien à tirer vraiment de ce petit vaurien,
qu'une faim qui ne sait plus grimper aux agrès de sa voix
une faim lourde et veule,
une faim ensevelie au plus profond de la Faim de ce morne famélique.

Au bout du petit matin, l'échouage hétéroclite, les puanteurs exacerbées de la corruption, les sodomies monstrueuses de l'hostie et du victimaire, les coltis infranchissables du préjugé et de la sottise, les prostitutions, les hypocrisies, les lubricités, les trahisons, les mensonges, les faux, les concussions—l'essoufflement des lâchetés insuffisantes, l'enthousiasme sans ahan aux poussis sur-

fall; or like a rapid sign of the cross without perceptive motive; or like the sudden grave animality of a peasant, urinating standing, her legs parted, stiff.

In this inert town, this desolate throng under the sun, not connected with anything that is expressed, asserted, released in broad earth daylight, its own. Neither with Josephine, Empress of the French, dreaming way up there above the nigger scum. Nor with the liberator fixed in his whitewashed stone liberation. Nor with the conquistador. Nor with this contempt, with this freedom, with this audacity.

At the end of the wee hours, this inert town and its beyond of lepers, of consumption, of famines, of fears squatting in the ravines, fears perched in the trees, fears dug in the ground, fears adrift in the sky, piles of fears and their fumaroles of anguish.

At the end of the wee hours, the morne forgotten, forgetful of leaping.

At the end of the wee hours, the morne in restless, docile hooves—its malarial blood routs the sun with its overheated pulse.

At the end of the wee hours, the restrained conflagration of the morne, like a sob gagged on the verge of a bloodthirsty burst, in quest of an ignition that slips away and ignores itself.

At the end of the wee hours, the morne crouching before bulimia on the lookout for tuns and mills, slowly vomiting out its human fatigue, the morne solitary and its blood shed, the morne bandaged in shades, the morne and its ditches of fear, the morne and its great hands of wind.

At the end of the wee hours, the famished morne and no one knows better than this bastard morne why the suicide choked with a little help from his hypoglossal jamming his tongue backward to swallow it; why a woman seems to float belly up on the Capot River (her chiaroscuro body submissively organized at the command of her navel) but she is only a bundle of sonorous water.

And neither the teacher in his classroom, nor the priest at catechism will be able to get a word out of this sleepy little nigger, no matter how energetically they drum on his shorn skull, for starvation has quicksanded his voice into the swamp of hunger (a word-one-single-word and we-will-forget-about-Queen-Blanche-of-Castille, a-word-one-single-word, you-should-see-this-little savage-who-doesn't-know-any-of-The-Ten-Commandments).
for his voice gets lost in the swamp of hunger,
and there is nothing, really nothing to squeeze out of this little brat,
other than a hunger which can no longer climb to the rigging of his voice
a sluggish flabby hunger,
a hunger buried in the depth of the Hunger of this famished morne.

At the end of the wee hours, the disparate stranding, the exacerbated stench of corruption, the monstrous sodomies of the host and the sacrificing priest, the impassable beakhead frames of prejudice and stupidity, the prostitutions, the hypocrisies, the lubricities, the treasons, the lies, the frauds, the concussions—the panting of a deficient cowardice, the heave-holess enthusiasm of

*See the *Notes* that follow the translation for commentary on words in lines marked by an asterisk.

numéraires, les avidités, les hystéries, les perversions, les arlequinades de la misère, les estropiements, les prurits, les urticaires, les hamacs tièdes de la dégénérescence. Ici la parade des risibles et scrofuleux bubons, les poutures de microbes très étranges, les poisons sans alexitère connu, les sanies de plaies bien antiques, les fermentations imprévisibles d'espèces putrescibles.

Au bout du petit matin, la grande nuit immobile, les étoiles plus mortes qu'un balafon crevé,

le bulbe tératique de la nuit, germé de nos bassesses et de nos renoncements.

Et nos gestes imbéciles et fous pour faire revivre l'éclaboussement d'or des instants favorisés, le cordon ombilical restitué à sa splendeur fragile, le pain, et le vin de la complicité, le pain, le vin, le sang des épousailles véridiques.

Et cette joie ancienne m'apportant la connaissance de ma présente misère, une route bossuée qui pique une tête dans un creux où elle éparpille quelques cases; une route infatigable qui charge à fond de train un morne en haut duquel elle s'enlise brutalement dans une mare de maisons pataudes, une route follement montante, témérairement descendante, et la carcasse de bois comiquement juchée sur de minuscules pattes de ciment que j'appelle "notre maison", sa coiffure de tôle ondulant au soleil comme une peau qui sèche, la salle à manger, le plancher grossier où luisent des têtes de clous, les solives de sapin et d'ombre qui courent au plafond, les chaises de paille fantomales, la lumière grise de la lampe, celle vernissée et rapide des cancrelats qui bourdonne à faire mal . . .

Au bout du petit matin, ce plus essentiel pays restitué à ma gourmandise, non de diffuse tendresse, mais la tourmentée concentration sensuelle du gras téton des mornes avec l'accidentel palmier comme son germe durci, la jouissance saccadée des torrents et depuis Trinité jusqu'à Grand-Rivière, la grand-lèche hystérique de la mer.

Et le temps passait vite, très vite.
Passés août où les manguiers pavoisent de toutes leurs lunules, septembre l'accoucheur des cyclones, octobre le flambeur de cannes, novembre qui ronronne aux distilleries, c'était Noël qui commençait.
Il s'était annoncé d'abord Noël par un picotement des désirs, une soif de tendresses neuves, un bourgeonnement de rêves imprécis, puis il s'était envolé tout à coup dans le froufrou violet de ses grandes ailes de joie, et alors c'était parmi le bourg sa vertigineuse retombée qui éclatait la vie des cases comme une grenade trop mûre.
Noël n'était pas comme toutes les fêtes. Il n'aimait pas à courir les rues, à danser sur les places publiques, à s'installer sur les chevaux de bois, à profiter de la cohue pour pincer les femmes, à lancer des feux d'artifice au front des tamariniers. Il avait l'agoraphobie, Noël. Ce qu'il lui fallait, c'était toute une journée d'affairements, d'apprêts, de cuisinages, de nettoyages, d'inquiétudes.
de-peur-que-ça-ne-suffise-pas,
de-peur-que-ça-ne-manque,
de-peur-qu'on-ne-s'embête,

puis le soir une petite église pas intimidante, qui se laissât emplir bienveillamment par les rires, les chuchotis, les confidences, les déclarations amoureuses, les médisances et la cacophonie gutturale d'un chantre bien d'attaque et aussi de gais copains et de franches luronnes et des cases aux entrailles riches en succulences, et pas regardantes, et l'on s'y parque une vingtaine, et la rue est déserte, et le

supernumerary sahibs, the greeds, the hysterias, the perversions, the clownings of poverty, the cripplings, the itchings, the hives, the tepid hammocks of degeneracy. Right here the parade of laughable and scrofulous buboes, the forced feedings of very strange microbes, the poisons without known alexins, the sanies of really ancient sores, the unforeseeable fermentations of putrescible species.

At the end of the wee hours, the great motionless night, the stars deader than a caved-in balafo,

the teratical bulb of night, sprouted from our vilenesses and our renunciations.

And our foolish and crazy stunts to revive the golden splashing of privileged moments, the umbilical cord restored to its ephemeral splendor, the bread, and the wine of complicity, the bread, the wine, the blood of honest weddings.

And this joy of former times making me aware of my present poverty, a bumpy road plunging into a hollow where it scatters a few shacks; an indefatigable road charging at full speed a morne at the top of which it brutally quicksands into a pool of clumsy houses, a road foolishly climbing, recklessly descending, and the carcass of wood, which I call "our house," comically perched on minute cement paws, its coiffure of corrugated iron in the sun like a skin laid out to dry, the main room, the rough floor where the nail heads gleam, the beams of pine and shadow across the ceiling, the spectral straw chairs, the grey lamp light, the glossy flash of cockroaches in a maddening buzz . . .

At the end of the wee hours, this most essential land restored to my gourmandise, not in diffuse tenderness, but the tormented sensual concentration of the fat tits of the mornes with an occasional palm tree as their hardened sprout, the jerky orgasm of torrents and from Trinité to Grand-Rivière, the hysterical grandsuck of the sea.

And time passed quickly, very quickly.

After August and mango trees decked out in all their little moons, September begetter of cyclones, October igniter of sugar-cane, November who purrs in the distilleries, there came Christmas.

It had come in at first, Christmas did, with a tingling of desires, a thirst for new tenderness, a burgeoning of vague dreams, then with a purple rustle of its great joyous wings it had suddenly flown away, and then its abrupt fall out over the village that made the shack life burst like an overripe pomegranate.

Christmas was not like other holidays. It didn't like to gad about the streets, to dance on public squares, to mount the wooden horses, to use the crowd to pinch women, to hurl fireworks in the faces of the tamarind trees. It had agoraphobia, Christmas did. What it wanted was a whole day of bustling, preparing, a cooking and cleaning spree, endless jitters
about-not-having-enough,
about-running-short,
about-getting-bored,

then at evening an unimposing little church, which would benevolently make room for the laughter, the whispers, the secrets, the love talk, the gossip and the guttural cacophony of a plucky singer and also boisterous pals and shameless hussies and shacks up to their guts in succulent

bourg n'est plus qu'un bouquet de chants, et l'on est bien à l'intérieur, et l'on en mange du bon, et l'on en boit du réjouissant et il y a du boudin, celui étroit de deux doigts qui s'enroule en volubile, celui large et trapu, le bénin à goût de serpolet, le violent à incandescence pimentée, et du café brûlant et de l'anis sucré et du punch au lait, et le soleil liquide des rhums, et toutes sortes de bonnes choses qui vous imposent autoritairement les muqueuses ou vous les distillent en ravissements ou vous les tissent de fragrances, et l'on rit, et l'on chante, et les refrains fusent à perte de vue comme des cocotiers:

ALLELUIA
KYRIE ELEISON . . . LEISON . . . LEISON
CHRISTE ELEISON . . . LEISON . . . LEISON.

Et ce ne sont pas seulement les bouches qui chantent, mais les mains, mais les pieds, mais les fesses, mais les sexes, et la créature tout entière qui se liquéfie en sons, voix et rythme.

Arrivée au sommet de son ascension, la joie crève comme un nuage. Les chants ne s'arrêtent pas, mais ils roulent maintenant inquiets et lourds par les vallées de la peur, les tunnels de l'angoisse et les feux de l'enfer.

Et chacun se met à tirer par la queue le diable le plus proche, jusqu'à ce que la peur s'abolisse insensiblement dans les fines sablures du rêve, et l'on vit comme dans un rêve véritablement, et l'on boit et l'on crie et l'on chante comme dans un rêve, et l'on somnole aussi comme dans un rêve avec des paupières en pétale de rose, et le jour vient velouté comme une sapotille, et l'odeur du purin des cacaoyers, et les dindons qui égrènent leurs pustules rouges au soleil, et l'obsession des cloches, et la pluie,

les cloches, . . . la pluie . . .
qui tintent, tintent, tintent . . .

Au bout du petit matin, cette ville plate-étalée . . .

Elle rampe sur les mains sans jamais aucune envie de vriller le ciel d'une stature de protestation. Les dos des maisons ont peur du ciel truffé de feu, leurs pieds des noyades du sol, elles ont opté de se poser superficielles entre les surprises et les perfidies. Et pourtant elle avance la ville. Même qu'elle paît tous les jours outre sa marée de corridors carrelés, de persiennes pudibondes, de cours gluantes, de peintures qui dégoulinent. Et de petits scandales étouffés, de petites hontes tues, de petites haines immenses pétrissent en bosses et creux les rues étroites où le ruisseau grimace longitudinalement parmi l'étron . . .

Au bout du petit matin, la vie prostrée, on ne sait où dépêcher ses rêves avortés, le fleuve de vie désespérément torpide dans son lit, sans turgescence ni dépression, incertain de fluer, lamentablement vide, la lourde impartialité de l'ennui, répartissant l'ombre sur toutes choses égales, l'air stagnant sans une trouée d'oiseau clair.

Au bout du petit matin, une autre petite maison qui sent très mauvais dans une rue très étroite, une maison minuscule qui abrite en ses entrailles de bois pourri des dizaines de rats et la turbulence de mes six frères et sœurs, une petite maison cruelle dont l'intransigeance affole nos fins de mois et mon père fantasque grignoté d'une seule misère, je n'ai jamais su laquelle, qu'une imprévisible sorcellerie assoupit en mélancolique tendresse ou exalte en hautes flammes de colère; et ma mère dont les jambes pour notre faim inlassable pédalent, pédalent de jour, de nuit, je suis même réveillé la nuit par ces jambes inlassables qui pédalent la nuit et la morsure âpre dans la chair molle de la nuit d'une Singer que ma mère pédale, pédale pour notre faim et de jour et de nuit.

goodies, and not stingy, and twenty people can crowd in, and the street is deserted, and the village turns into a bouquet of singing, and you are cozy in there, and you eat good, and you drink hearty and there are blood sausages, one kind only two fingers wide twined in coils, the other broad and stocky, the mild one tasting of wild thyme, the hot one spiced to an incandescence, and steaming coffee and sugared anise and milk punch, and the liquid sun of rums, and all sorts of good things which drive your taste buds wild or distill them to the point of ecstasy or cocoon them with fragrances, and you laugh, and you sing, and the refrains flare on and on like coco-palms:

ALLELUIA
KYRIE ELEISON . . . LEISON . . . LEISON
CHRISTE ELEISON . . . LEISON . . . LEISON.

And not only do the mouths sing, but the hands, the feet, the buttocks, the genitals, and your entire being liquefies into sounds, voices, and rhythm.

At the peak of its ascent, joy bursts like a cloud. The songs don't stop, but now anxious and heavy roll through the valleys of fear, the tunnels of anguish and the fires of hell.

And each one starts pulling the nearest devil by his tail, until fear imperceptibly fades in the fine sand lines of dream, and you really live as in a dream, and you drink and you shout and you sing as in a dream, and doze too as in a dream, with rose petal eyelids, and the day comes velvety as a sapodilla tree, and the liquid manure smell of the cacao trees, and the turkeys which shell their red pustules in the sun, and the obsessive bells, and the rain,

the bells . . . the rain . . .
that tinkle, tinkle, tinkle . . .

At the end of the wee hours, this town sprawled-flat . . .

It crawls on its hands without the slightest desire to drill the sky with a stature of protest. The backs of the houses are afraid of the sky truffled with fire, their feet of the drownings of the soil, they chose to perch shallowly between surprises and treacheries. And yet it advances, the town does. It even grazes every day further out into its tide of tiled corridors, prudish shutters, gluey courtyards, dripping paintwork. And petty hushed-up scandals, petty unvoiced guilts, petty immense hatreds knead the narrow streets into bumps and potholes where the waste-water grins longitudinally through turds . . .

At the end of the wee hours, life prostrate, you don't know how to dispose of your aborted dreams, the river of life desperately torpid in its bed, neither turgid nor low, hesitant to flow, pitifully empty, the impartial heaviness of boredom distributing shade equally on all things, the air stagnant, unbroken by the brightness of a single bird.

At the end of the wee hours, another little house very bad-smelling in a very narrow street, a miniscule house which harbors in its guts of rotten wood dozens of rats and the turbulence of my six brothers and sisters, a cruel little house whose demands panic the ends of our months and my temperamental father gnawed by one persistent ache, I never knew which one, whom an unexpected sorcery could lull to melancholy tenderness or drive to towering flames of anger; and my mother whose legs pedal, pedal, night and day, for our tireless hunger, I was even awakened at night by these tireless legs which pedal the night and the bitter bite in the soft flesh of the night of a Singer that my mother pedals, pedals for our hunger and day and night.

Au bout du petit matin, au-delà de mon père, de ma mère, la case gerçant d'ampoules, comme un pêcher tourmenté de la cloque, et le toit aminci, rapiécé de morceaux de bidon de pétrole, et ça fait des marais de rouillure dans la pâte grise sordide empuantie de la paille, et quand le vent siffle, ces disparates font bizarre le bruit, comme un crépitement de friture d'abord, puis comme un tison que l'on plonge dans l'eau avec la fumée des brindilles qui s'envole. Et le lit de planches d'où s'est levée ma race, tout entière ma race de ce lit de planches, avec ses pattes de caisses de Kérosine, comme s'il avait l'éléphantiasis le lit, et sa peau de cabri, et ses feuilles de banane séchées, et ses haillons, une nostalgie de matelas le lit de ma grand-mère. (Au-dessus du lit, dans un pot plein d'huile un lumignon dont la flamme danse comme un gros ravet . . . sur le pot en lettres d'or: MERCI.)

Et une honte, cette rue Paille,

un appendice dégoûtant comme les parties honteuses du bourg qui étend à droite et à gauche, tout au long de la route coloniale, la houle de ses toits d'essentes. Ici il n'y a que des toits de paille que l'embrun a brunis et que le vent épile.

Tout le monde la méprise la rue Paille. C'est là que la jeunesse du bourg se débauche. C'est là surtout que la mer déverse ses immondices, ses chats morts et ses chiens crevés. Car la rue débouche sur une plage, et la plage ne suffit pas à la rage écumante de la mer.

Une détresse cette plage elle aussi, avec ses tas d'ordure pourrissant, ses croupes furtives qui se soulagent, et le sable est noir, funèbre, on n'a jamais vu un sable si noir, et l'écume glisse dessus en glapissant, et la mer la frappe à grands coups de boxe, ou plutôt la mer est un gros chien qui lèche et mord la plage aux jarrets, et à force de la mordre elle finira par la dévorer, bien sûr, la plage et la rue Paille avec.

Au bout du petit matin, le vent de jadis qui s'élève, des fidélités trahies, du devoir incertain qui se dérobe et cet autre petit matin d'Europe . . .

Partir.
Comme il y a des hommes-hyènes et des hommes-panthères, je serais un homme-juif
un homme-cafre
un homme-hindou-de-Calcutta
un homme-de-Harlem-qui-ne-vote-pas

l'homme-famine, l'homme-insulte, l'homme-torture, on pouvait à n'importe quel moment le saisir, le rouer de coups, le tuer—parfaitement le tuer—sans avoir de compte à rendre à personne, sans avoir d'excuses à présenter à personne
un homme-juif
un homme-pogrom
un chiot
un mendigot
mais est-ce qu'on tue le Remords, beau comme la face de stupeur d'une dame anglaise qui trouverait dans sa soupière un crâne de Hottentot?

Je retrouverais le secret des grandes communications et des grandes combustions. Je dirais orage. Je dirais fleuve. Je dirais tornade. Je dirais feuille. Je dirais arbre. Je serais mouillé de toutes les pluies, humecté de toutes les rosées. Je roulerais comme du sang frénétique sur le courant lent de l'œil des mots en chevaux fous en enfants frais en caillots en couvre-feu en vestiges de temple en pierres

At the end of the wee hours, beyond my father, my mother, the shack chapped with blisters, like a peach tree afflicted with curl, and the thin roof patched with pieces of gasoline cans, which create swamps of rust in the stinking sordid grey straw pulp, and when the wind whistles, these odds and ends make a noise bizarre, first like the crackling of frying, then like a brand dropped into water the smoke of its twigs flying up. And the bed of boards from which my race arose, my whole entire race from this bed of boards, with its kerosene case paws, as if it had elephantiasis, that bed, and its kidskin, and its dry banana leaves, and its rags, yearning for a mattress, my grandmother's bed. (Above the bed, in a jar full of oil a dim light whose flame dances like a fat cockroach . . . on the jar in gold letters: MERCI.)

And this rue Paille, this disgrace,

an appendage repulsive as the private parts of the village which extends right and left, along the colonial highway, the grey surge of its shingled roofs. Here there are only straw roofs, spray browned and wind plucked.

Everybody despises rue Paille. It's there that the village youth go astray. It's there especially that the sea pours forth its garbage, its dead cats and its croaked dogs. For the street opens on to the beach, and the beach alone cannot satisfy the sea's foaming rage.

A blight this beach as well, with its piles of rotting muck, its furtive rumps relieving themselves, and the sand is black, funereal, you've never seen a sand so black, and the scum glides over it yelping, and the sea pummels it like a boxer, or rather the sea is a huge dog licking and biting the shins of the beach, biting them so fiercely that it will end up devouring it, the beach and rue Paille along with it.

At the end of the wee hours, the wind of long ago—of betrayed trusts, of uncertain evasive duty and that other dawn in Europe—arises . . .

To go away.
As there are hyena-men and panther-men, I would be a jew-man
a Kaffir-man
a Hindu-man-from-Calcutta
a Harlem-man-who-doesn't-vote

the famine man, the insult-man, the torture man you can grab anytime, beat up, kill—no joke, kill—without having to account to anyone, without having to make excuses to anyone
a jew-man
a pogrom-man
a puppy
a beggar
but *can* one kill Remorse, perfect as the stupefied face of an English lady discovering a Hottentot skull in her soup-tureen?

I would rediscover the secret of great communications and great combustions. I would say storm. I would say river. I would say tornado. I would say leaf. I would say tree. I would be drenched by all rains, moistened by all dews. I would roll like frenetic blood on the slow current of the eye of words turned into mad horses into fresh children into clots into curfew into vestiges of temples into

précieuses assez loin pour décourager les mineurs. Qui ne me comprendrait pas ne comprendrait pas davantage le rugissement du tigre.

Et vous fantômes montez bleus de chimie d'une forêt de bêtes traquées de machines tordues d'un jujubier de chairs pourries d'un panier d'huîtres d'yeux d'un lacis de lanières découpées dans le beau sisal d'une peau d'homme j'aurais des mots assez vastes pour vous contenir et toi terre tendue terre saoule
terre grand sexe levé vers le soleil
terre grand délire de la mentule de Dieu
terre sauvage montée des resserres de la mer avec dans la bouche une touffe de cécropies terre dont je ne puis comparer la face houleuse qu'à la forêt vierge et folle que je souhaiterais pouvoir en guise de visage montrer aux yeux indéchiffreurs des hommes
il me suffirait d'une gorgée de ton lait jiculi pour qu'en toi je découvre toujours à même distance de mirage—mille fois plus natale et dorée d'un soleil que n'entame nul prisme—la terre où tout est libre et fraternel, ma terre.

Partir. Mon cœur bruissait de générosités emphatiques. Partir . . . j'arriverais lisse et jeune dans ce pays mien et je dirais à ce pays dont le limon entre dans la composition de ma chair: "J'ai longtemps erré et je reviens vers la hideur désertée de vos plaies."
Je viendrais à ce pays mien et je lui dirais: "Embrassez- moi sans crainte . . . Et si je ne sais que parler, c'est pour vous que je parlerai."
Et je lui dirais encore:
"Ma bouche sera la bouche des malheurs qui n'ont point de bouche, ma voix, la liberté de celles qui s'affaissent au cachot du désespoir."
Et venant je me dirais à moi-même:
"Et surtout mon corps aussi bien que mon âme, gardez-vous de vous croiser les bras en l'attitude stérile du spectateur, car la vie n'est pas un spectacle, car une mer de douleurs n'est pas un proscenium, car un homme qui crie n'est pas un ours qui danse . . ."

Et voici que je suis venu!
De nouveau cette vie clopinante devant moi, non pas cette vie, cette mort, cette mort sans sens ni piété, cette mort où la grandeur piteusement échoue, l'éclatante petitesse de cette mort, cette mort qui clopine de petitesses en petitesses; ces pelletées de petites avidités sur le conquistador; ces pelletées de petits larbins sur le grand sauvage, ces pelletées de petites âmes sur le Caraïbe aux trois âmes,
et toutes ces morts futiles
absurdités sous l'éclaboussement de ma conscience ouverte
tragiques futilités éclairées de cette seule noctiluque
et moi seul, brusque scène de ce petit matin où fait le beau l'apocalypse des monstres puis, chavirée, se tait
chaude élection de cendres, de ruines et d'affaissements
—Encore une objection! une seule, mais de grâce une seule: je n'ai pas le droit de calculer la vie à mon empan fuligineux; de me réduire à ce petit rien ellipsoïdal qui tremble à quatre doigts au-dessus de la ligne, moi homme, d'ainsi bouleverser la création, que je me comprenne entre latitude et longitude!

Au bout du petit matin,
la mâle soif et l'entêté désir,

precious stones remote enough to discourage miners. Whoever would not understand me would not understand any better the roaring of a tiger.

And you ghosts rise blue from alchemy from a forest of hunted beasts of twisted machines of a jujube tree of rotten flesh of a basket of oysters of eyes of a network of straps in the beautiful sisal of human skin I would have words vast enough to contain you earth taut earth drunk
earth great vulva raised to the sun   *
earth great delirium of God's mentula
savage earth arisen from the storerooms of the sea a clump of Cecropia in your mouth earth whose tumultuous face I can only compare to the virgin and mad forest which were it in my power I would show in guise of a face to the undeciphering eyes of men
all I would need is a mouthful of jiculi milk to discover in you always as distant as a mirage—a   *
thousand times more native and made golden by a sun that no prism divides—the earth where everything is free and fraternal, my earth.

To go away. My heart was pounding with emphatic generosities. To go away . . . I would arrive sleek and young in this land of mine and I would say to this land whose loam is part of my flesh: "I have wandered for a long time and I am coming back to the deserted hideousness of your sores."
I would go to this land of mine and I would say to it: "Embrace me without fear . . . And if all I can do is speak, it is for you I shall speak."
And again I would say:
"My mouth shall be the mouth of those calamities that have no mouth, my voice the freedom of those who break down in the solitary confinement of despair."
And on the way I would say to myself:
"And above all, my body as well as my soul, beware of assuming the sterile attitude of a spectator, for life is not a spectacle, a sea of miseries is not a proscenium, a man screaming is not a dancing bear . . ."

And behold here I am!
Once again this life hobbling before me, what am I saying life, *this death*, this death without sense or piety, this death that so pathetically falls short of greatness, the dazzling pettiness of this death, this death hobbling from pettiness to pettiness; these shovelfuls of petty greeds over the conquistador; these shovelfuls of petty flunkies over the great savage, these shovelfuls of petty souls over the three-souled Carib,
and all these deaths futile
absurdities under the splashing of my open conscience
tragic futilities lit up by this single noctiluca
and I alone, sudden stage of these wee hours when the apocalypse of monsters cavorts then, capsized, hushes
warm election of cinders, of ruins and collapses
—One more thing! only one, but please make it only one: I have no right to measure life by my sooty finger span; to reduce myself to this little ellipsoidal nothing trembling four fingers above the line, I a man, to so overturn creation, that I include myself between latitude and longitude!

At the end of the wee hours,
the male thirst and the desire stubborn,

me voici divisé des oasis fraîches de la fraternité
ce rien pudique frise d'échardes dures
cet horizon trop sûr tressaille comme un geôlier.

      Ton dernier triomphe, corbeau tenace de la Trahison.
      Ce qui est à moi, ces quelques milliers de mortiférés qui tournent en rond dans la calebasse d'une
île et ce qui est à moi aussi, l'archipel arqué comme le désir inquiet de se nier, on dirait une anxiété
maternelle pour protéger la ténuité plus délicate qui sépare l'une de l'autre Amérique; et ses flancs qui
sécrètent pour l'Europe la bonne liqueur d'un Gulf Stream, et l'un des deux versants d'incandescence
entre quoi l'Equateur funambule vers l'Afrique. Et mon île non-clôture, sa claire audace debout à
l'arrière de cette polynésie, devant elle, la Guadeloupe fendue en deux de sa raie dorsale et de même
misère que nous, Haïti où la négritude se mit debout pour la première fois et dit qu'elle croyait à son
humanité et la comique petite queue de la Floride où d'un nègre s'achève la strangulation, et l'Afrique
gigantesquement chenillant jusqu'au pied hispanique de l'Europe, sa nudité où la mort fauche à larges
andains.

      Et je me dis Bordeaux et Nantes et Liverpool et New-York et San-Francisco.

pas un bout de ce monde qui ne porte mon empreinte digitale
et mon calcanéum sur le dos des gratte-ciel et ma crasse dans le scintillement des gemmes!
Qui peut se vanter d'avoir mieux que moi? Virginie.
Tennessee. Géorgie. Alabama
putréfactions monstrueuses de révoltes
inopérantes
marais de sang putrides
trompettes absurdement bouchées
terres rouges, terres sanguines, terres consanguines.

      Ce qui est à moi aussi: une petite
cellule dans le Jura,
une petite cellule, la neige la double de barreaux blancs
la neige est un geôlier blanc qui monte
la garde devant une prison

Ce qui est à moi
c'est un homme seul emprisonné de
blanc
c'est un homme seul qui défie les cris
blancs de la mort blanche
(TOUSSAINT, TOUSSAINT LOUVERTURE)

c'est un homme qui fascine
l'épervier blanc de la mort blanche
c'est un homme seul dans la mer
inféconde de sable blanc
c'est un moricaud vieux dressé contre
les eaux du ciel

here I am, severed from the cool oases of brotherhood
this so modest nothing bristles with hard splinters
this too safe horizon is startled like a jailer.

 Your last triumph, tenacious crow of Treason.
 What is mine, these few thousand deathbearers who mill in the calabash of an island and mine
too, the archipelago arched with an anguished desire to negate itself, as if from maternal anxiety to
protect this impossibly delicate tenuity separating one America from another; and these loins which
secrete for Europe the hearty liquor of a Gulf Stream, and one of the two slopes of incandescence
between which the Equator tightropewalks toward Europe. And my nonfence island, its brave
audacity standing at the stern of this Polynesia, before it, Guadeloupe, split in two down its dorsal
line and equal in poverty to us, Haiti where negritude rose for the first time and stated that it believed
in its humanity and the funny little tail of Florida where the strangulation of a nigger is being
completed, and Africa gigantically caterpillaring up to the Hispanic foot of Europe it nakedness
where Death scythes widely.

 And I say to myself Bordeaux and Nantes and Liverpool and New York and San Francisco

not an inch of this world devoid of my fingerprint
and my calcaneum on the spines of skyscrapers and my filth in the glitter of gems!
Who can boast of being better off than I? Virginia.
Tennessee. Georgia. Alabama
monstrous putrefactions of stymied
revolts
marshes of putrid blood
trumpets absurdly muted
land red, sanguineous, consanguineous land.

 What is mine also: a little
cell in the Jura,
a little cell, the snow lines it with white bars
the snow is a jailer mounting
guard before a prison

What is mine
a lonely man imprisoned in
whiteness
a lonely man defying the white
screams of white death
(TOUSSAINT, TOUSSAINT L'OUVERTURE)

a man who mesmerizes
the white hawk of white death
a man alone in the sterile
sea of white sand
a coon grown old standing up to
the waters of the sky

La mort décrit un cercle brillant
au-dessus de cet homme
la mort étoile doucement au-dessus de sa tête
la mort souffle, folle, dans la cannaie
mûre de ses bras
la mort galope dans la prison comme
un cheval blanc
la mort luit dans l'ombre comme des
yeux de chat
la mort hoquette comme l'eau sous les Cayes
la mort est un oiseau blessé
la mort décroît
la mort vacille
la mort est un patyura ombrageux
la mort expire dans un blanche mare
de silence.
Gonflements de nuit aux quatre coins
de ce petit matin
soubresauts de mort figée
destin tenace
cris debout de terre muette
la splendeur de ce sang n'éclatera-t-elle point?

      Au bout du petit matin ces pays sans stèle, ces chemins sans mémoire, ces vents sans tablette.
      Qu'importe?
      Nous dirions. Chanterions. Hurlerions.
      Voix pleine, voix large, tu serais notre bien, notre pointe en avant.
      Des mots?
      Ah oui, des mots!

Raison, je te sacre vent du soir.
Bouche de l'ordre ton nom?
Il m'est corolle du fouet.
Beauté je t'appelle pétition de la pierre.
Mais ah! la rauque contrebande
de mon rire
Ah! mon trésor de salpêtre!
Parce que nous vous haïssons vous
et votre raison nous nous réclamons
de la démence précoce de la folie flamboyante
du cannibalisme tenace

Trésor, comptons:
la folie qui se souvient
la folie qui hurle
la folie qui voit
la folie qui se déchaîne

Death traces a shining circle
above this man
death stars softly above his head
death breathes, crazed, in the ripened
cane field of his arms
death gallops in the prison like
a white horse
death gleams in the dark like the
eyes of a cat
death hiccups like water under the Keys
death is a struck bird
death wanes
death flickers
death is a very shy patyura
death expires in a white pool
of silence.
Swellings of night in the four corners
of this dawn
convulsions of congealed death
tenacious fate
screams erect from mute earth
the splendor of this blood will it not burst open?

      At the end of the wee hours this land without a stele, these paths without memory, these winds without a tablet.
      So what?
      We would tell. Would sing. Would howl.
      Full voice, ample voice, you would be our wealth, our spear pointed.
      Words?
      Ah yes, words!

Reason, I crown you evening wind.
Your name voice of order?
To me the whip's corolla.
Beauty I call you the false claim of the stone.
But ah! my raucous laughter
smuggled in
Ah! my saltpetre treasure!
Because we hate you
and your reason, we claim kinship
with dementia praecox with the flaming madness
of persistent cannibalism

Treasure, let's count:
the madness that remembers
the madness that howls
the madness that sees
the madness that is unleashed

Et vous savez le reste

Que 2 et 2 font 5
que la forêt miaule
que l'arbre tire les marrons du feu
que le ciel se lisse la barbe
et caetera et caetera . . .

Qui et quels nous sommes?
Admirable question!

A force de regarder les arbres je suis
devenu un arbre et mes longs pieds
d'arbre ont creusé dans le sol de larges
sacs à venin de hautes villes d'ossements
à force de penser au Congo
je suis devenu un Congo bruissant de
forêts et de fleuves
où le fouet claque comme un grand étendard
l'étendard du prophète
où l'eau fait
likouala-likouala
où l'éclair de la colère lance sa hache
verdâtre et force les sangliers de la
putréfaction dans la belle orée violente
des narines.

Au bout du petit matin le soleil qui
toussotte et crache ses poumons

Au bout du petit matin
un petit train de sable
un petit train de mousseline
un petit train de grains de maïs
Au bout du petit matin
un grand galop de pollen
un grand galop d'un petit train de
petites filles
un grand galop de colibris
un grand galop de dagues pour défoncer
la poitrine de la terre

douaniers anges qui montez aux portes
de l'écume la garde des prohibitions

je déclare mes crimes et il n'y a rien à
dire pour ma défense.
Danses. Idoles. Relaps. Moi aussi

And you know the rest

That 2 and 2 are 5
that the forest miaows
that the tree plucks the maroons from the fire
that the sky strokes its beard
etc. etc. . . .

Who and what are we?
A most worthy question!

From staring too long at trees I have
become a tree and my long tree
feet have dug in the ground large
venom sacs high cities of bone
from brooding too long on the Congo
I have become a Congo resounding with
forests and rivers
where the whip cracks like a great banner
the banner of a prophet
where the water goes
likouala-likouala
where the angerbolt hurls its greenish
axe forcing the boars of
putrefaction to the lovely wild edge
of the nostrils.

At the end of the wee hours the sun which
hacks and spits up its lungs

At the end of the wee hours
a slow gait of sand
a slow gait of gauze
a slow gait of corn kernels
At the end of the wee hours
a full gallop of pollen
a full gallop of a slow gait of
little girls
a full gallop of hummingbirds
a full gallop of daggers to stave in
the earth's breast

customs angels mounting guard over
prohibitions at the gates of foam

I declare my crimes and that there is nothing
to say in my defense.
Dances. Idols. An apostate. I too

J'ai assassiné Dieu de ma paresse de
mes paroles de mes gestes
de mes chansons obscènes

J'ai porté des plumes de perroquet des
dépouilles de chat musqué
J'ai lassé la patience des missionnaires
insulté les bienfaiteurs de l'humanité.
Défié Tyr. Défié Sidon.
Adoré le Zambèze.
L'étendue de ma perversité me confond!

Mais pourquoi brousse impénétrable encore cacher le vif zéro de ma mendicité et par un souci de
noblesse apprise ne pas entonner l'horrible bond de ma laideur pahouine?

voum rooh oh
voum rooh oh
à charmer les serpents à conjurer
les morts
voum rooh oh
à contraindre la pluie à contrarier
les raz de marée
voum rooh oh
à empêcher que ne tourne l'ombre
voum rooh oh que mes cieux à moi
s'ouvrent

—moi sur une route, enfant, mâchant
une racine de canne à sucre
—traîné homme sur une route sanglante
une corde au cou
—debout au milieu d'un cirque immense,
sur mon front noir une couronne de daturas
voum rooh
s'envoler
plus haut que le frisson plus haut
que les sorcières vers d'autres étoiles
exaltation féroce de forêts et
montagnes déracinées à l'heure
où nul n'y pense
les îles liées pour mille ans!

voum rooh oh
pour que revienne le temps de promission
et l'oiseau qui savait mon nom
et la femme qui avait mille noms
de fontaine de soleil et de pleurs

I have assassinated God with my laziness with
my words with my gestures
with my obscene songs

I have worn parrot plumes
musk cat skins
I have exhausted the missionaries' patience
insulted the benefactors of mankind.
Defied Tyre. Defied Sidon.
Worshipped the Zambezi.
The extent of my perversity overwhelms me!

But why impenetrable jungle are you still hiding the raw zero of my mendacity and from a
self-conscious concern for nobility not celebrating the horrible leap of my Pahouin ugliness?   *

voum rooh oh
voum rooh oh
to charm the snakes to conjure
the dead
voum rooh oh
to compel the rain to turn back
the tidal waves
voum rooh oh
to keep the shade from moving
voum rooh oh that my own skies
may open

—me on a road, a child, chewing
sugar cane root
—a dragged man on a bloodspattered road
a rope around his neck
—standing in the center of a huge circus,
on my black forehead a crown of daturas
voum rooh
to fly off
higher than quivering higher
than the sorceresses toward other stars
ferocious exultation of forests and
mountains uprooted at the hour
when no one expects it
the islands linked for a thousand years!

voum rooh oh
that the promised times may return
and the bird who knew my name
and the woman who had a thousand names
names of fountain sun and tears

et ses cheveux d'alevin
et ses pas mes climats
et ses yeux mes saisons
et les jours sans nuisance
et les nuits sans offense
et les étoiles de confidence
et le vent de connivence

Mais qui tourne ma voix? qui écorche
ma voix? Me fourrant dans la
gorge mille crocs de bambou. Mille
pieux d'oursin. C'est toi sale bout
de monde. Sale bout de petit matin.
C'est toi sale haine. C'est toi poids
de l'insulte et cent ans de coups
de fouet. C'est toi cent ans de ma
patience, cent ans de mes soins
juste à ne pas mourir.
rooh oh
nous chantons les fleurs vénéneuses
éclatant dans des prairies furibondes;
les ciels d'amour coupés d'embolie;
les matins épileptiques; le blanc embrasement
des sables abyssaux, les descentes
d'épaves dans les nuits foudroyées
d'odeurs fauves.

Qu'y puis-je?

Il faut bien commencer.

Commencer quoi?

La seule chose au monde qui vaille
la peine de commencer:
La Fin du monde parbleu.

Tourte
ô tourte de l'effroyable automne
où poussent l'acier neuf et le béton
vivace
tourte ô tourte
où l'air se rouille en grandes plaques
d'allégresse mauvaise
où l'eau sanieuse balafre les grandes
joues solaires
je vous hais

and her hair of minnows
and her steps my climates
and her eyes my seasons
and the days without injury
and the nights without offense
and the stars my confidence
and the wind my accomplice

But who misleads my voice? who grates
my voice? Stuffing my throat
with a thousand bamboo fangs. A thousand
sea urchin stakes. It is you dirty end
of the world. Dirty end of the wee hours.
It is you dirty hatred. It is you weight
of the insult and a hundred years of whip
lashes. It is you one hundred years of my
patience, one hundred years of my effort
simply to stay alive
rooh oh
we sing of venomous flowers
flaring in fury-filled prairies;
the skies of love cut with bloodclots;
the epileptic mornings; the white blaze
of abyssal sands, the sinking
of flotsam in nights electrified
with feline smells.

What can I do?

One must begin somewhere.

Begin what?

The only thing in the world
worth beginning:
The End of the world of course.

Torte
oh torte of the terrifying autumn
where the new steel and the perennial concrete
grow
torte oh torte
where the air rusts in great sheets
of evil glee
where the sanious water scars the great
solar cheeks
I hate you

on voit encore des madras aux reins
des femmes des anneaux à leurs oreilles
des sourires à leurs bouche des enfants
à leurs mamelles et j'en passe:

ASSEZ DE CE SCANDALE!

Alors voilà le grand défi et l'impulsion
sataniques et l'insolente
dérive nostalgique de lunes rousses,
de feux verts, de fièvres jaunes!

En vain dans la tiédeur de votre gorge
mûrissez-vous vingt fois la même pauvre
consolation que nous sommes des
marmonneurs de mots

Des mots? quand nous manions des
quartiers de monde, quand nous épousons
des continents en délire, quand
nous forçons de fumantes portes,
des mots, ah oui, des mots! mais
des mots de sang frais, des mots qui sont
des raz-de-marée et des érésipèles
des paludismes et des laves et des feux
de brousse, et des flambées de chair,
et des flambées de villes . . .

Sachez-le bien:
je ne joue jamais si ce n'est à l'an mil
je ne joue jamais si ce n'est à la Grande
Peur

Accommodez-vous de moi. Je ne m'accommode pas de vous!

Parfois on me voit d'un grand geste du cerveau,
happer un nuage trop rouge
ou une caresse de pluie, ou un prélude
du vent,
ne vous tranquillisez pas outre mesure:

Je force la membrane vitelline qui me
sépare de moi-même,
Je force les grandes eaux qui me ceinturent de sang

C'est moi rien que moi qui arrête ma
place sur le dernier train de la dernière
vague du dernier raz-de-marée

one still sees madras rags around the loins
of women rings in their ears
smiles on their lips babies
at their nipples, these for starters:

ENOUGH OF THIS OUTRAGE!

So here is the great challenge and the satanic
compulsion and the insolent
nostalgic drift of April moons,
of green fires, of yellow fevers!

Vainly in the tepidity of your throat
you ripen for the twentieth time the same indigent
solace that we are
mumblers of words

Words? while we handle
quarters of earth, while we wed
delirious continents, while
we force steaming gates,
words, ah yes, words! but
words of fresh blood, words that are
tidal waves and erysipelas
malarias and lava and brush
fires, and blazes of flesh,
and blazes of cities . . .

Know this:
the only game I play is the millenium
the only game I play is the Great
Fear

Put up with me. I won't put up with you!

Sometimes you see me with a great display of brains
snap up a cloud too red
or a caress of rain, or a prelude
of wind,
don't fool yourself:

I am forcing the vitelline membrane that separates
me from myself,
I am forcing the great waters which girdle me with blood

I and I alone choose
a seat on the last train of the last
surge of the last tidal wave

C'est moi rien que moi
qui prends langue avec la dernière
angoisse

C'est moi oh, rien que moi
qui m'assure au chalumeau
les premières gouttes de lait virginal!

Et maintenant un dernier zut:
au soleil (il ne suffit pas à soûler
ma tête très forte)
à la nuit farineuse avec les pondaisons
d'or des lucioles incertaines
à la chevelure qui tremble tout au
haut de la falaise
le vent y saute en inconstantes cavaleries
salées
je lis bien à mon pouls que l'exotisme
n'est pas provende pour moi

Au sortir de l'Europe toute révulsée de cris
les courants silencieux de la désespérance
au sortir de l'Europe peureuse qui se
reprend et fière se surestime
je veux cet égoïsme beau
et qui s'aventure
et mon labour me remémore d'une implacable étrave.

Que de sang dans ma mémoire! Dans ma mémoire sont les lagunes. Elles sont couvertes de têtes de
morts. Elles ne sont pas couvertes de nénuphars.
Dans ma mémoire sont des lagunes. Sur leurs rives ne sont pas étendus des pagnes de femmes.
Ma mémoire est entourée de sang. Ma mémoire a sa ceinture de cadavres!
et mitraille de barils de rhum génialement arrosant
nos révoltes ignobles, pâmoisons d'yeux doux d'avoir
lampé la liberté féroce

(les nègres-sont-tous-les-mêmes, je-vous-le-dis les vices-tous-les-vices, c'est-moi-qui-vous-le-dis
l'odeur-du-nègre, ça-fait-pousser-la-canne
rappelez-vous-le-vieux-dicton:
battre-un-nègre, c'est le nourrir)
autour des rockings-chairs méditant la volupté des rigoises
je tourne, inapaisée pouliche

Ou bien tout simplement comme on nous aime!
Obscènes gaiement, très doudous de jazz sur leur excès d'ennui.
Je sais le tracking, le Lindy-hop et les claquettes.
Pour les bonnes bouches la sourdine de nos plaintes enrobées de oua-oua. Attendez . . . Tout est dans
l'ordre. Mon bon ange broute du néon. J'avale des baguettes. Ma dignité se vautre dans les dégobille-
ments . . .

I and I alone
make contact with the latest
anguish

I and oh, only I
secure the first
drops of virginal milk through a straw!

And now a last boo:
to the sun (not strong enough to inebriate
my very tough head)
to the mealy night with its golden
hatchings of erratic fireflies
to the head of hair trembling at the very
top of the cliff
where the wind leaps in bursts of salty
cavalries
I clearly read in my pulse that for me
exoticism is no provender

Leaving Europe utterly twisted with screams
the silent currents of despair
leaving timid Europe which
collects and proudly overrates itself
I summon this egotism beautiful
and bold
and my ploughing reminds me of an implacable cutwater.

So much blood in my memory! In my memory are lagoons. They are covered with death's-heads.
They are not covered with water lilies.
In my memory are lagoons. No women's loincloths spread out on their shores.
My memory is encircled with blood. My memory has a belt of corpses!
and machine gun fire of rum barrels brilliantly sprinkling
our ignominious revolts, amorous glances swooning from having
swigged too much ferocious freedom

(niggers-are-all-alike, I-tell-you vices-all-the-vices-believe-you-me
nigger-smell, that's-what-makes-cane-grow
remember-the-old-saying:
beat-a-nigger, and you feed him)
among "rocking chairs" contemplating the voluptuousness of quirts   *
I circle about, an unappeased filly

Or else quite simply as they like to think of us!
Cheerfully obscene, completely nuts about jazz to cover their extreme boredom
I can boogie-woogie, do the Lindy-hop and tap-dance.   *
And for a special treat the muting of our cries muffled with wah-wah. Wait . . . Everything is as it
should be. My good angel grazes the neon. I swallow batons. My dignity wallows in puke . . .

Soleil, Ange Soleil, Ange frisé du Soleil
    pour un bond par-delà la nage verdâtre
et douce des eaux de l'abjection!

Mais je me suis adressé au mauvais sorcier, sur cette terre exorcisée, larguée à la dérive de sa précieuse intention maléfique, cette voix qui crie, lentement enrouée, vainement, vainement enrouée,

et il n'y a que les fientes accumulées de nos mensonges—et qui ne répondent pas. Quelle folie le merveilleux entrechat par moi rêvé au-dessus de la bassesse!
Parbleu les Blancs sont de grands guerriers hosannah pour le maître et pour le châtre-nègre!
Victoire! Victoire, vous dis-je: les vaincus sont contents!
Joyeuses puanteurs et chants de boue!

Par une inattendue et bienfaisante révolution intérieure, j'ignore maintenant mes laideurs repoussantes.

A la Saint-Jean-Baptiste, dès que tombent les premières ombres sur le bourg du Gros-Morne, des centaines de maquignons se réunissent dans la rue "De PROFUNDIS", dont le nom a du moins la franchise d'avertir d'une ruée des bas-fonds de la Mort. Et c'est de la mort véritablement, de ses mille mesquines formes locales (fringales inassouvies d'herbe de Para et rond asservissement des distilleries) que surgit vers la grand-vie déclose l'étonnante cavalerie des rosses impétueuses. Et quels galops! quels hennissements! quelles sincères urines! quelles fientes mirobolantes! "Un beau cheval difficile au montoir!"—"Une altière jument sensible à la molette!"—"Un intrépide poulain vaillamment jointé!"

Et le malin compère dont le gilet se barre d'une fière chaîne de montre, refile au lieu de pleines mamelles, d'ardeur juvénile, de rotondités authentiques, ou les boursouflures régulières de guêpes complaisantes, ou les obscènes morsures du gingembre, ou la bienfaisante circulation d'un décalitre d'eau sucrée.

Je refuse de me donner mes boursouflures comme d'authentiques gloires.
Et je ris de mes anciennes imaginations puériles.
Non, nous n'avons jamais été Amazones du roi du Dahomey, ni princes du Ghana avec huit cents chameaux, ni docteurs à Tombouctou Askia le Grand étant roi, ni architectes de Djénné, ni Madhis, ni guerriers. Nous ne nous sentons pas sous l'aisselle la démangeaison de ceux qui tinrent jadis la lance. Et puisque j'ai juré de ne rien celer de notre histoire (moi qui n'admire rien tant que le mouton broutant son ombre d'après-midi), je veux avouer que nous fûmes de tout temps d'assez piètres laveurs de vaisselle, des cireurs de chaussures sans envergure, mettons les choses au mieux, d'assez consciencieux sorciers et le seul indiscutable record que nous ayons battu est celui d'endurance à la chicotte . . .

Et ce pays cria pendant des siècles que nous sommes des bêtes brutes; que les pulsations de l'humanité s'arrêtent aux portes de la négrerie; que nous sommes un fumier ambulant hideusement prometteur de cannes tendres et de coton soyeux et l'on nous marquait au fer rouge et nous dormions dans nos excréments et l'on nous vendait sur les places et l'aune de drap anglais et la viande salée d'Irlande coûtaient moins cher que nous, et ce pays était calme, tranquille, disant que l'esprit de Dieu était dans ses actes.

Nous vomissure de négrier
Nous vénerie des Calabars

Sun, Angel Sun, curled Angel of the Sun
for a leap beyond the sweet and greenish
treading of the waters of abjection!

But I approached the wrong sorcerer, on this exorcised earth, cast adrift from its precious malignant purpose, this voice that cries, little by little hoarse, vainly, vainly hoarse,
and there remains only the accumulated droppings of our lies—and they do not respond.
What madness to dream up a marvelous caper above the baseness!
Oh Yes the Whites are great warriors hosannah to the master and to the nigger-gelder!
Victory! Victory, I tell you: the defeated are content!
Joyous stenches and songs of mud!
By a sudden and beneficent inner revolution, I now ignore my repugnant ugliness.

On Midsummer Day, as soon as the first shadows fall on the village of Gros-Morne, hundreds of horse dealers gather on rue "De PROFUNDIS," a name at least honest enough to announce an onrush from the shoals of Death. And it truly is from Death, from its thousand petty local forms (cravings unsatisfied by Para grass and tipsy bondage to the distilleries) that the astonishing cavalry of impetuous nags surges unfenced toward the great-life. What a galloping! what neighing! what sincere urinating! what prodigious droppings! "A fine horse difficult to mount!"—"A proud mare sensitive to the spur"—"A fearless foal superbly pasterned!"
And the shrewd fellow whose waistcoat displays a proud watch chain, palms off instead of full udders, youthful mettle and genuine contours, either the systematic puffiness from obliging wasps, or the obscene stings from ginger, or the helpful distribution of several gallons of sugared water.

I refuse to pass off my puffiness for authentic glory.
And I laugh at my former childish fantasies.
No, we've never been Amazons of the king of Dahomey, nor princes of Ghana with eight hundred camels, nor wise men in Timbuktu under Askia the Great, nor the architects of Djenne, nor Madhis, nor warriors. We don't feel under our armpit the itch of those who in the old days carried a lance. And since I have sworn to leave nothing out of our history (I who love nothing better than a sheep grazing his own afternoon shadow), I may as well confess that we were at all times pretty mediocre dishwashers, shoeblacks without ambition, at best conscientious sorcerers and the only unquestionable record that we broke was that of endurance under the chicote . . .   *

And this land screamed for centuries that we are bestial brutes; that the human pulse stops at the gates of the slave compound; that we are walking compost hideously promising tender cane and silky cotton and they would brand us with red-hot irons and we would sleep in our excrement and they would sell us on the town square and an ell of English cloth and salted meat from Ireland cost less than we did, and this land was calm, tranquil, repeating that the spirit of the Lord was in its acts.

We the vomit of slave ships
We the venery of the Calabars
what? Plug up our ears?
We, so drunk on jeers and inhaled fog that we rode the roll to death!
Forgive us fraternal whirlwind!

I hear coming up from the hold the enchained curses, the gasps of the dying, the noise of someone thrown into the sea . . . the baying of a woman in labor . . . the scrape of fingernails

quoi? Se boucher les oreilles?
Nous, soûlés à crever le roulis, de risées, de brume humée!
Pardon tourbillon partenaire!

J'entends de la cale monter les malédictions enchaînées, les hoquettements des mourants, le bruit d'un qu'on jette à la mer . . . les abois d'une femme en gésine . . . des raclements d'ongles cherchant des gorges . . . des ricanements de fouet . . . des farfouillis de vermine parmi les lassitudes . . .

Rein ne put nous insurger jamais vers quelque noble aventure désespérée.
Ainsi soit-il. Ainsi soit-il.
Je ne suis d'aucune nationalité prévue par les chancelleries.
Je défie le craniomètre. Homo sum etc.
Et qu'ils servent et trahissent et meurent.
Ainsi soit-il. Ainsi soit-il. C'était écrit dans la forme de leur bassin.

Et moi, et moi,
moi qui chantais le poing dur.
Il faut savoir jusqu'où je poussai la lâcheté. Un soir, dans un tramway en face de moi, un nègre.
C'était un nègre grand comme un pongo qui essayait de se faire tout petit sur un banc de tramway. Il essayait d'abandonner sur ce banc crasseux de tramway ses jambes gigantesques et ses mains tremblantes de boxeur affamé. Et tout l'avait laissé, le laissait. Son nez qui semblait une péninsule en dérade et sa négritude même qui se décolorait sous l'action d'une inlassable mégie. Et le mégissier était la Misère. Un gros oreillard subit dont les coups de griffes sur ce visage s'étaient cicatrisés en îlots scabieux. Ou plutôt, c'était un ouvrier infatigable, la Misère, travaillant à quelque cartouche hideux. On voyait très bien comment le pouce industrieux et malveillant avait modelé le front en bosse, percé le nez de deux tunnels parallèles et inquiétants, allongé la démesure de la lippe, et par un chef-d'œuvre caricatural, raboté, poli, verni la plus minuscule mignonne petite oreille de la création.
C'était un nègre dégingandé sans rythme ni mesure.
Un nègre dont les yeux roulaient une lassitude sanguinolente.
Un nègre sans pudeur et ses orteils ricanaient de façon assez puante au fond de la tanière entrebâillée de ses souliers.
La misère, on ne pouvait pas dire, s'était donné un mal fou pour l'achever.
Elle avait creusé l'orbite, l'avait fardée d'un fard de poussière et de chassie mêlées.
Elle avait tendu l'espace vide entre l'accrochement solide des mâchoires et les pommettes d'une vieille joue décatie. Elle avait planté dessus les petits pieux luisants d'une barbe de plusieurs jours. Elle avait affolé le cœur, voûté le dos.
Et l'ensemble faisait parfaitement un nègre hideux, un nègre grognon, un nègre mélancolique, un nègre affalé, ses mains réunies en prière sur un bâton noueux. Un nègre enseveli dans une vieille veste élimée. Un nègre comique et laid et des femmes derrière moi ricanaient en le regardant.
Il était COMIQUE ET LAID,
COMIQUE ET LAID pour sûr.
J'arborai un grand sourire complice . . .
Ma lâcheté retrouvée!
Je salue les trois siècles qui soutiennent mes droits civiques et mon sang minimisé.
Mon héroïsme, quelle farce!
Cette ville est à ma taille.
Et mon âme est couchée. Comme cette ville dans la crasse et dans la boue couchée.

seeking throats . . . the flouts of the whip . . . the seethings of vermin amid the weariness . . .

Nothing could ever lift us toward a noble hopeless adventure.
So be it. So be it.
I am of no nationality recognized by the chancelleries.
I defy the craniometer. Homo sum etc.
Let them serve and betray and die
So be it. So be it. It was written in the shape of their pelvis.

And I, and I,
I was singing the hard fist
You must know the extent of my cowardice. One evening on the streetcar facing me, a nigger.

A nigger big as a pongo trying to make himself small on the streetcar bench. He was trying to leave behind, on this grimy bench, his gigantic legs and his trembling famished boxer hands. And everything had left him, was leaving him. His nose which looked like a drifting peninsula and even his negritude discolored as a result of untiring tawing. And the tawer was Poverty. A big unexpected lop-eared bat whose claw marks in his face had scabbed over into crusty islands. Or rather, it was a tireless worker, Poverty was, working on some hideous cartouche. One could easily see how that industrious and malevolent thumb had kneaded bumps into his brow, bored two bizarre parallel tunnels in his nose, overexaggerated his lips, and in a masterpiece of caricature, planed, polished and varnished the tiniest cutest little ear in all creation.

He was a gangly nigger without rhythm or measure.

A nigger whose eyes rolled a bloodshot weariness.

A shameless nigger and his toes sneered in a rather stinking way at the bottom of the yawning lair of his shoes.

Poverty, without any question, had knocked itself out to finish him off.

It had dug the socket, had painted it with a rouge of dust mixed with rheum.

It had stretched an empty space between the solid hinge of the jaw and bone of an old tarnished cheek. Had planted over it the small shiny stakes of a two- or three-day beard. Had panicked his heart, bent his back.

And the whole thing added up perfectly to a hideous nigger, a grouchy nigger, a melancholy nigger, a slouched nigger, his hands joined in prayer on a knobby stick. A nigger shrouded in an old threadbare coat. A comical and ugly nigger, with some women behind me sneering at him.

He was COMICAL AND UGLY,

COMICAL AND UGLY for sure.

I displayed a big complicitous smile . . .

My cowardice rediscovered!

Hail to the three centuries which uphold my civil rights and my minimized blood!
My heroism, what a farce!
This town fits me to a t.
And my soul is lying down. Lying down like this town in its refuse and mud.
This town, my face of mud.
For my face I demand the vivid homage of spit! . . .
So, being what we are, ours the warrior thrust, the triumphant knee, the well-plowed plains of the future?
Look, I'd rather admit to uninhibited ravings, my heart in my brain like a drunken knee.
My star now, the funereal menfenil.   *

Cette ville, ma face de boue.

Je réclame pour ma face la louange éclatante du crachat! . . .

Alors, nous étant tels, à nous l'élan viril, le genou vainqueur, les plaines à grosses mottes à l'avenir?

Tiens, je préfère avouer que j'ai généreusement déliré, mon cœur dans ma cervelle ainsi qu'un genou ivre.

Mon étoile maintenant, le menfenil funèbre.

Et sur ce rêve ancien mes cruautés cannibales:

(Les balles dans la bouche salive épaisse

notre cœur de quotidienne bassesse éclate les continents rompent la frêle attache des isthmes

des terres sautent suivant la division fatale des fleuves

et le morne qui depuis des siècles retient son cri au-dedans de lui-même, c'est lui qui à son tour écartèle

le silence et ce peuple vaillance rebondissante

et nos membres vainement disjoints par les plus raffinés supplices

et la vie plus impétueuse jaillissant de ce fumier—comme le corossolier imprévu parmi la décomposition des fruits du jacquier!)

Sur ce rêve vieux en moi mes cruautés cannibales

Je me cachais derrière une vanité stupide le destin m'appelait j'étais caché derrière et voici l'homme par terre, sa très fragile défense dispersée,

ses maximes sacrées foulées aux pieds, ses déclamations pédantesques rendant du vent par chaque blessure.

Voici l'homme par terre

et son âme est comme nue

et le destin triomphe qui contemple se muer en l'ancestral bourbier cette âme qui le défiait.

Je dis que cela est bien ainsi.

Mon dos exploitera victorieusement la chalasie des fibres.

Je pavoiserai de reconnaissance mon obséquiosité naturelle

Et rendra des points à mon enthousiasme le boniment gallonné d'argent du postillon de la Havane, lyrique babouin entremetteur des splendeurs de la servitude.

Je dis que cela est bien ainsi.

Je vis pour le plus plat de mon âme.

Pour le plus terne de ma chair!

   Tiède petit matin de chaleur et de peur ancestrales

je tremble maintenant du commun tremblement que notre sang docile chante dans le madrépore.

Et ces têtards en moi éclos de mon ascendance prodigieuse!

Ceux qui n'ont inventé ni la poudre ni la boussole

ceux qui n'ont jamais su dompter la vapeur ni l'électricité

ceux qui n'ont exploré ni les mers ni le ciel mais ils savent

en ses moindres recoins le pays de souffrance

ceux qui n'ont connu de voyages que de déracinements

And on this former dream my cannibalistic cruelties:

(The bullets in the mouth thick saliva
our heart from daily lowness bursts the continents break the fragile bond of isthmuses
lands leap in accordance with the fatal division of rivers
and the morne which for centuries kept its scream within itself, it is its turn to draw and quarter the
silence and this people an ever-rebounding spirit
and our limbs vainly disjointed by the most refined tortures
and life even more impetuously jetting from this compost—unexpected as a soursop amidst the
decomposition of jack tree fruit!)

On this dream so old in me my cannibalistic cruelties

I was hiding behind a stupid vanity destiny called me I was hiding behind it and suddenly there was a
man on the ground, his feeble defenses scattered,
his sacred maxims trampled underfoot, his pedantic rhetoric oozing air through each wound.
There is a man on the ground
and his soul is almost naked
and destiny triumphs in watching this soul which defied its metamorphosis in the ancestral slough.

I say that this is right.
My back will victoriously exploit the chalaza of fibers.
I will deck my natural obsequiousness with gratitude
And the silver-braided bullshit of the postillion of Havana, lyrical baboon pimp for the glamour of
slavery, will be more than a match for my enthusiasm.

I say that this is right.
I live for the flattest part of my soul.
For the dullest part of my flesh!

      Tepid dawn of ancestral heat and fear
I now tremble with the collective trembling that our docile blood sings in the madrepore.

And these tadpoles hatched in me by my prodigious ancestry!
Those who invented neither powder nor compass
those who could harness neither steam nor electricity
those who explored neither the seas nor the sky but who know
in its most minute corners the land of suffering
those who have known voyages only through uprootings
those who have been lulled to sleep by so much kneeling
those whom they domesticated and Christianized
those whom they inoculated with degeneracy
tom-toms of empty hands
inane tom-toms of resounding sores
burlesque tom-toms of tabetic treason

ceux qui se sont assoupis aux agenouillements
ceux qu'on domestiqua et christianisa
ceux qu'on inocula d'abâtardissement
tam-tams de mains vides
tam-tams inanes de plaies sonores
tam-tams burlesques de trahison tabide

      Tiède petit matin de chaleurs et de peurs ancestrales
par-dessus bord des richesses pérégrines
par-dessus bord mes faussetés authentiques
Mais quel étrange orgueil tout soudain m'illumine?
vienne le colibri
vienne l'épervier
vienne le bris de l'horizon
vienne le cynocéphale
vienne le lotus porteur du monde
vienne de dauphins une insurrection perlière
brisant la coquille de la mer
vienne un plongeon d'îles
vienne la disparition des jours de chair
morte dans la chaux vive des rapaces
viennent les ovaires de l'eau où le futur agite ses petites têtes
viennent les loups qui pâturent dans les orifices sauvages du corps à l'heure où à l'auberge écliptique se
rencontrent ma lune et ton soleil

il y a sous la réserve de ma luette une bauge de sangliers
il y a tes yeux qui sont sous la pierre grise du jour un conglomérat frémissant de coccinelles
il y a dans le regard du désordre cette hirondelle de menthe et de genêt qui fond pour toujours renaître
dans le raz-de-marée de ta lumière
Calme et berce ô ma parole l'enfant qui ne sait pas que la carte du printemps est toujours à refaire
les herbes balanceront pour le bétail vaisseau doux de l'espoir
le long geste d'alcool de la houle
les étoiles du chaton de leur bague jamais vue couperont les tuyaux de l'orgue de verre du soir
puis répandront sur l'extrémité riche de ma fatigue
des zinnias
des coryanthes
et toi veuille astre de ton lumineux fondement tirer lémurien du sperme insondable de l'homme la
forme non osée

que le ventre tremblant de la femme porte tel un minerai!

ô lumière amicale
ô fraîche source de la lumière
ceux qui n'ont inventé ni la poudre ni la boussole
ceux qui n'ont jamais su dompter ni la vapeur ni l'électricité
ceux qui n'ont exploré ni les mers ni le ciel mais ceux
sans qui la terre ne serait pas la terre

Tepid dawn of ancestral heat and fears
overboard with alien riches
overboard with my genuine falsehoods
But what strange pride suddenly illuminates me!
let the hummingbird come
let the sparrow hawk come
the breach in the horizon
the cynocephalus
let the lotus bearer of the world come
the pearly upheaval of dolphins
cracking the shell of the sea
let a plunge of islands come
let it come from the disappearing of days of dead
flesh in the quicklime of birds of prey
let the ovaries of the water come where the future stirs its testicles
let the wolves come who feed in the untamed openings of the body at the hour when my moon and
your sun meet at the ecliptic inn

under the reserve of my uvula there is a wallow of boars
under the grey stone of the day there are your eyes which are a shimmering conglomerate of
coccinella
in the glance of disorder there is this swallow of mint and broom which melts always to be reborn in
the tidal wave of your light
Calm and lull oh my voice the child who does not know that the map of spring is always to be
drawn again
the tall grass will sway gentle ship of hope for the cattle
the long alcoholic sweep of the swell
the stars with the bezels of their rings never in sight will cut the pipes of the glass organ of evening
zinnias
coryanthas
will then pour into the rich extremity of my fatigue
and you star please from your luminous foundation draw lemurian being—of man's unfathomable
sperm the yet undared form

carried like an ore in woman's trembling belly!

oh friendly light
oh fresh source of light
those who have invented neither powder nor compass
those who could harness neither steam nor electricity
those who explored neither the seas nor the sky but those
without whom the earth would not be the earth
gibbosity all the more beneficent as the bare earth even more earth
silo where that which is earthiest about earth ferments and ripens
my negritude is not a stone, its deafness hurled against the clamor of the day
my negritude is not a leukoma of dead liquid over the earth's dead eye
my negritude is neither tower nor cathedral

gibbosité d'autant plus bienfaisante que la terre déserte davantage la terre
silo où se préserve et mûrit ce que la terre a de plus terre
ma négritude n'est pas une pierre, sa surdité ruée contre la clameur du jour
ma négritude n'est pas une taie d'eau morte sur l'œil mort de la terre
ma négritude n'est ni une tour ni une cathédrale
elle plonge dans la chair rouge du sol
elle plonge dans la chair ardente du ciel
elle troue l'accablement opaque de sa droite patience

Eia pour le Kaïlcédrat royal!
Eia pour ceux qui n'ont jamais rien inventé
pour ceux qui n'ont jamais rien exploré
pour ceux qui n'ont jamais rien dompté

mais ils s'abandonnent, saisis, à l'essence de toute chose
ignorants des surfaces mais saisis par le mouvement de toute chose
insoucieux de dompter, mais jouant le jeu du monde
véritablement les fils aînés du monde
poreux à tous les souffles du monde
aire fraternelle de tous les souffles du monde
lit sans drain de toutes les eaux du monde
étincelle du feu sacré du monde
chair de la chair du monde palpitant du mouvement même du monde!
        Tiède petit matin de vertus ancestrales

Sang! Sang! tout notre sang ému par le cœur mâle du soleil
ceux qui savent la féminité de la lune au corps d'huile
l'exaltation réconciliée de l'antilope et de l'étoile
ceux dont la survie chemine en la germination de l'herbe!
Eia parfait cercle du monde et close concordance!

Ecoutez le monde blanc
horriblement las de son effort immense
ses articulations rebelles craquer sous les étoiles dures
ses raideurs d'acier bleu transperçant la chair mystique
écoute ses victoires proditoires trompeter ses défaites
écoute aux alibis grandioses son piètre trébuchement

Pitié pour nos vainqueurs omniscients et naïfs!

Eia pour la douleur aux pis de larmes réincarnées
pour ceux qui n'ont jamais rien exploré
pour ceux qui n'ont jamais rien dompté

Eia pour la joie
Eia pour l'amour
Eia pour la douleur aux pis de larmes réincarnées

it takes root in the red flesh of the soil
it takes root in the ardent flesh of the sky
it breaks through the opaque prostration with its upright patience

Eia for the royal Cailcedra!
Eia for those who have never invented anything
for those who never explored anything
for those who never conquered anything

but yield, captivated, to the essence of all things
ignorant of surfaces but captivated by the motion of all things
indifferent to conquering, but playing the game of the world
truly the eldest sons of the world
porous to all the breathing of the world
fraternal locus for all the breathing of the world
drainless channel for all the water of the world
spark of the sacred fire of the world
flesh of the world's flesh pulsating with the very motion of the world!
        Tepid dawn of ancestral virtues

Blood! Blood! all our blood aroused by the male heart of the sun
those who know about the femininity of the moon's oily body
the reconciled exultation of antelope and star
those whose survival travels in the germination of grass!
Eia perfect circle of the world, enclosed concordance!

Hear the white world
horribly weary from its immense efforts
its stiff joints crack under the hard stars
hear its blue steel rigidity pierce the mystic flesh
its deceptive victories tout its defeats
hear the grandiose alibis of its pitiful stumblings

Pity for our omniscient and naive conquerors!

Eia for grief and its udders of reincarnated tears
for those who have never explored anything
for those who have never conquered anything

Eia for joy
Eia for love
Eia for grief and its udders of reincarnated tears

and here at the end of these wee hours is my virile prayer that I hear neither the laughter nor the screams, my eyes fixed on this town which I prophesy, beautiful,

grant me the savage faith of the sorcerer

et voici au bout de ce petit matin ma prière virile que je n'entende ni les rires ni les cris, les yeux fixés sur
cette ville que je prophétise, belle,

donnez-moi la foi sauvage du sorcier
donnez à mes mains puissance de modeler
donnez à mon âme la trempe de l'épée
je ne me dérobe point. Faites de ma tête une tête de proue
et de moi-même, mon cœur, ne faites ni un père ni un frère
ni un fils, mais le père, mais le frère, mais le fils
ni un mari, mais l'amant de cet unique peuple.

Faites-moi rebelle à toute vanité, mais docile à son génie comme le poing à l'allongée du bras!

Faites-moi commissaire de son sang
faites-moi dépositaire de son ressentiment
faites de moi un homme de terminaison
faites de moi un homme d'initiation
faites de moi un homme de recueillement
mais faites aussi de moi un homme d'ensemencement

faites de moi l'exécuteur de ces œuvres hautes
voici le temps de se ceindre les reins comme un vaillant homme—

Mais les faisant, mon cœur, préservez-moi de toute haine
ne faites point de moi cet homme de haine
pour qui je n'ai que haine
car pour me cantonner en cette unique race
vous savez pourtant mon amour tyrannique
vous savez que ce n'est point par haine des autres races
que je m'exige bêcheur de cette unique race
que ce que je veux
c'est pour la faim universelle
pour la soif universelle

la sommer libre enfin
de produire de son intimité close
la succulence des fruits.

Et soyez l'arbre de nos mains!
il tourne, pour tous, les blessures incises
en son tronc
pour tous le sol travaille
et griserie vers les branches de précipitation parfumée!

Mais avant d'aborder aux futurs vergers
donnez-moi de les mériter sur leur ceinture de mer
donnez-moi mon cœur en attendant le sol

grant my hands power to mold
grant my soul the sword's temper
I won't flinch. Make my head into a figurehead
and as for me, my heart, do not make me into a father nor a brother,
nor a son, but into the father, the brother, the son,
nor a husband, but the lover of this unique people.

Make me resist any vanity, but espouse its genius as the fist the extended arm!

Make me a steward of its blood
make me trustee of its resentment
make me into a man for the ending
make me into a man for the beginning
make me into a man of meditation
but also make me into a man of germination

make me into the executor of these lofty works
the time has come to gird one's loins like a brave man—

But in doing so, my heart, perserve me from all hatred
do not make me into that man of hatred for whom I feel only hatred
for entrenched as I am in this unique race
you still know my tyrannical love
you know that it is not from hatred of other races
that I demand a digger for this unique race
that what I want
is for universal hunger
for universal thirst

to summon it to generate,
free at last, from its intimate closeness
the succulence of fruit.

And be the tree of our hands!
it turns, for all, the wounds cut
in its trunk
the soil works for all
and toward the branches a headiness of fragrant precipitation!

But before stepping on the shores of future orchards
grant that I deserve those on their belt of sea
grant me my heart while awaiting the earth
grant me on the ocean sterile
but somewhere caressed by the promise of the clew-line
grant me on this diverse ocean
the obstinacy of the fierce pirogue
and its marine vigor.

donnez-moi sur l'océan stérile
mais où caresse la promesse de l'amure
donnez-moi sur cet océan divers
l'obstination de la fière pirogue
et sa vigueur marine.
La voici avancer par escalades et retombées sur le flot pulvérisé
la voici danser la danse sacrée devant la grisaille du bourg
la voici barrir d'un lambi vertigineux

voici galoper le lambi jusqu'à l'indécision des mornes

et voici par vingt fois d'un labour vigoureux
la pagaie
forcer l'eau
la pirogue se cabre sous l'assaut de la lame,
dévie un instant,
tente de fuir, mais la caresse rude de la pagaie la vire,
alors elle fonce, un frémissement parcourt l'échine de la vague,
la mer bave et gronde
la pirogue comme un traîneau file sur le sable.

        Au bout de ce petit matin, ma prière virile:

donnez-moi les muscles de cette pirogue sur la mer démontée
et l'allégresse convaincante du lambi de la bonne nouvelle!
Tenez je ne suis plus qu'un homme, aucune dégradation, aucun crachat ne le conturbe, je ne suis plus
qu'un homme qui accepte n'ayant plus de colère
(il n'a plus dans le cœur que de l'amour immense, et qui brûle)

J'accepte . . . j'accepte . . . entièrement, sans réserve . . .
ma race qu'aucune ablution d'hypsope et de lys mêlés ne pourrait purifier
ma race rongée de macules
ma race raisin mûr pour pieds ivres
ma reine des crachats et des lèpres
ma reine des fouets et des scrofules
ma reine des squasmes et des chloasmes (oh ces reines que j'aimais jadis aux jardins printaniers et
lointains avec derrière l'illumination de toutes les bougies de marronniers!)
J'accepte. J'accepte.
et le nègre fustigé qui dit: "Pardon mon maître"
et les vingt-neuf coups de fouet légal
et le cachot de quatre pieds de haut
et le carcan à branches
et le jarret coupé à mon audace marronne
et la fleur de lys qui flue du fer rouge sur le gras de mon épaule
et la niche de Monsieur VAULTIER MAYENCOURT, où j'aboyai six mois de caniche
et Monsieur BRAFIN
et Monsieur de FOURNIOL

See it advance rising and falling on the pulverized wave
see it dance the sacred dance before the greyness of the village
see it trumpet from a vertiginous conch

see the conch gallop up to the uncertainty of the morne

and see twenty times over the paddle
vigorously
plow the water
the pirogue rears under the attack of the swells
deviates for an instant
tries to escape, but the paddle's rough caress turns it,
then it charges, a shudder runs along the wave's spine,
the sea slobbers and rumbles
the pirogue like a sleigh glides onto the sand.

      At the end of these wee hours, my virile prayer:

grant me pirogue muscles on this raging sea
and the irresistible gaiety of the conch of good tidings!
Look, now I am only a man, no degradation, no spit perturbs him, now I am only a man who
accepts emptied of anger
(nothing left in his heart but immense love, which burns)

I accept . . . I accept . . . totally, without reservation . . .
my race that no ablution of hyssop mixed with lilies could purify
my race pitted with blemishes
my race a ripe grape for drunken feet
my queen of spittle and leprosy
my queen of whips and scrofula
my queen of squasma and chloasma (oh those queens I once loved in the remote gardens of spring
against the illumination of all the candles of the chestnut trees!)
I accept. I accept.
and the flogged nigger saying: "Forgive me master"
and the twenty-nine legal blows of the whip
and the four-feet-high cell
and the spiked iron-collar
and the hamstringing of my runaway audacity
and the fleur de lys flowing from the red iron into the fat of my shoulder
and Monsieur VAULTIER MAYENCOURT'S dog house where I barked
six poodle months
and Monsieur BRAFIN
and Monsieur FOURNIOL
and Monsieur de la MAHAUDIERE
and the yaws
the mastiff
the suicide

et Monsieur de la MAHAUDIERE
et le pian
le molosse
le suicide
la promiscuité
le brodequin
le cep
le chevalet
le cippe
le frontal

Tenez, suis-je assez humble? Ai-je assez de cals aux genoux? De muscles aux reins?
Ramper dans les boues. S'arc-bouter dans le gras de la boue. Porter.
Sol de boue. Horizon de boue. Ciel de boue.
Morts de boue, ô noms à réchauffer dans la paume d'un souffle fiévreux!

Siméon Piquine, qui ne s'était jamais connu ni père ni mère; qu'aucune mairie n'avait jamais connu et qui toute une vie s'en était allé—cherchant son nom.

Grandvorka—celui-là je sais seulement qu'il est mort, broyé par un soir de récolte, c'était paraît-il son travail de jeter du sable sous les roues de la locomotive en marche, pour lui permettre, aux mauvais endroits, d'avancer.

Michel qui m'écrivait signant d'un nom étrange. Michel Deveine adresse *Quartier Abandonné* et vous leurs frères vivants Exélie Vêté Congolo Lemké Boussolongo quel guérisseur de ses lèvres épaisses sucerait tout au fond de la plaie béante le tenace secret du venin?

quel précautionneux sorcier déferait à vos chevilles la tiédeur visqueuse des mortels anneaux?

Présences je ne ferai pas avec le monde ma paix sur votre dos

Iles cicatrices des eaux
Iles évidences de blessures
Iles miettes
Iles informes

Iles mauvais papier déchiré sur les eaux
Iles tronçons côte à côte fichés sur l'épée flambée du Soleil
Raison rétive tu ne m'empêcheras pas de lancer absurde sur les eaux au gré des courants de ma soif
votre forme, îles difformes,
votre fin, mon défi.

Iles annelées, unique carène belle
Et je te caresse de mes mains d'océan. Et je te vire
de mes paroles alizées. Et je te lèche de mes langues d'algues.
Et je te cingle hors-flibuste

the promiscuity
the bootkin
the shackles
the rack
the cippus
the head screw

Look, am I humble enough? Have I enough calluses on my knees? Muscles on my loins?
Grovel in mud. Brace yourself in the thick of the mud. Carry.
Soil of mud. Horizon of mud. Sky of mud.
Dead of the mud, oh names to thaw in the palm of a feverish breathing!

Siméon Piquine, who never knew his father or mother; unheard of in any town hall and who
wandered his whole life—seeking a new name.

Grandvorka—of him I only know that he died, crushed one harvest evening, it was his job,
apparently, to throw sand under the wheels of the running locomotive, to help it across bad spots.

Michel who used to write me signing a strange name. Lucky Michel address *Condemned
District* and you their living brothers Exélie Vêté Congolo Lemké Boussolongo what healer with his
thick lips would suck from the depths of the gaping wound the tenacious secret of venom?

what cautious sorcerer would undo from your ankles the viscous tepidity of mortal rings?

Presences it is not on your back that I will make my peace with the world

Islands scars of the water
Islands evidence of wounds
Islands crumbs
Islands unformed

Islands cheap paper shredded upon the water
Islands stumps skewered side by side on the flaming sword of the Sun
Mulish reason you will not stop me from casting on the waters at the mercy of the currents of my
thirst
your form, deformed islands,
your end, my defiance.

Annulose islands, single beautiful hull
And I caress you with my oceanic hands. And I turn you
around with the tradewinds of my speech. And I lick you with my seaweed tongues.
And I sail you unfreebootable!

O death your mushy marsh!
Shipwreck your hellish debris! I accept!

O mort ton palud pâteux!
Naufrage ton enfer de débris! j'accepte!

Au bout du petit matin, flaques perdues, parfums errants, ouragans échoués, coques démâtées, vieilles plaies, os pourris, buées, volcans enchaînés, morts mal racinés, crier amer. J'accepte!

Et mon originale géographie aussi; la carte du monde faite à mon usage, non pas teinte aux arbitraires couleurs des savants, mais à la géométrie de mon sang répandu, j'accepte et la détermination de ma biologie, non prisonnière d'un angle facial, d'une forme de cheveux, d'un nez suffisamment aplati, d'un teint suffisamment mélanien, et la négritude, non plus un indice céphalique, ou un plasma, ou un soma, mais mesurée au compas de la souffrance
et le nègre chaque jour plus bas, plus lâche, plus stérile, moins profond, plus répandu au dehors, plus séparé de soi-même, plus rusé avec soi-même, moins immédiat avec soi-même,

j'accepte, j'accepte tout cela

et loin de la mer de palais qui déferle sous la syzygie suppurante des ampoules, merveilleusement couché le corps de mon pays dans le désespoir de mes bras, ses os ébranlés et, dans ses veines, le sang qui hésite comme la goutte de lait végétal à la pointe blessée du bulbe . . .

Et voici soudain que force et vie m'assaillent comme un taureau et l'onde de vie circonvient la papille du morne, et voilà toutes les veines et veinules qui s'affairent au sang neuf et l'énorme poumon des cyclones qui respire et le feu thésaurisé des volcans et le gigantesque pouls sismique qui bat maintenant la mesure d'un corps vivant en mon ferme embrasement.

Et nous sommes debout maintenant, mon pays et moi, les cheveux dans le vent, ma main petite maintenant dans son poing énorme et la force n'est pas en nous, mais au-dessus de nous, dans une voix qui vrille la nuit et l'audience comme la pénétrance d'une guêpe apocalyptique. Et la voix prononce que l'Europe nous a pendant des siècles gavés de mensonges et gonflés de pestilences,

car il n'est point vrai que l'œuvre de l'homme est finie
que nous n'avons rien à faire au monde
que nous parasitons le monde
qu'il suffit que nous nous mettions au pas du monde
mais l'œuvre de l'homme vient seulement de commencer
et il reste à l'homme à conquérir toute interdiction immobilisée aux coins de sa ferveur et aucune race ne possède le monopole de la beauté, de l'intelligence, de la force

et il est place pour tous au rendez-vous de la conquête et nous savons maintenant que le soleil tourne autour de notre terre éclairant la parcelle qu'a fixée notre volonté seule et que toute étoile chute de ciel en terre à notre commandement sans limite.

Je tiens maintenant le sens de l'ordalie: mon pays est la "lance de nuit" de mes ancêtres Bambaras. Elle se ratatine et sa pointe fuit désespérément vers le manche si c'est de sang de poulet qu'on l'arrose et elle dit que c'est du sang d'homme qu'il faut à son tempérament, de la graisse, du foie, du cœur d'homme, non du sang de poulet.

At the end of the wee hours, lost puddles, wandering scents, beached hurricanes, demasted hulls, old sores, rotted bones, vapors, shackled volcanoes, shallow-rooted dead, bitter cry. I accept!

And my special geography too; the world map made for my own use, not tinted with the arbitrary colors of scholars, but with the geometry of my spilled blood, I accept both the determination of my biology, not a prisoner to a facial angle, to a type of hair, to a well-flattened nose, to a clearly Melanian coloring, and negritude, no longer a cephalic index, or plasma, or soma, but measured by the compass of suffering
and the Negro every day more base, more cowardly, more sterile, less profound, more spilled out of himself, more separated from himself, more wily with himself, less immediate to himself,

I accept, I accept it all

and far from the palatial sea that foams beneath the suppurating syzygy of blisters, miraculously lying in the despair of my arms the body of my country, its bones shocked and, in its veins, the blood hesitating like a drop of vegetal milk at the injured point of the bulb . . .

Suddenly now strength and life assail me like a bull and the water of life overwhelms the papilla of the morne, now all the veins and veinlets are bustling with new blood and the enormous breathing lung of cyclones and the fire hoarded in volcanoes and the gigantic seismic pulse which now beats the measure of a living body in my firm conflagration.

And we are standing now, my country and I, hair in the wind, my hand puny in its enormous fist and now the strength is not in us but above us, in a voice that drills the night and the hearing like the penetrance of an apocalyptic wasp. And the voice proclaims that for centuries Europe has force-fed us with lies and bloated us with pestilence,

for it is not true that the work of man is done
that we have no business being on earth
that we parasite the world
that it is enough for us to heel to the world
whereas the work has only begun
and man still must overcome all the interdictions wedged in the recesses of his fervor and no race has a monopoly on beauty, on intelligence, on strength

and there is room for everyone at the convocation of conquest and we know now that the sun turns around our earth lighting the parcel designated by our will alone and that every star falls from sky to earth at our omnipotent command.

I now see the meaning of this trial by the sword: my country is the "lance of night" of my Bambara ancestors. It shrivels and its point desperately retreats toward the haft when it is sprinkled with chicken blood and it says that its nature requires the blood of man, his fat, his liver, his heart, not chicken blood.

And I seek for my country not date hearts, but men's hearts which, in order to enter the silver cities through the great trapezoidal gate, beat with warrior blood, and as my eyes sweep my

Et je cherche pour mon pays non des cœurs de datte, mais des cœurs d'homme qui, c'est pour entrer aux villes d'argent par la grand'porte trapézoïdale, qu'ils battent le sang viril, et mes yeux balayent mes kilomètres carrés de terre paternelle et je dénombre les plaies avec une sorte d'allégresse et je les entasse l'une sur l'autre comme rares espèces, et mon compte s'allonge toujours d'imprévus monnayages de la bassesse.

Et voici ceux qui ne se consolent point de n'être pas faits à la ressemblance de Dieu mais du diable, ceux qui considèrent que l'on est nègre comme commis de seconde classe: en attendant mieux et avec possibilité de monter plus haut; ceux qui battent la chamade devant soi-même, ceux qui vivent dans un cul de basse fosse de soi-même; ceux qui se drapent de pseudomorphose fière; ceux qui disent à l'Europe: "Voyez, je sais comme vous faire des courbettes, comme vous présenter mes hommages, en somme, je ne suis pas différent de vous; ne faites pas attention à ma peau noire: c'est le soleil qui m'a brûlé."

Et il y a le maquereau nègre, l'askari nègre, et tous zèbres se secouent à leur manière pour faire tomber leurs zébrures en une rosée de lait frais. Et au milieu de tout cela je dis hurrah! mon grand-père meurt, je dis hurrah! la vieille négritude progressivement se cadavérise.

Il n'y a pas à dire: c'était un bon nègre. Les Blancs disent que c'était un bon nègre, un vrai bon nègre, le bon nègre à son bon maître. Je dis hurrah!

C'était un très bon nègre,
la misère lui avait blessé poitrine et dos et on avait fourré dans sa pauvre cervelle qu'une fatalité pesait sur lui qu'on ne prend pas au collet; qu'il n'avait pas puissance sur son propre destin; qu'un Seigneur méchant avait de toute éternité écrit des lois d'interdiction en sa nature pelvienne; et d'être le bon nègre; de croire honnêtement à son indignité, sans curiosité perverse de vérifier jamais les hiéroglyphes fatidiques.

C'était un très bon nègre

et il ne lui venait pas à l'idée qu'il pourrait houer, fouir, couper tout, tout autre chose vraiment que la canne insipide

C'était un très bon nègre.

Et on lui jetait des pierres, des bouts de ferraille, des tessons de bouteille, mais ni ces pierres, ni cette ferraille, ni ces bouteilles . . . O quiètes années de Dieu sur cette motte terraquée!

et le fouet disputa au bombillement des mouches la rosée sucrée de nos plaies.

Je dis hurrah! La vieille négritude
progressivement se cadavérise
l'horizon se défait, recule et s'élargit
et voici parmi des déchirements de nuages la fulgurance d'un signe
le négrier craque de toute part . . . Son ventre se convulse et résonne . . . L'affreux ténia de sa cargaison ronge les boyaux fétides de l'étrange nourrisson des mers!

kilometers of paternal earth I number its sores almost joyfully and I pile one on top of the other like rare species, and my total is ever lengthened by unexpected mintings of baseness.

And there are those who will never get over not being made in the likeness of God but of the devil, those who believe that being a nigger is like being a second-class clerk; waiting for a better deal and upward mobility; those who beat the drum of compromise in front of themselves, those who live in their own dungeon pit; those who drape themselves in proud pseudomorphosis; those who say to Europe: "You see, I *can* bow and scrape, like you I pay my respects, in short, I am no different from you; pay no attention to my black skin: the sun did it."

And there is the nigger pimp, the nigger askari, and all the zebras shaking themselves in various ways to get rid of their stripes in a dew of fresh milk. And in the midst of all that I say right on! my grandfather dies, I say right on! the old negritude progressively cadavers itself.

No question about it: he was a good nigger. The Whites say he was a good nigger, a really good nigger, massa's good ole darky. I say right on!

He was a good nigger, indeed,
poverty had wounded his chest and back and they had stuffed into his poor brain that a fatality impossible to trap weighed on him; that he had no control over his own fate; that an evil Lord had for all eternity inscribed Thou Shall Not in his pelvic constitution; that he must be a good nigger; must sincerely believe in his worthlessness, without any perverse curiosity to check out the fatidic hieroglyphs.

He was a very good nigger

and it never occurred to him that he could hoe, burrow, cut anything, anything else really than insipid cane

He was a very good nigger.

And they threw stones at him, bits of scrap iron, broken bottles, but neither these stones, nor this scrap iron, nor these bottles . . . O peaceful years of God on this terraqueous clod!

and the whip argued with the bombilation of the flies over the sugary dew of our sores.

I say right on! The old negritude
progressively cadavers itself
the horizon breaks, recoils and expands
and through the shredding of clouds the flashing of a sign
the slave ship cracks everywhere . . . Its belly convulses and resounds . . . The ghastly tapeworm of its cargo gnaws the fetid guts of the strange suckling of the sea!

And neither the joy of sails filled like a pocket stuffed with doubloons, nor the tricks played on the dangerous stupidity of the frigates of order prevent it from hearing the threat of its intestinal rumblings

Et ni l'allégresse des voiles gonflées comme une poche de doublons rebondie, ni les tours joués à la sottise dangereuse des frégates policières ne l'empêchent d'entendre la menace de ses grondements intestins

En vain pour s'en distraire le capitaine pend à sa grand' vergue le nègre le plus braillard ou le jette à la mer, ou le livre à l'appétit de ses molosses

La négraille aux senteurs d'oignon frit retrouve dans son sang répandu le goût amer de la liberté

Et elle est debout la négraille

la négraille assise
inattendument debout
debout dans la cale
debout dans les cabines
debout sur le pont
debout dans le vent
debout sous le soleil
debout dans le sang
   debout
     et
       libre
debout et non point pauvre folle dans sa liberté et son dénuement maritimes girant en la dérive parfaite
et la voici:
plus inattendument debout
debout dans les cordages
debout à la barre
debout à la boussole
debout à la carte
debout sous les étoiles
   debout
     et
       libre
et le navire lustral s'avancer impavide sur les eaux écroulées.

Et maintenant pourrissent nos flocs d'ignominie!
par la mer cliquetante de midi
par le soleil bourgeonnant de minuit
écoute épervier qui tiens les clefs de l'orient
par le jour désarmé
par le jet de pierre de la pluie

écoute squale qui veille sur l'occident

écoutez chien blanc du nord, serpent noir du midi qui achevez le ceinturon du ciel
Il y a encore une mer à traverser
oh encore une mer à traverser

In vain to ignore them the captain hangs the biggest loudmouth nigger from the main yard or throws him into the sea, or feeds him to his mastiffs

Reeking of fried onions the nigger scum rediscovers the bitter taste of freedom in its spilled blood

And the nigger scum is on its feet

the seated nigger scum
unexpectedly standing
standing in the hold
standing in the cabins
standing on deck
standing in the wind
standing under the sun
standing in the blood
   standing
     and
       free
standing and no longer a poor madwoman in her maritime freedom and destitution gyrating in perfect drift
and there she is:
most unexpectedly standing
standing in the rigging
standing at the tiller
standing at the compass
standing at the map
standing under the stars
   standing
     and
       free
and the lustral ship fearlessly advances on the crumbling water.

And now our ignominous plops are rotting away!
by the clanking noon sea
by the burgeoning midnight sun
listen sparrow hawk who holds the keys to the orient
by the disarmed day
by the stony spurt of the rain

listen dogfish that watches over the occident

listen white dog of the north, black serpent of the south that cinches the sky girdle
There still remains one sea to cross
oh still one sea to cross

pour que j'invente mes poumons
pour que le prince se taise
pour que la reine me baise
encore un vieillard à assassiner
un fou à délivrer
pour que mon âme luise aboie luise
aboie aboie aboie
et que hulule la chouette mon bel ange curieux.
Le maître des rires?
Le maître du silence formidable?
Le maître de l'espoir et du désespoir?
Le maître de la paresse? Le maître des danses?
        C'est moi!
et pour ce, Seigneur
les hommes au cou frêle
reçois et perçois fatal calme triangulaire

Et à moi mes danses
mes danses de mauvais nègre
à moi mes danses
la danse brise-carcan
la danse saute-prison
la danse il-est-beau-et-bon-et-légitime-d'être-nègre
A moi mes danses et saute le soleil sur la raquette de mes mains

mais non l'inégal soleil ne me suffit plus
enroule-toi, vent, autour de ma nouvelle croissance
pose-toi sur mes doigts mesurés
je te livre ma conscience et son rythme de chair
je te livre les feux où brasille ma faiblesse
je te livre le chain-gang
je te livre le marais
je te livre l'intourist du circuit triangulaire
dévore vent
je te livre mes paroles abruptes
dévore et enroule-toi
et t'enroulant embrasse-moi d'un plus vaste frisson
embrasse-moi jusqu'au nous furieux
embrasse, embrasse NOUS
mais nous ayant également mordus
jusqu'au sang de notre sang mordus!
embrasse, ma pureté ne se lie qu'à ta pureté
mais alors embrasse
comme un champ de justes filaos
le soir
nos multicolores puretés
et lie, lie-moi sans remords

that I may invent my lungs
that the prince may hold his tongue
that the queen may lay me
still one old man to murder
one madman to deliver
that my soul may shine bark shine
bark bark bark
and the owl my beautiful inquisitive angel may hoot.
The master of laughter?
The master of ominous silence?
The master of hope and despair?
The master of laziness? Master of the dance?
        It is I!
and for this reason, Lord,
the frail-necked men
receive and perceive deadly triangular calm

Rally to my side my dances
you bad nigger dances
the carcan-cracker dance
the prison-break dance
the it-is-beautiful-good-and-legitimate-to-be-a-nigger-dance
Rally to my side my dances and let the sun bounce on the racket of my hands

but no the unequal sun is not enough for me
coil, wind, around my new growth
light on my cadenced fingers
to you I surrender my conscience and its fleshy rhythm
to you I surrender the fire in which my weakness smolders
to you I surrender the "chain-gang"
to you the swamps
to you the nontourist of the triangular circuit
devour wind
to you I surrender my abrupt words
devour and encoil yourself
and self-encoiling embrace me with a more ample shudder
embrace me unto furious us
embrace, embrace US
but after having drawn from us blood
drawn by our own blood!
embrace, my purity mingles only with yours
so then embrace
like a field of even filagos
at dusk
our multicolored purities
and bind, bind me without remorse

lie-moi de tes vastes bras à l'argile lumineuse
lie ma noire vibration au nombril même du monde
lie, lie-moi, fraternité âpre
puis, m'étranglant de son lasso d'étoiles
monte,
Colombe
monte
monte
monte
Je te suis, imprimée en mon ancestrale cornée blanche.
monte lécheur de ciel
et le grand trou noir où je voulais me noyer l'autre lune c'est là que je veux pêcher maintenant la langue
maléfique de la nuit en son immobile verrition!

bind me with your vast arms to the luminous clay
bind my black vibration to the very navel of the world
bind, bind me, bitter brotherhood
then, strangling me with your lasso of stars
rise,
Dove
rise
rise
rise
I follow you who are imprinted on my ancestral white cornea.
rise sky licker
and the great black hole where a moon ago I wanted to drown it is there I will now fish the malevolent tongue of the night in its motionless veerition!

LES ARMES MIRACULEUSES
*
THE MIRACULOUS WEAPONS

Wifredo Lam, "The Antillean Parade," 1945, 49½ × 43½"

Avis de tirs

J'attends au bord du monde les-voyageurs-qui-ne-viendront-pas
donnez-m'en
du lait d'enfance des pains de pluie des farines de mi-nuit et de baobab
mes mains piquées aux buissons d'astres mais cueillies d'écume
délacent avant temps
le corsage des verrous
et la foudroyante géométrie du trigonocéphale
pour mon rêve aux jambes de montre en retard
pour ma haine de cargaison coulée
pour mes 6 arbres géants de Tasmanie
pour mon château de têtes en Papouasie
pour mes aurores boréales mes sœurs mes bonnes amies
pour mon amie ma femme mon otarie
ô vous toutes mes amitiés merveilleuses, mon amie, mon amour
ma mort, mon accalmie, mes choléras
mes lévriers
mes tempes maudites
et les mines de radium enfouies dans l'abysse de mes innocences
sauteront en grains
dans la mangeoire des oiseaux
(et le stère d'étoiles
sera le nom commun du bois de chauffage
recueilli aux alluvions des veines chanteuses de nuit)
à la 61e minute de la dernière heure
la ballerine invisible exécutera des tirs au cœur
à boulets rouges d'enfer et de fleurs pour la première fois
à droite les jours sans viande sans yeux sans méfiance sans lacs
à gauche les feux de position des jours tout court et des avalanches
le pavillon noir à dents blanches du Vomito-Negro
sera hissé pendant la durée illimitée
du feu de brousse de la fraternité.

Gunnery Warning

At the edge of the world I wait for the-travelers-who-will-not-come
give me
some milk of childhood some loaves of rain some meal of midnight and of the baobab
my hands pricked in thickets of stars but gathered from the foam
unlace prematurely
the bodice of bolts
and the lightning geometry of the fer-de-lance   *
for my dream with the legs of a slow watch
for my sunken cargo hatred
for my 6 giant Tasmanian trees
for my castle of Papuan heads
for my northern lights my sisters my girlfriends
for my friend my wife my sea lion
oh all of you marvelous friendships, my friend, my love
my death, my lull, my choleras
my hounds
my cursed human temples
and the radium mines buried in the abyss of my innocences
will jump like grain
into the bird feeder
(and a cord of stars
will be the common name for firewood
gathered in the alluvium of veins singers of night)
at the 61st minute of the final hour
the invisible ballerina will perform shots in the heart
with cannonballs red from hell and from flowers for the first time
to the right the days without meat without eyes without distrust without lakes
to the left the navigation lights of days—period—and of avalanches
the white-toothed black flag of Vomito Negro
will be hoisted for the unlimited duration
of the brush fire of brotherhood.

Les pur-sang

Et voici par mon ouïe tramée de crissements
et de fusées syncoper des laideurs rêches
les cent pur-sang hennissant du soleil
parmi la stagnation.

Ah! je sens l'enfer des délices
et par les brumes nidoreuses imitant de floches
chevelures—respirations touffues de vieillards
imberbes—la tiédeur mille fois féroce
de la folie hurlante et de la mort.
Mais comment comment ne pas bénir
telle que ne l'ont point rêvée mes logiques
dure à contre-fil lézardant leur pouacre ramas
et leur saburre et plus pathétique
que la fleur fructifiante
la gerce lucide des déraisons?

Et j'entends l'eau qui monte
la nouvelle l'intouchée l'éternelle
vers l'air renouvelé.

Ai-je dit l'air?

Une flueur de cadmium avec géantes élevures
expalmées de céruse de blanches mèches
de tourmente.

Essentiel paysage.

Taillés à même la lumière de fulgurants nopals
des aurores poussantes d'inouïs blanchoiements
d'enracinées stalagmites porteuses de jour

O ardentes lactescences prés hyalins
neigeuses glanes

vers les rivières de néroli docile des haies
incorruptibles mûrissent de mica lontain
leur longue incandescence.
La paupière des brisants se referme—Prélude—
audiblement des youcas tintent
dans une lavande d'arcs-en-ciel tièdes
des huettes picorent des mordorures.

The Thoroughbreds

And behold through my ear woven with crunchings
and with rockets the hundred whinnying
thoroughbreds of the sun syncopate harsh uglinesses
amidst the stagnation.

Ah! I scent the hell of delights
and through nidorous mists mimicking flaxen
hair—bushy breathing of beardless
old men—the thousandfold ferocious tepidity
of howling madness and death.
But how how not bless
unlike anything dreamt by my logics
hard against the grain cracking their licy piles
and their saburra and more pathetic
than the fruit-bearing flower
the lucid chap of unreasons?

And I hear the water mounting
the new the untouched the timeless water
toward the renewed air.

Did I say air?

A discharge of cadmium with gigantic weals
expalmate in ceruse white wicks
of anguish.

Essence of a landscape.

Carved out of light itself fulgurating nopals
burgeoning dawns unparalleled whitescence
deep-rooted stalagmites carriers of day

O blazing lactescences hyaline meadows
snowy gleanings

toward streams of docile necroli incorruptible
hedges ripen with distant mica
their long incandescence.
The eyelids of breakers shut—Prelude—
yuccas tinkle audibly
in a lavender of tepid rainbows
owlettes peck at bronzings.

Qui
rifle,
rifle
le vacarme par delà le cœur brouillé de ce troisième jour?

Qui se perd et se déchire et se noie
dans les ondes rougies du Siloé?
Rafale.
Les lumières flanchent. Les bruits rhizulent
la rhizule
fume
silence.

Le ciel bâille d'absence noire

et voici passer
vagabondage sans nom
vers les sûres nécropoles du couchant
les soleils les pluies les galaxies
fondus en fraternel magma
et la terre oubliée la morgue des orages
qui dans son roulis ourle des déchirures
perdue patiente debout
durcifiant sauvagement l'invisible falun
s'éteignit

et la mer fait à la terre un collier de silence
la mer humant la paix sacrificielle
où s'enchevêtrent nos râles immobile avec
d'étranges perles et de muets mûrissements
d'abysse

la terre fait à la mer un bombement de silence
dans le silence

et voici la terre seule
sans tremblement et sans trémulement
sans fouaillement de racine
et sans perforation d'insecte

vide

vide comme au jour d'avant le jour . . .
—Grâce! grâce!
Qu'est-ce qui crie grâce?
Poings avortés amassements taciturnes jeûnes
hurrah pour le départ lyrique

Who
riffles,
riffles
the uproar beyond the muddled heart of this third day?

Who gets lost and rips and drowns
in the reddened waves of the Siloam?
Rifle fire.
The lights flinch. The noises rhizulate
the rhizule
smokes
silence.

                                                          *

The sky yawns from black absence

behold—
nameless wanderings
the suns the rains the galaxies
fused in fraternal magma
pass by toward the safe necropolises of the sunset
and the earth the morgue of storms forgotten
which stitches rips in its rolling
lost patient arisen
savagely hardening the invisible falun
blew out

and the sea makes a necklace of silence for the earth
the sea inhaling the sacrificial peace
where our death rattles entangle motionless with
strange pearls and abyssal mute
maturations

the earth makes a bulge of silence for the sea
in the silence

behold the earth alone
without its trembling nor tremoring
without the lashing of roots
nor the perforations of insects

empty

empty as on the day before day . . .
—Mercy! mercy!
What cries mercy?
Aborted fists taciturn amassings fasts
hurrah for the lyrical departure

brûlantes métamorphoses
dispenses foudroyantes
feu, ô feu
éclair des neiges absolues
cavalerie de steppe chimique
retiré de mer à la marée d'ibis
le sémaphore anéanti
sonne aux amygdales du cocotier
et vingt mille baleines soufflant
à travers l'éventail liquide
un lamantin nubile mâche la braise des orients

La terre ne joue plus avec les blés
la terre ne fait plus l'amour avec le soleil
la terre ne réchauffe plus des eaux dans le creux de sa main.

La terre ne se frotte plus la joue avec des touffes d'étoiles.
Sous l'œil du néant suppurant une nuit
la terre saquée doucement dérive
éternellement

La grisaille suinte à mes yeux, alourdit
mes jarrets paresse affreusement le long de mes bras
Moi à moi
Fumée
fumée
de la terre

Entendez-vous parmi le vétiver le cri fort de la sueur?
        Je n'ai point assassiné mon ange. C'est sûr.
à l'heure des faillites frauduleuses nourri d'enfants occultes
et de rêves de terre il y a notre oiseau de clarinette,
luciole crêpue au front fragile des éléphants
et les amazones du roi de Dahomey de leur pelle restaurent
le paysage déchu des gratte-ciel de verre déteint
de voies privées de dieux pluvieux voirie et hoirie de roses brouillées
—des mains du soleil cru des nuits lactées.
Mais Dieu? comment ai-je pu oublier Dieu?
je veux dire la Liberté

ô Chimborazo violent
prendre aux cheveux la tête du soleil
36 flûtes n'insensibiliseront point les mains d'arbre à pain
de mon désir de pont de cheveux sur l'abîme
de bras de pluies de sciure de nuit
de chèvres aux yeux de mousse remontant les abîmes sans rampe
de sang bien frais de voilures au fond du volcan des lentes termitières

burning metamorphoses
thundering dispensations
fire, oh fire
flash of absolute snows
cavalry of a chemical steppe
plucked from the sea at ibis tide
the wiped-out semaphore
sounds in the tonsils of the coco-palm
and twenty thousand whales blow
through the liquid fan
a nubile manatee chews the ember of the easts

The earth no longer plays with the wheat
the earth no longer makes love with the sun
the earth no longer warms up waters in the hollow of its palm.

The earth no longer rubs its cheek with clumps of stars.
Under the eye of nothingness suppurating a night
the sacked earth softly drifts
forever

Colorlessness oozes from my eyes, slows
my joints idles hideously along my arms
I to myself
Smoke
smoke
of the earth

Do you hear amidst the vetiver the loud scream of sweat?
            I have not murdered my angel. For sure.
at the hour of fraudulent bankruptcies feeding on hidden children
and on dreams of earth there is our clarinet bird,
crinkled firefly in the fragile foreheads of elephants
and the amazons of the king of Dahomey with their spades retrieve
the blighted landscape of skyscrapers of faded glass
of private drives of rainy gods dump and dowry of blurred roses
—from the hands of harsh sun from the milky nights.
But God? how could I forget God?
I mean, Freedom

oh violent Chimborazo
to grab the sun's head by its hair
36 flutes will not anesthetize the breadfruit tree's hands
of my yearning for bridges of hair over the abyss
for arms of rain for nightdust
for mossy-eyed goats climbing railless abysses
for really fresh blood for sails at the bottom of the volcano of slow termitariums

mais moi homme! rien qu'homme!
Ah! ne plus voir avec les yeux.
N'être plus une oreille à entendre!
N'être plus la brouette à évacuer le décor!
N'être plus une machine à déménager
les sensations!

Je veux le seul le pur trésor,
celui qui fait largesse des autres.

Homme!
Mais ce début me fait moins qu'homme!
Quelle torpeur! ma tête stupidement
ballotte.
Ma tête rongée est déglutie par mon corps.
mon œil coule à pic dans la chose
non plus regardée mais regardante.

Homme!
Et voici l'assourdissement violet
qu'officie ma mémoire terrestre
mon désir frappe aux états simples
je rêve d'un bec étourdi d'hibiscus
et de vierges sentences violettes
s'alourdissant aux lézards avaleurs de soleil
l'heure bat comme un remords la neige d'un soleil
aux caroncules crève la patte levée
le monde . . .

Ça y est. Atteint. Comme frappe
la mort brutale. Elle ne fauche pas.
Elle n'éclate pas. Elle frappe silencieusement
au ras du sang au ras du cœur,
comme un ressentiment
comme un retour de sang
floc

médullairement
C'est bon
Je veux un soleil plus brillant et de plus pures étoiles
Je m'ébroue en une mouvance d'images
de souvenirs nérétiques de possibles
en suspension de tendances-larves
d'obscurs devenirs

les habitudes font à la vase liquide
de traînantes algues—mauvaisement,

but I a man! just a man!
Ah! to stop seeing with my eyes.
No longer to be an ear for hearing!
No longer to be the wheelbarrow for vacating the scenery!
No longer to be a machine for unhinging
sensations!

I want the only the pure treasure,
the one which endlessly generates others.

Man!
But this debut makes me less than man!
What torpor! my head stupidly
tosses about.
My gnawed head is swallowed by my body.
my eye flows perpendicularly into the thing
no longer looked at but looking.

Man!
Behold the violet deafening
which my terrestrial memory officiates
my desire knocks at simple states
I dream of a beak drunk on hibiscus
and of purple virgin proverbs
growing heavy with sun-swallowing lizards
the hour beats like a remorse the snow of a caruncular sun
its leg lifted bursts
the world . . .

That's it. Stricken. Like ruthless
death strikes. It does not reap.
Does not burst. It strikes silently
flush with the blood flush with the heart,
like a resentment
like a stroke
plop

medullarily
All right
I want a shinier sun and purer stars
I splash about in a movance of images
of neritic memories of possibles
in suspension of larva-tendencies
of obscure becomings

habits form drifting seaweed
for the liquid slime—wickedly,

des fleurs éclatent
floc

On enfonce, on enfonce comme dans
une musique.
Radiolaires nous dérivons à travers votre sacrifice

d'un dodelinement de vague je saute
ancestral aux branches de ma végétation
Je m'égare aux complications
fructueuses
Je nage aux vaisseaux
Je plonge aux écluses

Où où où vrombissent les hyènes
fienteuses du désespoir?

Non. Toujours ici torrentueuses
cascadent les paroles.

Silence
Silence par delà les rampes
sanguinolentes

par cette grisaille et cette calcination inouïe.

Enfin lui
ce vent des méplats bonheur
le silence   ·
mon cerveau meurt dans une illumination
avec de fumantes aigrettes d'or fauve
un bourrelet tiédi de circonvolution
par un ricanement de palmes strié
fond
une titillation duvetée nage nage nage
brindilles forêt lac
aérienne une biche

Oh un vide d'incendie Tortures

Où où où
vrombissent les hyènes fienteuses du désespoir?

Renversé sur ma lassitude,
à travers la gaze des bouffées tièdes
irradient mon inexistence fluide
une saveur meurt à ma lèvre
une flèche file je ne sais pas.

flowers shatter
plop

One sinks, one sinks as into
a music.
Radiolarians we drift across your sacrifice

with a wavelike doddling I leap
ancestral to the branches of my vegetation
I stray through fertile
complications
I swim to the vessels
I plunge to the locks

Where where where hum the bedunged
hyenas of despair?

No. Words still cascade
torrentially here.

Silence
Silence beyond the blood-tinged
ramps

through this colorlessness and this outrageous calcination.

At last it
this wind from flats happiness
the silence
my brain dies in an incandescence
with smoking aigrettes of fulvous gold
a tepid fold of circumvolution
streaked by a sneer of palm trees
melts
a downy titillation swims swims swims
twigs forest lake
aerial a doe

O an emptiness of fire Tortures

Where where where
hum the bedunged hyenas of despair?

Laid back on my weariness,
across the gauze warm puffs
irradiate my fluid non-existence
a flavor dies on my lip
an arrow flies I don't know

Frisson. Tout le vécu pétarade avec des reprises.

Les bruits se donnent la main et s'embrassent
par-dessus moi.
J'attends. Je n'attends plus.
Délire.

Néant de jour
Néant de nuit
une attirance douce
à la chair même des choses
éclabousse.

Jour nocturne
nuit diurne
qu'exsude
la Plénitude

Ah

Le dernier des derniers soleils tombe

Où se couchera-t-il sinon en Moi?

A mesure que se mourait toute chose,
Je me suis, je me suis élargi—comme le monde—
et ma conscience plus large que la mer!
Dernier soleil.
J'éclate. Je suis le feu, je suis la mer.
Le monde se défait mais je suis le monde

La fin, la fin disions-nous.

Quelle sottise une paix proliférante
d'obscures puissances. Branchies opacules
palmes syrinx pennes. Il me pousse
invisibles et instants par tout le corps,
secrètement exigés des sens,

et nous voici pris dans le sacré
tourbillonnant ruissellement primordial
au recommencement de tout.

La sérénité découpe l'attente en prodigieux cactus.
Tout le possible sous la main.
Rien d'exclu.

A shudder. All one has lived sputters on and off.

The noises join hands and embrace
above me.
I wait. No longer wait.
Delirium.

Nothingness of a day
Nothingness of a night
a soft enticement
to the very flesh of things
spatters.

Nocturnal day
diurnal night
exuded by
Plenitude

Ah

The last last sun falls

Where will it lie if not in Me?

As everything was dying,
I did, I did grow—as big as the world—
and my conscience wider than the sea!
Last sun.
I explode. I am the fire, I am the sea.
The world is dissolving but I am the world

The end, the end did we say.

What nonsense a peace proliferating
with obscure powers. Gills opacules
palm branches syrinx quills. Invisible and instant
secretly required, senses
grow all over me,

and here we are caught in the sacred
whirling primordial streaming
at the second beginning of everything.

Serenity carves the suspense into prodigious cacti.
The whole possible at hand.
Nothing excluded.

et je pousse moi l'Homme
stéatopyge assis
en mes yeux des reflets de marais de honte
d'acquiescement
—pas un pli d'air ne bougeant aux
échancrures de ses membres—
sur les épines séculaires

Je pousse comme une plante
sans remords et sans gauchissement
vers les heures dénouées du jour
pur et sûr comme une plante
sans crucifiement
vers les heures dénouées du soir

La fin!
Mes pieds vont le vermineux cheminement
plante
mes membres ligneux conduisent d'étranges sèves
plante plante

et je dis
et ma parole est paix
et je dis et ma parole est terre
et je dis
et
la Joie
éclate dans le soleil nouveau
et je dis:
par de savantes herbes le temps glisse
les branches picoraient une paix de flammes vertes
et la terre respira sous la gaze des brumes
et la terre s'étira. Il y eut un craquement
à ses épaules nouées. Il y eut dans ses veines
un pétillement de feu.
Son sommeil pelait comme un goyavier d'août
sur de vierges îles assoiffées de lumière
et la terre accroupie dans ses cheveux
d'eau vive
au fond de ses yeux attendit
les étoiles.

"dors, ma cruauté", pensai-je

l'oreille collée au sol, j'entendis
passer Demain

and I grow I the seated
steatopygous Man
reflections of swamps of shame of acquiescence
in my eyes
—not a wrinkle of air moving about
the notches of his limbs—
on age-old thorns

I grow like a plant
remorseless and unwarped
toward the ungnarled hours of day
pure and confident as a plant
uncrucifiable
toward the ungnarled hours of evening

The end!
My feet follow the wormy meandering
plant
my woody limbs circulate strange saps
plant plant

and I speak
and my word is peace
and I speak and my word is earth
and I speak
and
Joy
bursts in the new sun
and I speak:
through knowing grasses time glides
the branches were pecking at a peace of green flames
and the earth breathed under the gauze of mists
and the earth stretched. There was a cracking
in its knotted shoulders. There was in it veins
a crackling of fire
Its sleep peeled off like an August guava tree
on virgin islands thirsty for light
and squatting in its hair
of running water
at the back of its eye the earth awaited
the stars.

"rest, my cruelty," I thought

my ear against the ground, I heard Tomorrow
pass

N'ayez point pitié

Fumez marais

les images rupestres de l'inconnu
vers moi détournent le silencieux crépuscule
de leur rire

Fumez ô marais cœur d'oursin
les étoiles mortes apaisées par des mains merveilleuses jaillissent
de la pulpe de mes yeux
Fumez fumez
l'obscurité fragile de ma voix craque de cités flamboyantes
et la pureté irrésistible de ma main appelle
de loin de très loin du patrimoine héréditaire
le zèle victorieux de l'acide dans la chair de la vie—marais—

telle une vipère née de la force blonde de l'éblouissement.

Soleil serpent

Soleil serpent œil fascinant mon œil
et la mer pouilleuse d'îles craquant aux doigts des roses lance-flamme et mon corps intact de foudroyé
l'eau exhausse les carcasses de lumière perdues dans le couloir sans pompe
des tourbillons de glaçons auréolent le cœur fumant des corbeaux
nos cœurs
c'est la voix des foudres apprivoisées tournant sur leurs gonds de lézarde
transmission d'anolis au paysage de verres cassés c'est les fleurs vampires à la relève des orchidées
élixir du feu central
feu juste feu manguier de nuit couvert d'abeilles
mon désir un hasard de tigres surpris aux soufres
mais l'éveil stanneux se dore des gisements enfantins
et mon corps de galet mangeant poisson mangeant colombes et sommeils
le sucre du mot Brésil au fond du marécage.

Have No Mercy

Keep smoking swamp

the rupestral images of the unknown
turn the silent dusk of their laughter
toward me

Keep smoking oh swamp sea urchin core
dead stars calmed by marvelous hands gush
from the pulp of my eyes
Smoke smoke
the frail darkness of my voice crackles with blazing cities
and the irresistible purity of my hand summons
out of vast distance from a genetic inheritance
the victorious zeal of the acid in the flesh of life—swamp—

like a viper born from the blonde force of resplendence.

Serpent Sun

Serpent sun eye bewitching my eye
and the sea flea-ridden with islands cracking in the fingers of flamethrower roses and my intact body
        of one thunderstruck
the water raises the carcasses of light lost in the pompless corridor
whirlwinds of ice floes halo the steaming hearts of ravens
our hearts
it is the voice of tamed thunderbolts turning on their crack hinges
a transfer of anolis to the landscape of broken glasses it is the vampire flowers relaying the orchids
elixir of the central fire
fire just fire night mango tree swarming with bees
my desire a throw of tigers caught in the sulphurs
but the stannous awakening gilds itself with infantine deposits
and my pebble body eating fish eating doves and slumbers
the sugar in the word Brazil deep in the marsh.

Phrase

Et pourquoi pas la haie de geysers les obélisques des heures le cri lisse des nuages la mer en écart vert
pâle fienté d'oiseaux vauriens et l'espérance roulant ses billes sur les faîtes et entrefaîtes des
maisons et les déchirures en dorades des surgeons bananiers

dans les hautes branches du soleil sur le cœur heurté des matins sur le tableau âcre du ciel un jour de
craie de faucon de pluie et d'acacia sur un portulan d'îles premières secouant leurs cheveux de sel
interjetés de doigts de mâts en toute main à toute fin sous le battement de cil du hasard aux délices
chantées d'ombre un assassin vêtu d'étamines riches et calmes comme un chant de vin dur

Poème pour l'aube

les fougues de chair vive
aux étés éployés de l'écorce cérébrale
ont flagellé les contours de la terre
les ramphorinques dans le sarcasme de leur queue prennent le vent
le vent qui n'a plus d'épée
le vent qui n'est plus qu'une gaule à cueillir
        les fruits de toutes les saisons du ciel
mains ouvertes
mains vertes
pour les fêtes belles des fonctions anhydrides
il neigera d'adorables crépuscules sur les mains coupées des mémoires respirantes
et voici
sur les rhagades de nos lèvres d'Orénoque désespéré
l'heureuse tendresse des îles bercées par la poitrine adolescente des sources de la mer
et dans l'air et le pain toujours renaissant des efforts musculaires
l'aube irrésistible ouverte sous la feuille
telle clarteux l'élan épineux des belladones

Sentence

And why not the hedge of geysers the obelisk of hours the smooth scream of clouds the sea's
    quartered pale green spattered by good-for-nothing birds and hope playing marbles on the
    beams and betweens of houses and the dolphin-like rips of banana tree suckers

in the top branches of the sun on the stubbed heart of mornings on the acrid canvas of the sky a day of
    chalk of falcons of rain and acacia on a portulan of primeval islands shaking their saline hair
    interposed by fingers of masts handwritten for any purpose under the blink of chance with its
    shadow sung delights an assassin clad in rich and calm muslins like a chant of hard wine

Poem for the Dawn

the mettles of vivid flesh
with summers spread from the cerebral cortex
have flogged the contours of the earth
the Rhamphorynchi in the sarcasm of their tails take to the wind
the wind which has no more sword
the wind no more now than a pole to gather
       the fruit of all seasons of the sky
hands open
hands green
for the beautiful feasts of anhydrid functions
delightful dusks will snow onto the lopped hands of breathing memories
behold
in the rhagades of our lips of a desperate Orinoco
the blissful tenderness of islands rocked by the adolescent breast of the sources of the sea
and in the air and the ever reborn bread of muscular efforts
the dawn irresistible open under the leaf
claritous as the thorny pluck of belladonnas

Visitation

ô houle annonciatrice sans nombre sans poussière de toute parole vineuse
houle et ma poitrine salée des anses des anciens jours et la jeune couleur
tendre aux seins du ciel et des femmes électriques de quels diamants

forces éruptives tracez vos orbes
communications télépathiques reprenez à travers la matière réfractaire
messages d'amour égarés aux quatre coins du monde revenez-nous ranimés
par les pigeons voyageurs de la circulation sidérale

pour moi je n'ai rien à craindre je suis d'avant Adam je ne relève ni du même lion
ni du même arbre je suis d'un autre chaud et d'un autre froid

ô mon enfance lait de luciole et frisson de reptile
mais déjà la veille s'impatientait vers l'astre et la poterne et nous fuyions
sur une mer cambrée incroyablement plantée de poupes de naufrages
vers une rive où m'attendait un peuple agreste et pénétreur de forêts avec aux mains
des rameaux de fer forgé—le sommeil camarade sur la jetée—le chien bleu de la métamorphose
l'ours blanc des icebergs et Ta très sauvage disparition
tropicale comme une apparition de loup nocturne en plein midi

Mythologie

à larges coups d'épée de sisal de tes bras fauves
à grands coups fauves de tes bras libres de pétrir l'amour à ton gré batéké
de tes bras de recel et de don qui frappent de clairvoyance les espaces aveugles baignés d'oiseaux
je profère au creux ligneux de la vague infantile de tes seins le jet du grand mapou
né de ton sexe où pend le fruit fragile de la liberté

Visitation

O surge without number without dust harbinger of each vinous word
surge and my chest salted by the coves of ancient days and the young color
tender on the breasts of the sky and of women electric with what diamonds

eruptive forces trace your orbs
telepathic communications resume across recalcitrant matter
messages of love strayed to the four corners of the world return to us rekindled
by the carrier pigeons of sidereal traffic

as for me I have nothing to fear I am from before Adam I do not come under the same lion
nor under the same tree I am from a different hot and a different cold

O my childhood of firefly milk and reptile quivering
but already the vigil was straining toward the star and the postern and we were racing
across an arched sea incredibly planted with shipwrecked sterns
toward a shore where I was welcomed by a rustic people penetrators of forests with wrought-iron
boughs in their hands—the comradely sleep on the jetty—the blue dog of metamorphosis
the white bear of icebergs and Your truly wild disappearance
tropical as an apparition of a nocturnal wolf at high noon

Mythology

with deep sisal sword thrusts of your feline arms
with great feline blows of your arms free to knead love to your liking batéké
of your arms of concealed goods and of gifts which strike with clarity the blind bird bathed spaces
into the woody hollow of the infantile swell of your breasts I bring forth the jet of the great mapau
born to your sex from which hangs liberty's fragile fruit

Perdition

nous frapperons l'air neuf de nos têtes cuirassées
nous frapperons le soleil de nos paumes grandes ouvertes
nous frapperons le sol du pied nu de nos voix
les fleurs mâles dormiront aux criques des miroirs
et l'armure même des trilobites
s'abaissera dans le demi-jour de toujours
sur des gorges tendres gonflées de mines de lait
et ne franchirons-nous pas le porche
le porche des perdition?
un vigoureux chemin aux veineuses jau issures
tiède
où bondissent les buffles des colères insoumises
court
avalant la bride des tornades mûres
aux balisiers sonnants des riches crépuscules

Perdition

we will strike the new air with our armor-plated heads
we will strike the sun with our wide-open palms
we will strike the soil with the bare foot of our voices
the male flowers will sleep in coves of mirrors
and even the armor of trilobites
will sink in the half-light of forever
over the tender breasts swollen with lodes of milk
and will we not cross the porch
the porch of perditions?
a vigorous road with veiny jaunders
tepid
where the buffaloes of irrepressible angers bound
runs
full-tilting the ripe tornados
in the tolling balisiers of crepuscular riches

*

Survie

Je t'évoque
bananier pathétique agitant mon cœur nu
dans le jour psalmodiant
je t'évoque
vieux hougan des montagnes sourdes la nuit
juste la nuit qui précède la dernière
et ses roulements d'ennui frappant à la poterne folle des villes enfouies
mais ce n'est que le prélude des forêts en marche au cou sanglant du monde
c'est ma haine singulière
dérivant ses icebergs dans l'haleine des vraies flammes
donnez-moi
ah donnez-moi l'œil immortel de l'ambre
et des ombres et des tombes en granit équarri
car l'idéale barrière des plans moites et les herbes aquatiques
écouteront aux zones vertes
les truchements de l'oubli se nouant et se dénouant
et les racines de la montagne
levant la race royale des amandiers de l'espérance
fleuriront par les sentiers de la chair
(le mal de vivre passant comme un orage)
cependant qu'à l'enseigne du ciel
un feu d'or sourira
au chant ardent des flammes de mon corps

Survival

I conjure you
pathetic plantain tossing my naked heart
in the daylight with my psalm
I conjure you
old hougan of nocturnally deaf mountains
only the night before the last one
and its rumblings of boredom knocking at the insane postern of buried cities
but this is only a prelude to forests on their way to the bloody neck of the world
it is my singular hatred
drifting its icebergs in the breath of real flames
give me
ah give me the immortal eye of amber
and of shadows and of tombs squared in granite
for the ideal barrier of damp planes and aquatic grasses
will hear in the green zones
the spokesmen of oblivion knotting and unknotting
and roots of the mountain
raising the royal descent of the almond trees of hope
will blossom through the paths of flesh
(the sickness of living passing over like a storm)
while at the Sign of the Sky
a golden fire will smile
at the ardent song of my body in flames

Au-delà

d'en bas de l'entassement furieux des songes épouvantables
les aubes nouvelles
montaient
roulant leurs têtes de lionceaux libres
le néant niait ce que je voyais à la lumière
plus fraîche de mes yeux naufragés
mais—des sirènes sifflant de puissance sourde—
la faim des heures manquées agaça l'aigle farouche du sang
les bras trop courts s'allongèrent de flammes
les désirs éclatèrent en grisou violent dans la ténèbre des cœurs lâches
le poids de rêve bascula dans le vent des flibustes
—merveille de pommes douces pour les oiseaux des branches—
et des bandes réconciliées se donnèrent richesse dans
la main d'une femme assassinant le jour

Beyond

from the depth of the furious piling up of appalling dreams
new dawns were
rising
rolling their free lion cub heads
nothingness denied what I was seeing by the fresher
light of my shipwrecked eyes
but—sirens hissing from a secret power—
the hunger of botched hours vexed the fierce eagle of blood
arms too short lengthened into flames
desires exploded like violent pit-gas in the dark of cowardly hearts
the weight of dream teetered in the freebooting wind
—wonder of sweet apples for birds of the branches—
and reconciled bands shared riches in
the hand of a woman assassinating the day

Les armes miraculeuses

Le grand coup de machette du plaisir rouge en plein front il y avait du sang et cet arbre qui s'appelle
    flamboyant et qui ne mérite jamais mieux ce nom-là que les veilles de cyclone et de villes mises à
    sac le nouveau sang la raison rouge tous les mots de toutes les langues qui signifient mourir de soif
    et seul quand mourir avait le goût du pain et la terre et la mer un goût d'ancêtre et cet oiseau qui
    me crie de ne pas me rendre et la patience des hurlements à chaque détour de ma langue

(la plus belle arche et qui est un jet de sang
la plus belle arche et qui est un cerne lilas
la plus belle arche et qui s'appelle la nuit
et la beauté anarchiste de tes bras mis en croix
et la beauté eucharistique et qui flambe de ton sexe au nom duquel je saluais le barrage des mes lèvres
    violentes)

il y avait la beauté des minutes qui sont les bijoux au rabais du bazar de la cruauté le soleil des minutes
    et leur joli museau de loup que la faim fait sortir du bois la croix-rouge des minutes qui sont les
    murènes en marche vers les viviers et les saisons et les fragilités immenses de la mer qui est un
    oiseau fou cloué feu sur la porte des terres cochères il y avait jusqu'à la peur telle que le récit de
    juillet des crapauds de l'espoir et du désespoir élagués d'astres au-dessus des eaux là où la fusion
    des jours qu'assure le borax fait raison des veilleuses gestantes les fornications de l'herbe à ne pas
    contempler sans précaution les copulations de l'eau reflétées par le miroir des mages les bêtes
    marines à prendre dans le creux du plaisir les assauts de vocables tous sabords fumants pour fêter la
    naissance de l'héritier mâle en instance parallèle avec l'apparition des prairies sidérales au flanc de
    la bourse aux volcans

scolopendre scolopendre
jusqu'à la paupière des dunes sur les villes interdites frappées de la colère de Dieu
scolopendre scolopendre
jusqu'à la déblâcle crépitante et grave qui jette les villes naines à la tête des chevaux les plus fougueux
    quand en plein sable elles lèvent
leur herse sur les forces inconnues du déluge
scolopendre scolopendre
crête crête cimaise déferle déferle en sabre en crique en village
endormi sur ses jambes de pilotis et des saphènes d'eau lasse
dans un moment il y aura la déroute des silos flairés de près
le hasard face de puits de condottière à cheval avec pour armure les flaques artésiennes et les petites
    cuillers des routes libertines
face de vent
face utérine et lémure avec des doigts creusés dans les monnaies et la nomenclature chimique
et la chair retournera ses grandes feuilles bananières que le vent des bouges hors les étoiles qui signalent
    la marche à reculons des blessures de la nuit vers les déserts de l'enfance feindra de lire

The Miraculous Weapons

The great machete blow of red pleasure right in the face there was blood and that tree called
flamboyant and which never deserves this name more than just before a cyclone or pillaged
cities the new blood the red reason all words in all tongues which mean to die of thirst and
alone when dying tasted like bread and the earth and the sea like ancestors and this bird
shrieking at me not to surrender and the patience of screams at each detour of my tongue

(the finest arch and it is a spurt of blood
the finest arch and it is a lilac ring about the eye
the finest arch and it is called night
and the anarchistic beauty of your arms made into a cross
and the eucharistic beauty—and how it blazes—of your sex in the name of which I hailed the
barrage with my violent lips)

there was the beauty of minutes which are the marked-down trinkets from the bazaar of cruelty the
sun of minutes and their pretty wolf snouts which hunger drives out of the woods the red cross
of minutes which are moray eels on their way toward breeding grounds and the seasons and the
immense fragilities of the sea which is an insane bird nailed dead on the gateway of carriage
crossed lands there were to the point of fear as with the July report of toads of hope and of
despair pruned from the stars over waters right where the fusion of days guaranteed by borax
justifies the gestant watchwoman the fornications of grass not to be observed without precau-
tion the copulations of water reflected by the mirror of magi the marine beasts to be taken in the
trough of pleasure the assaults of vocables all gun ports smoking in order to celebrate the birth
of the male heir simultaneously with the apparition of sidereal prairies on the flank of volcanic
scrotums

scolopendra scolopendra
until the eyelid of dunes over forbidden cities struck by the anger of God
scolopendra scolopendra
until the crackling and ponderous defeat which drives dwarf cities to take command of the fieriest
horses when in the thick of the sand they raise
their portcullis over the unknown forces of the deluge
scolopendra scolopendra
crest crest cyma unfurl unfurl as a sword as a cove as a village
asleep on its leg-like pilings and on saphenas of tired water
in a moment there will be a rout of silos sniffed close up
chance pit face of a mounted condottiere armored in artesian puddles and the little spoons of
libertine roads
face of wind
lemur and uterine face with fingers dug into coins and chemical nomenclature
and the flesh will turn over its great plantain leaves which the wind of dives outside the stars
signalling the backward march of the night's wounds toward the deserts of childhood will
pretend to read

dans un instant il y aura le sang versé où les vers luisants tirent les chaînettes des lampes électriques
   pour la célébration des compitales
et les enfantillages de l'alphabet des spasmes qui fait les grandes ramures de l'hérésie ou de la
   connivence
il y aura le désintéressement des paquebots du silence qui sillonnent
jour et nuit les cataractes de la catastrophe aux environs des tempes savantes en transhumance
et la mer rentrera ses petites paupières de faucon et tu tâcheras de saisir le moment le grand feudataire
   parcourra son fief à la vitesse d'or fin du désir sur les routes à neurones regarde bien le petit oiseau
   s'il n'a pas avalé l'étole le grand roi ahuri dans la salle pleine d'histoires adorera ses mains très
   nettes ses mains dressées au coin du désastre alors la mer rentrera dans ses petits souliers prends
   bien garde de chanter pour ne pas éteindre la morale qui est la monnaie obsidionale des villes
   privées d'eau et de sommeil alors la mer se mettra à table tout doucement et les oiseaux chanteront
   tout doucement dans les bascules du sel la berceuse congolaise que les soudards m'ont désapprise
   mais que la mer très pieuse des boîtes crâniennes conserve sur ses feuillets rituels

scolopendre scolopendre

jusqu'à ce que les chevauchées courent la prétentaine aux prés salés d'abîmes avec aux oreilles riche de
   préhistoire le bourdonnement humain

scolopendre scolopendre

tant que nous n'aurons pas atteint la pierre sans dialecte la feuille sans donjon l'eau frêle sans fémur le
   péritoine séreux des soirs de source

in an instant there will be blood shed where the glowworms pull their little electric lamp-chains to
  celebrate the Compitalia
and the childish tricks of the alphabet of spasms which constitutes the great boughs of heresy or
  complicity
there will be the indifference of the ocean liners of silence that furrow
day and night the cataracts of the catastrophe in the proximity of wise human temples in
  transhumance
and the sea will roll back its tiny falcon eyelids and you will try to grasp the moment the great feudal
  lord will ride though its fief at the speed of fine gold of desire along the neuron roads look at the
  birdie if it has not swallowed the stole the great king bewildered in the hall full of stories will
  adore his very pure hands his hands raised in the corner of the disaster then the sea will once
  again be on pins and needles be sure to sing so as not to extinguish the morals which are the
  obsidianal coin of cities deprived of water and sleep then the sea will very softly spill the beans
  and the birds will very softly sing in the seasaws of salt the Congolese lullaby which the tough
  old troopers made me unlearn but which the very pious sea of cranial boxes preserves on its
  ritual leaves

scolopendra scolopendra

until the cavalcades sow their wild oats in the salt meadows of abysses their ears filled with the
  human humming rich in prehistory

scolopendra scolopendra

as long as we do not reach the stone without a dialect the leaf without a dungeon the frail water
  without a femur the serous peritoneum of springhead evenings

Prophétie

là où l'aventure garde les yeux clairs
là où les femmes rayonnent de langage
là où la mort est belle dans la main comme un oiseau saison de lait
là où le souterrain cueille de sa propre génuflexion un luxe de prunelles plus violent que des chenilles
là où la merveille agile fait flèche et feu de tout bois

là où la nuit vigoureuse saigne une vitesse de purs végétaux

là où les abeilles des étoiles piquent le ciel d'une ruche plus ardente que la nuit
là où le bruit de mes talons remplit l'espace et lève à rebours la face du temps
là où l'arc-en-ciel de ma parole est chargé d'unir demain à l'espoir et l'infant à la reine

d'avoir injurié mes maîtres mordu les soldats du sultan
d'avoir gémi dans le désert
d'avoir crié vers mes gardiens
d'avoir supplié les chacals et les hyènes pasteurs de caravanes

je regarde
la fumée se précipite en cheval sauvage sur le devant de la scène ourle un instant sa lave de sa fragile
        queue de paon puis se déchirant la chemise s'ouvre d'un coup la poitrine et je la regarde en îles
        britanniques en îlots en rochers déchiquetés se fondre peu à peu dans la mer lucide de l'air
où baignent prophétiques
ma gueule
        ma révolte
                mon nom

Tam-tam de nuit

train d'okapis facile aux pleurs la rivière aux doigts charnus
fouille dans le cheveu des pierres mille lunes miroirs tournants
mille morsures de diamants mille langues sans oraison
fièvre entrelacs d'archet caché à la remorque des mains de pierre
chatouillant l'ombre des songes plongés aux simulacres de la mer

Prophecy

there where adventure remains clear-sighted
where women radiate language
where death in the hand is beautiful like a milk season bird
where the tunnel gathers from its own genuflexion a profusion of wild plums fiercer than caterpillars
where the agile wonder leaves no stone nor fire unturned

there where the vigorous night bleeds a speed of pure vegetation

where the bees of the stars sting the sky with a hive more ardent than the night
where the noise of my heels fills space and raises the face of time backwards
where the rainbow of my speech is charged to unite tomorrow with hope and the infant with the
    queen,

for having insulted my masters bitten the sultan's men
for having cried in the wilderness
for having screamed at my jailers
for having begged from the jackals and the hyenas shepherds of caravans

I watch
the smoke rushes like a mustang to the front of the stage briefly hems its lava with its fragile peacock
    tail then tearing its shirt suddenly opens its chest and I watch it dissolve little by little into
    British isles into islets into jagged rocks in the limpid sea of the air
where my mug
my revolt
    my name
        prophetically bathe

Night Tom-Tom

file of okapis easily in tears the river with fleshy fingers
searches in the hair of stones a thousand moons mirrors revolving
a thousand diamond bites a thousand prayerless tongues
a fever loopings of a hidden violin bow towed by stone hands
tickling the shade of dreams plunged into the simulacra of the sea

Nostalgique

ô lances de nos corps de vin pur
vers la femme d'eau passée de l'autre côté d'elle-même
aux sylves des nèfles amollies
davier des lymphes mères
nourrissant d'amandes douces d'heures mortes de stipes d'orage
de grands éboulis de flamme ouverte
la lovée massive des races nostalgiques

Le cristal automatique

allo allo encore une nuit pas la peine de chercher c'est moi l'homme des cavernes il y a les cigales qui
étourdissent leur vie comme leur mort il y a aussi l'eau verte des lagunes même noyé je n'aurai
jamais cette couleur-là pour penser à toi j'ai déposé tous mes mots au mont-de-piété un fleuve de
traîneaux de baigneuses dans le courant de la journée blonde comme le pain et l'alcool de tes seins
allo allo je voudrais être à l'envers clair de la terre le bout de tes seins a la couleur et le goût de cette
terre-là allo allo encore une nuit il y a la pluie et ses doigts de fossoyeur il y a la pluie qui met ses
pieds dans le plat sur les toits la pluie a mangé le soleil avec des baguettes de chinois allo allo
l'accroissement du cristal c'est toi . . . c'est toi ô absente dans le vent et baigneuse de lombric
quand viendra l'aube c'est toi qui poindras tes yeux de rivière sur l'émail bougé des îles et dans ma
tête c'est toi le maguey éblouissant d'un ressac d'aigles sous le banian

Nostalgic

oh spears of our pure wine bodies
toward the water woman gone to the other side of herself
to sylvas of softened medlars
a forceps of mother lymphs
feeding with sweet almonds with dead hours with culms of storms
with great screes of open flame
the massive coil of nostalgic races

The Automatic Crystal

hullo hullo one more night stop guessing it's me the cave man there are cicadas which deafen both
their life and their death there also is the green water of lagoons even drowned I will never be
that color to think of you I left all my words at the pawn shop a river of sleds of women bathing
in the course of the day blonde as bread and the alcohol of your breasts hullo hullo I would like
to be on the clear other side of the earth the tips of your breasts have the color and the taste of
that earth hullo hullo one more night there is rain and its gravedigger fingers there is rain
putting its foot in its mouth on the roofs the rain ate the sun with chopsticks hullo hullo the
enlargement of the crystal that's you . . . that is you oh absent one in the wind an earthworm
bathing beauty when day breaks it is you who will dawn your riverine eyes on the stirred enamel
of the islands and in my mind it is you the dazzling maguey of an undertow of eagles under the
banyan

Conquête d'une aube

Nous mourons notre mort dans des forêts d'eucalyptus géants dorlotant des échouages de paquebots
        saugrenus
dans le pays où croître
drosera irrespirable
patûrant aux embouchures des clartés somnambules
ivre
très ivre guirlande arrachant démonstrativement
nos pétales sonores
dans la pluie campanulaire de sang bleu

Nous mourons
avec des regards croissant en amours extatiques dans des salles vermoulues
sans parole de barrage dans nos poches, comme une île qui sombre dans l'explosion brumeuse de ses
        polypes—le soir

Nous mourons
parmi les substances vivantes renflées anecdotiquement de préméditations
arborisées qui seulement jubilent qui seulement s'insinuent au cœur même
de nos cris qui seulement se feuillent de voix d'enfants qui seulement
rampent au large des paupières dans la marche percée des sacrés myriapodes
des larmes silencieuses

Nous mourons d'une mort blanche fleurissant de mosquées son poitrail d'absence splendide où
        l'araignée de perles salive son ardente mélancolie de monère convulsive

dans l'inénarrable conversion de la Fin

Merveilleuse mort de rien
une écluse alimentée aux sources les plus secrètes de l'arbre du voyageur
s'évase en croupe de gazelle inattentive

Merveilleuse mort de rien

les sourires échappés au lasso des complaisances
écoulent sans prix les bijoux de leur enfance
au plus fort de la foire des sensitives en tablier d'ange
dans la saison liminaire de ma voix
sur la pente douce de ma voix
à tue-tête
pour s'endormir
Merveilleuse mort de rien
Ah! l'aigrette déposée des orgueils puérils

Conquest of a Dawn

We die our death in giant eucalyptus forests coddling the wreckage of preposterous steamers
in that country where unbreathable
drosera are grown
grazing in the estuaries of somnambulistic clarities
drunk
very drunk garland demonstratively tearing off
our sonorous petals
in the campanularian rain of blue blood

We die
with glances expanding into ecstatic loves in worm-eaten halls
without a damming word in our pockets, like an island foundering in the foggy explosion of its
        polyps—in the evening

We die
among living substances anecdotally swollen with arborized premeditations
which merely gloat which merely worm their way into the very heart
of our screams which merely foliate with children's voices which merely
crawl some distance from eyelids in the dotted progress of the sacred myriapods
of silent tears

We die a white death decking out its breast of respendent absence with mosques where the
        spider-of-pearls drools its ardent melancholy of a convulsive moneron

in the untellable conversion of the End

A marvelous two-bit death
a canal lock fed by the most secretive sources of the traveler's tree
flares wide as the croup of a heedless gazelle

A marvelous two-bit death

smiles escaped from the lasso of complacencies
quickly liquidate the jewels of their childhoods
at the peak of the fair sensitives in angel smocks
in the liminal season of my voice
on the gentle slope of my voice
at the top of my voice
to go to sleep
A marvelous two-bit death
Ah! the aigrette of childish pride deposed

les tendresses devinéés
voici aux portes plus polies que les genoux de la prostitution—
le château des rosées—mon rêve
où j'adore
du dessèchement des cœurs inutiles

(sauf du triangle orchidal qui saigne violent comme le silence des basses terres)
jaillir

dans une gloire de trompettes libres à l'écorce écarlate
cœur non crémeux dérobant à la voix large des précipices
d'incendiaires et capiteux tumultes de cavalcade.

the tenderness divined
here at gates more polished than the knees of prostitution—
the castle of dews—my dream
where I adore
out of the desiccation of useless hearts

(saved from the orchidal triangle which bleeds violently like the silence of lowlands)
to spring up

in a halo of free trumpets with scarlet bark
a noncreamy heart stealing from the great voice of precipices
incendiary and heady cavalcadic tumults.

Débris

Et merde comme aucune la mer sans sape sans poste d'écoute sans pare-éclats
sans boyaux excoriée de lunes rompues sur les genoux de fer de la nuit
si céphalopode ex-voto des houillères je dressais contre son sein mon gueuloir
d'Antille verte
corymbe des jours corymbe des nuits
vers l'hermaphrodite Rien grand erre cultivant son âme prieure et porteuse de croix
merde entre veille et sommeil de sensitive moi debout dans les champs de sang et du couchant tapant
leurs chansons d'hernandia sonora
et ta langue bifide que ma pureté révère Révolte
dans les débris
c'est la mer baveuse de gorgones et d'isis de mes yeux et l'air harnaché
pluie et or des balles de l'orgasme tes yeux
merde c'est la mer sans allèle qui ouvre ses éventails et fait bruire ses noix c'est la mer qui abat toutes ses
cartes chromosiennes c'est la mer qui imprime un fleuve de troupeaux et de langues par en
dessous la paume des terres létales et le vent la poche pleine de naufrages à la bouche de source
aussi fraîche que ta pensée que je perds et que je traque entre veille et sommeil
c'est la mer ma chère cariophylle et vierge moussant vers l'hermaphrodite Rien ses excellentes feuilles
de femme et de renoncule où s'accomplissent des spermatozoïdes d'oiseau parfait

comme le soleil ma chère comme le soleil grenouille éclaboussée dans son nid de boue sèche.

Investiture

vol de cayes de mancenilliers de galets de ruisseau baliste intimité du souffle
toute l'eau de Kananga chavire de la Grande Ourse à mes yeux
mes yeux d'encre de Chine de Saint-Pierre assassiné
mes yeux d'exécution sommaire et de dos au mur
mes yeux qui s'insurgent contre l'édit de grâce
mes yeux de ville bravant les assassins sous la cendre morte
des purs mille défis des roses de Jéricho
O mes yeux sans baptême et sans rescrit
mes yeux de scorpène frénétique et de poignard sans roxelane
je ne lâcherai pas l'ibis de l'investiture folle de mes mains en flammes.

Debris

And shit like none other the sea without a sap without a listening post without a splinter shield
without communication trenches peeled of moons broken on the iron knees of the night
if a cephalopodic ex-voto from the coal mines I raised against its breast my mugpiece
of a green Antille
corymb of days corymb of nights
toward the hermaphroditic Nothing full sail cultivating its prioress and cross-bearing soul
shit between waking and sleeping of a sensitive plant I standing in the fields of blood and sunset
      thumping their hernandia sonora songs
and your forked tongue which my purity reveres Revolt
in the debris
it is the gorgon and isis drooling sea of my eyes and the harnessed air
rain and gold from the bullets of orgasm your eyes
shit it is the sea without an allelomorph opening its fans and rustling its nuts it is the sea laying down
      its entire chromosian hand it is the sea imprinting a river of herds and tongues way under the
      palm of lethal lands and the wind its pocket full of shipwrecks with its mouth a source as fresh as
      your thought which I lose and which I hunt down between waking and sleeping
it is the sea my darling caryophyllaceous and virgin frothing toward the hermaphroditic Nothing its
      excellent woman's and ranunculus leaves in which spermatazoids of perfect birds are achieved

like the sun my darling like the sun a frog spattered in its nest with dry mud.

Investiture

flight of cays of manchineels of pebbles of a stream ballista intimacy of the breath
all the water of Kananga capsizes from Ursa Major into my eyes
my eyes of Indian ink of Saint-Pierre assassinated
my eyes of summary execution and of back against the wall
my eyes which riot against the edict of mercy
my eyes defying the assassins from under the dead ash
of a thousand pure challenges of Jericho roses
O my eyes unbaptized unrescripted
my eyes of a frantic scorpaena and of a dagger without a roxelane
I will not let the ibis of the incredible investiture go from my blazing hands.

La forêt vierge

je ne suis pas de ceux qui croient qu'une ville ne doit pas s'élever jusqu'à la catastrophe encore un tour
de rein de cou d'étage ce sera le déclic du promontoire je ne suis pas de ceux qui luttent contre la
propagation du taudis encore une tache de merde ce sera le marais vrai. Vrai la puissance d'une
cité n'est pas en raison inverse de la saleté de ses ménagères pour moi je sais bien le panier où ne
roulera jamais plus ma tête. Vrai la puissance d'un regard n'est pas en fonction inverse de sa cécité
pour moi je sais bien où la lune ne viendra pas poser sa jolie tête d'affaire étouffée. Au coin du
tableau le désespoir inférieur et ma gueule de primate caressée depuis trois cents ans. Au centre la
centrale téléphonique et l'usine à gaz en pleine anthèse (trahison des houilles et des maréchaux).
Au coin ouest-ouest le métabolisme floral et ma gueule de primate démantelée depuis trois cents
ans la fumée nopal nopal au paysage repu les figuiers étrangleurs font leur apparition salivée de ma
gueule de mufle de sphinx démuselée depuis le néant.

Autre saison

où allez-vous ma femme marron ma restituée ma cimarronne les morts pour la patrie défont leurs
tranquilles oreillers de jungle au creux des pièges à dormir; les volcans émettent leur gueule
silencieuse de veuve et de laboratoire, les jolis parachutes des années sautent dans le vide et
lancent à la petite semaine leurs tracts de rue de blé-de-rue de femmes à prendre et à quitter car il y
a toujours l'air et ses moraines l'œstre de l'air les avalanches de l'air et les empires paternes
claquant au vent galant de la justice mais les femmes du matin trébuchent dans leurs cauchemars
de nuit et viennent s'écraser sur le trottoir où il n'y a plus ni police ni crime mais des dieux à
confirmer et le docteur angélique forçant sa face de pas géométriques à travers les champs de
sabotage Où allez-vous ma femme marron ma restituée ma cimarronne il vit à pierre fendre et la
limaille et la grenaille tremblent leur don de sabotage dans les eaux et les saisons Où allez-vous ma
femme marron ma restituée ma cimarronne le cœur rouge des pierres les plus sombres s'arrête de
battre quand passent les cavaliers du sperme et du tonnerre.

The Virgin Forest

I am not one of those who believe that a city must not rise to catastrophe one more back twisting neck twisting twist of stairs it will be the snap of the promontory I am not one of those who fight against the propagation of slums one more shit stain it will be a real swamp. Really the power of a city is not in inverse ratio to the sloppiness of its housekeepers as for me I know very well into what basket my head will never again roll. Really the power of a glance is not an inverse function of its blindness as for me I know very well where the moon will not come to rest its pretty head of a hushed-up affair. In the corner of the canvas the lower-class despair and my mug of a primate stoked for three hundred years. In the middle the telephone exchange and the gas plant in full anthesis (betrayal of coal and field-marshals). In the west-west corner the floral metabolism and my mug of a primate dismantled for three hundred years the nopal smoke a nopal in the gorged landscape the strangler fig trees make an appearance salivated from my mug of a sphinx muzzle unmuzzled since nothingness.

Another Season

where are you going my maroon wife my restored one my cimarron those who died for the fatherland are pulling apart their quiet jungle pillows in the hollow of sleep traps; the volcanoes give off their silent mugs of widows and laboratories, the pretty parachutes of years leap into the void and float at high interest their leaflets of rue of wheat-of-rue of women to take and to leave for there is always the air and its moraines the oestrus of the air the avalanches of air and the benevolent empires flapping in the gallant wind of justice but the women of the morning stagger in their foul dreams at night and end up collapsing on the sidewalk where there no longer are police or crimes but gods to be confirmed and the angelic doctor forcing his face of geometrical steps across the fields of sabotage Where are you going my maroon wife my restored one my cimarron it is so alive the stones are freezing and the filings and the pellets tremble their gift of sabotage in the waters and the seasons Where are you going my maroon wife my restored one my cimarron the red hearts of the darkest stones stop beating when the horsemen of sperm and thunder pass.

Jour et nuit

le soleil le bourreau la poussée des masses la routine de mourir et mon cri de bête blessée et c'est ainsi jusqu'à l'infini des fièvres la formidable écluse de la mort bombardée par mes yeux à moi-même aléoutiens qui de terre de ver cherchent parmi terre et vers tes yeux de chair de soleil comme un négrillon la pièce dans l'eau où ne manque pas de chanter la forêt vierge jaillie du silence de la terre de mes yeux à moi-même aléoutiens et c'est ainsi le saute-mouton salé des pensées hermaphrodites des appels de jaguars de source d'antilope de savanes cueillies aux branches à travers leur première grande aventure: la cyathée merveilleuse sous laquelle s'effeuille une jolie nymphe parmi le lait des mancenilliers et les accolades des sangsues fraternelles.

Annonciation / à André Breton

Des sangs nouveaux de mokatine sonnant à la viande s'accrochent aux branches du soleil végétal; ils attendent leur tour.

Un mouvement de palmes dessine le corps futur des porteuses aux seins jaunes moisson germante de tous les cœurs révélés.

Le pitt du flambeau descendant jusqu'à l'extrême pointe fait à la faiblesse de la ville une rosace amicale amarrée de lianes jeunes au vrai soleil de vrai feu de terre vraie: annonciation.

Pour l'annonciation des porteuses de palmiers de mokatine amarrés au soleil du pitt de flambeaux— œil vert bagué de jaune d'oxyde chargé de lunes œil de lune chargé de torches—œil de torche tordez l'engrais discret des lacs dénoués.

Day and Night

the sun the executioner the shoving of masses the routine of dying and my cry of a wounded beast
and that's the way it is until the infinite of fevers the awesome canal lock of death bombarded by
my eyes Aleutian to myself which made of earth and worms search amidst the earth and worm
toward your eyes of flesh and sun like a little nigger for the coin in the water where the virgin
forest does not fail to sing sprung up from the silence from the earth from my eyes Aleutian to
myself and that's the way it is the salty leap-frog of hermaphroditic thoughts of jaguar calls of a
springhead of an antelope of savannas plucked from the branches in the midst of their first great
venture: the marvelous cyathus under which a pretty nymph sheds her leaves amidst the
manchineel milk and the accolades of fraternal leeches.

Annunciation / for André Breton

New mokatine blood ringing at the meat hangs from branches of the vegetal sun; awaiting its turn.

A sway of palm fronds suggests the future body of yellow-breasted porters a harvest germinant with
all hearts revealed.

The pitt of the flaming torches descending to the very end makes for the weakness of the city a *
benevolent rose window moored by young lianas to the true sun of the true fire of a sincere
earth: annunciation.

For the annunciation of the porters of the mokatine palm trees moored to the sun of the pitt of
flaming torches—a green eye ringed with yellow oxide loaded with moons moon eye loaded
with torches—a torch eye contorts the discrete manure of unknotted snares.

Tam-tam I / à Benjamin Péret

à même le fleuve de sang de terre
à même le sang de soleil brisé
à même le sang d'un cent de clous de soleil
à même le sang du suicide des bêtes à feu
à même le sang de cendre le sang de sel le sang des sangs d'amour
à même le sang incendié d'oiseau feu
hérons et faucons
montez et brûlez

Tam-tam II / pour Wifredo

à petits pas de pluie de chenilles
à petits pas de gorgée de lait
à petits pas de roulements à billes
à petits pas de secousse sismique
les ignames dans le sol marchent à grands pas de trouées d'étoiles
de trouée de nuit de trouée de Sainte
Mère de Dieu
à grands pas de trouée de parole dans un gosier de bègue
orgasme des pollutions saintes
alleluiah

Tom-Tom I / *for Benjamin Péret*

bareback on the river of blood of earth
on the blood of broken sun
on the blood of a hundred sun nails
on the blood of the suicide of fire beasts
on the blood of an ember the blood of salt the blood of bloods of love
on the fire bird inflamed blood
herons and falcons
ride and burn

Tom-Tom II / *for Wifredo*

with baby steps like a rain of caterpillars
with baby steps like a gulp of milk
with baby steps like ball bearings
with baby steps like a seismic tremor
the yams in the soil advance with giant steps like a breach of stars
like a breach of night like a Holy
Mother of God breach
with giant steps like a breach of words in a stutterer's throat
orgasm of the holy pollutions
hallelujah

Le grand midi

—Halte, halte d'auberge! Plus outre! Plus bas! Halte d'auberge! L'impatient devenir fléchant de réveils
      et de fumées
orteils sanglants se dressant en coursiers

insurrection
se lève!

Reine du vent fondu
—au cœur des fortes paix—
gravier brouhaha d'hier
reine du vent fondu mais tenace mémoire
c'est une épaule qui se gonfle
c'est une main qui se desserre
c'est une enfant qui tapote les joues de son sommeil
c'est une eau qui lèche ses babines d'eau
vers des fruits de noyés succulents
gravier brouhaha d'hier reine du vent fondu . . .

Essaim dur. Guerriers ivres ô mandibules caïnites
éblouissements rampants paradisiaques thaumalées
jets croisements et dépouillements
ô poulpe
crachats des rayonnements
pollen secrètement bavant les quatre coins cardinaux
moi moi seul flottille nolisée
m'agrippant à moi-même
dans l'effarade et l'effroyante gueulée vermiculaire.

Seul et nu!

Les messages d'atomes frappent à même et d'incroyables
baisers gargouillant leurs errances qui se délitent
et des vagissements et des agonisements comme des lys
perfides éclatant dans la rosace et l'ensablement et la farouche occultation des solitudes.

Je bourlingue
à travers le lait tendre des lumières et des lichens
et les mitoses et l'épaisse myéline
et l'éozoon
et les brouillards et les mites de la chaleur hurlante.

High Noon

—Stop, stop for rest! Onward! Downward! Stop for rest! The impatient becoming tupping from
    awakenings and fumes
bloody toes bristling like chargers

insurrection
rises!

Queen of the melted down wind
—at the heart of forceful peaces—
gravel yesterday's hum
queen of the melted down wind but tenacious memory
it is a shoulder swelling up
it is a fist unclenching
it is a baby girl tapping the cheeks of her sleep
it is a water licking its water chops
toward the fruit of the succulent drowned
gravel yesterday's hum queen of the melted down wind . . .

Cruel swarm. Drunk warriors oh kainite mandibles
rampant bedazzlements paradisiac Chrysolophi
spurts crossings and strippings
oh octopus
spittle of radiances
pollen secretly drooling the four cardinal points
I I alone freighted flotilla
clinging to myself
in the frightation and the terrifying vermicular mugful.

Alone and naked!

The atomic messages hit home and incredible
kisses gurgling their roamings which slake
and wailings and agonizings like lilies
perfidiously bursting in the rose window and the sand piling up and the fierce occultation of
    solitudes.

I toss about
amidst the tender milk of lights and lichen
and the mitoses and the thick myelin
and the eozoon
and the fogs and the mites of the bellowing heat.

O immense frai du jour aux yeux verts broutant des fleurs
de cervelles éclatantes

l'œil nu non sacré de la nuit récite en son opacité même le genêt de mes profondeurs et de ma haine!

Mon beau pays aux hautes rives de sésame
où fume de noirceurs adolescentes la flèche de mon sang de bons sentiments!

Je bourlingue
gorge tendue à travers les mystérieux rouissements les atolls enroulés
les têtards à face de molosse les levures réticentes et les délires de tonnerre bas
et la tempête sacrée des chromosomes
gorge tendue tête levée et l'épouvante première et les délires secrets
incendiant dans mon crâne des frénésies d'or gorge tendue tête levée
à travers les patiences, les attentes, les montées les girations,
les métamorphoses les coalescences l'écaillement ictérique des futurs paysages
gorge lourde tête levée tel un nageur têtu
à travers les pluvieuses mitraillades de l'ombre
à travers le trémail virevoltant du ciel
à travers le ressac et l'embrun pépiant neuf
à travers le pertuis désemparé des peurs
tête levée
sous les pavois
dans le frisselis des naissances et des aubes . . .

Le sang du monde une lèvre salée
vertement à mon oreille aiguë
sanglote
gréée de foudres
ses fenaisons marines

O embrassements sans portulan.
Qu'importe?
jaillissant palmier
fontaine irrésistible ombelle
ma hourque
lourde
écrase
la
vase
avance
et
monte!
Ah! cime demain flexible,
virgule d'eau ma hourque lourde sans chamulque à contre-flot
écrase la cime qui s'amenuise

O immense spawning of the green-eyed day grazing flowers
of glittering brains

the night's naked nonsacred eye recites in its very opacity the gorse of my depths and my hatred!

My beautiful country with its high sesame shores
where the arrow of my good-natured blood smokes with base and adolescent schemes!

I toss about
throat stretched amidst the mysterious rettings the coiled atolls
the mastiff-faced tadpoles the reticent yeasts and the deliriums of low thunder
and the sacred tempest of chromosomes
throat stretched head raised and the primal terror and the secret deliriums
setting fire in my skull to golden frenzies throat stretched head raised
amidst the patiences, the expectations, the surges the gyrations,
the metamorphoses the coalescings the icteric scaling of future landscapes
throat heavy head raised like a stubborn swimmer
amidst the rainy shot exchange of the dark
amidst the twirling trammel of the sky
amidst the undertow and the sea spray chirping anew
amidst the disabled strait of fears
head raised
under the pavis
in the shiverance of births and dawns . . .

The blood of the world a salty lip
rigged with lightning
sobs sharply
its marine haymakings
into my keen ear

O chartless embracings.
Does it matter?
jetting up palm tree
irresistible fountain umbel
my heavy
hooker
crushes
the
sludge
lurches ahead
and
ascends!
Ah! peak flexible tomorrow,
comma of water my heavy hooker with no chamulcus against the current
crushes the attenuating peak

*

Ecume!

Je ne cherche plus : j'ai trouvé!

L'amour s'accroche aux branches
l'amour perce les narines du soleil l'amour, d'une dent bleue
happe la blanche mer.

Je suis la colonne du matin terrassé
Je suis la flamme juste de l'écorce brûlée;
dans le blocage de mes cinq doigts toute la forêt debout rougit oui
rougit au-dessus des abîmes les cent mille pointes des danses impavides.
Large, ah! plus large! disperser au carrefour de mes reins les cavaleries frappées d'amour!
broutantes fongosités
l'abîme a soufflé la bulle vivantes des collines
broutantes fongosités
élan assassiné
ne partirez-vous point?
Suivrais-je déjà les lourds chemins bis des pluies et des coxalgies?
Mon amour sans pourquoi fait une roue de serpent tiède
mon amour sans pourquoi fait un tour de soleil blanc
mon amour aux entrailles de temps dans une désolation brusque
de sauge et de glaucome gratte sabot inquiet le bombax de la savane sourde.

M'avancerais-je caressé déjà de soleil pâle vers les ciels
où mes crimes et le long effilochement d'herbes de mes enfers colonisés
luiront comme des oreilles trépassées dans la caverne des Requiems?
O oiseau du soleil aux durs becs renaissants
fraternel minuit seul estuaire où bouillir ma darne indifférence
j'entends le souffle des aralies
la creuse lumière des plages
le tisonnement des soleils marins
et les silences
et les soirs chevelus aux ricanements noueux
et sur la clapotante batterie des grenouilles l'âcre persévérance nocturne!
Qui fêle ma joie? Qui soupire vers le jour?
Qui conspire sur la tour?
Mon sang miaule
des cloches tintent dans mes genoux.
O l'aptère marche de l'homme dans le sable hérissée.
Demain? Mais déjà cet aujourd'hui me fuit s'effondre muette divinité que gorge
une lasse noyade à travers la bonace!

—Lâche, lâche soupir! et ceinturant la nucelle
de son gargouillement, la mort l'autre mort lambruche aigre et vivace!
misère

Spume!

I no longer search: I've got it!

Love clings to the branches
love pierces the nostrils of the sun love, with a blue tooth
snaps up the white sea.

I am the column of the floored morning
I am the just flame from the burned bark;
in the blockage of my five fingers the whole standing forest reddens yes
reddens above the abysses the hundred thousand tips of fearless dances.
Large, ah! larger! to scatter at the crossroads of my loins the love-struck cavalries!
grazing fungosities
the abyss has burst the living bubble of the hills
grazing fungosities
assassinated ardor
will you not leave?
Am I already following the heavy grayish-brown paths of rains and coxalgias?
My whyless love struts about like a tepid snake
my whyless love strolls about like a white sun
my love with the guts of time in an abrupt desolation
of sage and glaucoma scrapes, an anxious hoof, the bombax of the mute savanna.

Stroked by a pale sun am I by chance already advancing toward the skies
where my crimes and the long grass-like shredding of my colonized hells
will gleam like deceased ears in the cavern of Requiems?
O sun bird with hard renaissant beaks
fraternal midnight sole estuary in which to boil my dazzled indifference
I hear the breathing of aralies
the hollow light of beaches
the fanning of marine suns
and the silences
and the shaggy evenings with their gnarled sniggers
and over the lapping percussion of frogs the acrid nocturnal perseverance!
Who cracks my joy? Who sighs for daylight?
Who conspires on the tower?
My blood miaows
bells ring in my knees.
O the apterous walk of man bristling in the sand.
Tomorrow? But already this today escapes me collapses mute divinity on which a weary
drowning gorges amidst the calm!

—Cowardly, cowardly sigh! and encircling the nucellus
of its gurgling, death the other death bitter hardy wild vine!
misery

Ah! Je défaille, ce son! Il entre par mes talons racle mes os,
étoile rose et gris parmi le bouillonnement de mon crâne.
Arrête! j'avoue j'avoue tout. Je ne suis pas un Dieu. Cicindelle!
Cicindelle! Cicindelle!

Lumière. Ah! pourquoi ce refus?
Quel ruissellement de sang!
Sur ma face.
En épaisse glu le long de mes épaules!
Ma décrépitude à genoux sanglote éperdument.

Ding!

D'incroyables sorties se précipitent! Sur des biseaux de voie lactée
j'accroche la fleur foudroyée en oiseau
j'incendie aux mille et une cloche inefficaces
le puissant tocsin de mes neuves salives

Tiédeur.
Souffle vireux Morsures caïeu sanglant à travers les névroses...
Quelque part dans le monde un tam-tam bat ma défaite
Des tiges de lumière brute sous les machettes
et dans le dérèglement tombent

Arums d'amour
me bercerez-vous plus docile que l'agami
mes lèpres et mes ennuis?

Tam-tam de sang
papayers de l'ombre
Mumbo-jumbo dur tipoyeur
Kolikombo dur tipoyeur
Kolikombo goutte de nuit au cœur jaune de pensée
Kolikombo aux larges yeux de cassave claire
Kolikombo milan de feu tassé dans l'oreille des années
Kolikombo
Kolikombo
Kolikombo
dans les tourbillonnants beuglements des crécopies...

Un panache de monde
tranquillement s'installe et parfile la pariade métallique dans ce boulottement d'incendie. Pluie!
(je ne comprends pas car je n'ai point convoqué d'onde)
pluie
(je ne comprends pas car je n'ai point envoyé mes messages pariétaux)
pluie pluie pluie
éclatant parmi moi ses épaules électriques.

Ah! I faint, this sound! It enters by my heels scrapes my bones,
pink and grey studding among the seething of my skull.
Stop! I confess I confess all. I am not a God. Cicindela!
Cicindela! Cicindela!

Light. Ah! why this refusal?
What a streaming of blood!
On my face.
In thick birdlime along my shoulders!
My decrepitude on its knees sobs frantically.

Ding!

Incredible sorties rush forth! On beveled edges of milky way
I hang the flower thunderstruck into a bird
I ignite with a thousand and one useless bells
the powerful tocsin of my new salivas

Tepidity.
Noxious breath Bites bloody bulbil amidst the neuroses . . .
Somewhere in the world a tom-tom beats my defeat
Under the machetes and in the disorder
stems of raw light fall

Arums of love
will you rock more docile than the agami
my leprosies and my ennuis for me?

Tom-tom of blood
papaw-trees of darkness
Mumbo-jumbo tough tipoyeur
Kolikombo tough tipoyeur
Kolikombo a drop of night with a pansy's yellow heart
Kolikombo with the big eyes of a clear cassava
Kolikombo fiery kite packed in the ear of years
Kolikombo
Kolikombo
Kolikombo
in the whirling bawlings of cecropias . . .

A panache of a world
quietly settles and unravels the metallic mating in the noshing of the blaze. Rain!
(I don't understand for I've not summoned water)
rain
(I don't understand for I've not sent out parietal messages)
rain rain rain
bursting its electric shoulders about me.

—Enos! Toute ma vie trouverai-je aux statiques carrefours
foisonnant aux mains pâles des tremblements et des silences
ta monarchie nocturne et ta paix violacée?
Arrière! je suis debout; mon pied hihane vers de moins plats pays!

Je marcherai plein d'une dernière et plantureuse ivresse mon or
et mes sanglots dans mon poing couchés contre mon cœur!

Ah! jeter l'ancre de nos ongles nets dans la pouture du jour!

Attendre? Pourquoi attendre?

le palmier à travers ses doigts s'évade comme un remords
et voici le martèlement et voici le piétinement
et voici le souffle vertigineux de la négation sur ma face de charrascal
Je pars. Je n'arriverai point. C'est égal, mais je pars sur la route des arrivées avec mon rire prognathe.
Je pars. Le trisme du désespoir ne déforme point ma bouche.
Tant pis pour les corbeaux: très loin jouent les pibrochs.

Je pars, je pars. Mer sans ailleurs, ô recreux sans départ
je vous dis que je pars: dans la clarté aréneuse vers mon hostie vivace
se cabrent des centaures.
Je pars. Le vent d'un museau dur fouine dans ma patience
O terre de cimaise dénuée
terre grasse gorgée d'eau lourde
votre jour est un chien qui jappe après une ombre.

Adieu!

Quand la terre acagnardée scalpera le soleil
dans la mer violette vous trouverez mon œil fumant comme un tison.

Fournaise rude tendresse
salut!

Les étoiles pourrissent dans les marais du ciel
mais j'avance plus sûr et plus secret et plus terrible que l'étoile pourrissante

O vol courbe de mes pas!
posez-vous dans la forêt ardente

et déjà les bossettes de mon front et la rose de mon pouls catapultent le Grand Midi.

—Enos! All my life will I find at the static crossroads
swarming in the pale hands of tremblings and silences
your nocturnal monarchy and your violaceous peace?
Back off! I'm standing; my foot heehaws toward less flat lands!

I will walk filled with a last and copious drunkenness my gold
and my sobs in my fist lying down against my heart!

Ah! to drop the anchor of our clean fingernails into the starchy fodder of the day!

Wait? Why wait?

the palm tree escapes through its fingers like a remorse
behold the hammering behold the stamping
behold the vertiginous breath of negation on my carrascal face   *
I'm leaving. I will not arrive. Never mind, but I'm leaving on the road of arrivals with my
          prognathous laughter.
I'm leaving. The trismus of despair does not distort my mouth.
Too bad for the crows: the pibrochs are playing very far away.

Leaving, leaving. Sea without elsewhere, oh replunge without departure
leaving I tell you: in the sandy clarity toward my undying host
centaurs are rearing.
I'm leaving. The wind forages my patience with a hard snout
O land of a stripped cyma
rich land gorged on sluggish water
your day is a dog yapping at a shadow.

Farewell!

When the land grown lazy scalps the sun
you will find my eye in the purple sea smoking like a brand.

Furnace rough tenderness
hail!

The stars are rotting in the swamps of the sky
but I advance more sure and more secret and more awesome than the rotting star

O curved flight of my steps!
alight in the blazing forest

and already the little bumps on my forehead and the rose of my pulse are catapulting the High
          Noon.

Batouque

Les rizières de mégots de crachat sur l'étrange sommation
de ma simplicité se tatouent de pitons.
Les mots perforés dans ma salive ressurgissent en villes
d'écluse ouverte, plus pâle sur les faubourgs
O les villes transparentes montées sur yaks
sang lent pissant aux feuilles de filigrane le dernier souvenir
le boulevard comète meurtrie brusque oiseau traversé
se frappe en plein ciel
noyé de flèches
C'est la nuit comme je l'aime très creuse et très nulle
éventail de doigts de boussole effondrés au rire blanc des sommeils.

batouque
quand le monde sera nu et roux
comme une matrice calcinée par les grands soleils de l'amour
batouque
quand le monde sera sans enquête
un cœur merveilleux où s'imprime le décor
des regards brisés en éclats
pour la première fois

quand les attirances prendront au piège les étoiles
quand l'amour et la mort seront
un même serpent corail ressoudé autour d'un bras sans joyau
sans suie
sans défense

batouque du fleuve grossi de larmes de crocodiles et de fouets à la dérive
batouque de l'arbre aux serpents des danseurs de la prairie
des roses de Pennsylvanie regardent aux yeux au nez aux oreilles
aux fenêtres de la tête sciée
du supplicié
batouque de la femme aux bras de mer aux cheveux de source sous-marine
la rigidité cadavérique transforme les corps
en larmes d'acier
tous les phasmes feuillus font une mer de youcas bleus et de radeaux
tous les fantasmes névrotiques ont pris le mors aux dents

batouque
quand le monde sera d'abstraction séduite
de pousses de sel gemme
les jardins de la mer

Batouque *

The rice fields of cigarette butts of spit on the strange summons
of my simplicity are tattooing themselves with sharp peaks.
Floodgate open, the words perforated in my saliva
paler above the cities, resurface as cities
O transparent cities mounted on yaks
slow blood pissing the last memory into filigreed leaves
the boulevard bruised comet brusque crossed bird
strikes itself right in the sky
drowned in arrows
It's my kind of night most hollow and most null
a fan of compass fingers collapsed into the white laughter of slumbers.

batouque
once the world is naked and russet
like a womb burned to a cinder by the great suns of love
batouque
once the world is without inquest
a wondrous heart where the scenery of glances
splintered to bits is embossed
for the first time

once the attractions entrap the stars
once love and death are
a single coral snake resoldered around a gemless arm
without soot
without defense

batouque of the river swollen with crocodile tears and drifting whips
batouque of the serpent tree of the dancers of the prairie
Pennsylvania roses peep at the eyes at the nose at the ears
at the windows of the tortured man's
sawed head
batouque of the woman with arms made of sea her hair an underwater source
rigor mortis turns bodies
into tears of steel
all the leafy phasmas make a sea of blue yuccas and rafts
all the neurotic phantasms have taken the bit between their teeth

batouque
once the world is turned into seduced abstraction
into shoots of rock salt
into the gardens of the sea

pour la première et la dernière fois
un mât de caravelle oubliée flambe amandier du naufrage
un cocotier un baobab une feuille de papier
un rejet de pourvoi
batouque
quand le monde sera une mine à ciel découvert
quand le monde sera du haut de la passerelle
mon désir
ton désir
conjugués en un saut dans le vide respiré
à l'auvent de nos yeux déferlent
toutes les poussières de soleils peuplées de parachutes
d'incendies volontaires d'oriflammes de blé rouge
batouque des yeux pourris
batouque des yeux de mélasse
batouque de mer dolente encroûtée d'îles
le Congo est un saut de soleil levant au bout d'un fil
un seau de villes saignantes
une touffe de citronnelle dans la nuit forcée
batouque
quand le monde sera une tour de silence
où nous serons la proie et le vautour
toutes les pluies de perroquets
toutes les démissions de chinchillas
batouque de trompes cassées de paupière d'huile de pluviers virulents
batouque de la pluie tuée fendue finement d'oreilles rougies
purulence et vigilance

ayant violé jusqu'à la transparence le sexe étroit du crépuscule
le grand nègre du matin
jusqu'au fond de la mer de pierre éclatée
attente les fruits de faim des villes nouées
batouque
Oh! sur l'intime vide
—giclant giclé—
jusqu'à la rage du site
les injonctions d'un sang sévère!
et le navire survola le cratère aux portes mêmes de l'heure labourée d'aigles
le navire marcha à bottes calmes d'étoiles filantes
à bottes fauves de wharfs coupés et de panoplies
et le navire lâcha une bordée de souris
de télégrammes de cauris de houris
un danseur wolof faisait des pointes et des signaux
à la pointe du mât le plus élevé
toute la nuit on le vit danser chargé d'amulettes et d'alcool
bondissant à la hauteur des étoiles grasses
une armée de corbeaux

for the first and the last time
the mast of a forgotten caravel blazes an almond tree in the wreckage
a coco-palm a baobab a sheet of paper
the dismissal of an appeal
batouque
once the world is a strip mine
once the world from the height of the upper bridge is
my desire
your desire
conjugated in a leap into the inhaled void
under the awning of our eyes unfurls
all the sundust thronged with parachutes
with deliberate fires with oriflammes of red wheat
batouque of rotted eyes
batouque of molasses eyes
batouque of a doleful sea encrusted with islands
the Congo is a leap of sun raising at the end of a thread
a pail of bloody cities
a tuft of citronella in the wrenched open night
batouque
once the world is a tower of silence
when we are prey and vulture
all the rains of parrots
all the resignations of chinchillas
batouque of broken trumpets of an oily eyelid of virulent plovers
batouque of the rain killed split finely by reddened ears
purulence and vigilance

having raped to the point of transparency the narrow sex of the dusk
the tall Negro of the morning
to the depths of the cracked stone sea
takes on the hunger fruit of knotted cities
batouque
Oh! over the intimate void
—spurted spurting—
to the very rage of the site
the injunctions of a severe blood!
and the ship flew over the crater at the very threshold of the eagle plowed hour
the ship walked in calm boots of shooting stars
in wild boots of chopped off wharves and dress armor
and the ship let fly a volley of mice
of telegrams of cowries of houris
a Wolof dancer was dancing on points and signaling
from the point of the highest mast
all night long he was seen dancing laden with amulets and alcohol
bounding to the level of the fattened stars
an army of ravens

une armée de couteaux
une armée de paraboles
et le navire cambré lâcha une armée de chevaux
A minuit la terre s'engagea dans le chenal du cratère
et le vent de diamants tendu de soutanes rouges
hors l'oubli
souffla des sabots de cheval chantant l'aventure de la mort à voix de lait
sur les jardins de l'arc-en-ciel planté de caroubiers

batouque
quand le monde sera un vivier où je pêcherai mes yeux à la ligne de tes yeux
batouque
quand le monde sera le latex au long cours des chairs de sommeil bu
batouque
batouque de houles et de hoquets
batouque de sanglots ricanés
batouque de buffles effarouchés
batouque de défis de guêpiers carminés

dans la maraude du feu et du ciel en fumée
batouque des mains
batouque des seins
batouque des sept péchés décapités
batouque du sexe au baiser d'oiseau à la fuite de poisson
batouque de princesse noire en diadème de soleil fondant
batouque de la princesse tisonnant mille gardiens inconnus
mille jardins oubliés sous le sable et l'arc-en-ciel
batouque de la princesse aux cuisses de Congo
de Bornéo
de Casamance

batouque de nuit sans noyau
de nuit sans lèvres
cravatée du jet de ma galère sans nom
de mon oiseau de boomerang
j'ai lancé mon œil dans le roulis dans la guinée du désespoir et de la mort
tout l'étrange se fige île de Pâques île de Pâques
tout l'étrange coupé des cavaleries de l'ombre
un ruisseau d'eau fraîche coule dans ma main sargasse de cris fondus

Et le navire dévêtu creusa dans la cervelle des nuits têtues
mon exil-minaret-soif-des-branches
batouque
les courants roulèrent des touffes de sabres d'argent
et de cuillers à nausée
et le vent troué des doigts du SOLEIL
tondit de feu l'aisselle des îles à cheveux d'écumes

an army of knives
an army of parabolas
and the arched ship let fly an army of horses
At midnight the earth entered the channel of the crater
and the diamond wind hung with red cassocks
out of oblivion
blew the hooves of horses singing the adventure of milky voiced death
over the gardens of the carob planted rainbow

batouque
once the world is a breeding pond where I angle for my eyes on the line of your eyes
batouque
once the world is the far-sailing latex drunk from the flesh of sleep
batouque
batouque of swells and hiccups
batouque of sneered sobs
batouque of startled buffaloes
batouque of defiances of carmined wasp nests

in the pilfering of the fire and the smoking sky
batouque of hands
batouque of breasts
batouque of the seven beheadly sins
batouque of the sex with a bird-like peck a fish-like flight
batouque of a black princess in a diadem of melting sun
batouque of the princess stoking up a thousand unknown guardians
a thousand gardens forgotten under the sand and the rainbow
batouque of the princess with thighs like the Congo
like Borneo
like Casamance

batouque of night without a seed pit
of night without lips
cravatted by the jetsam of my nameless slave galley
by my boomerang bird
I threw my eye into the rolling into the guinea of despair and death
all strangeness solidifies Easter Island Easter Island
all strangeness cut off from the cavalries of darkness
a fresh brook flows in my hand a sargasso of melted screams

And the stripped-down ship dug my thirst-for-branches-minaret-exile
out of the brain of stubborn nights
batouque
the currents churned wisps of silver sabers
and nausea spoons
and the wind pierced by SOLAR fingers
sheared with fire the armpits of foam haired islands

batouque de terres enceintes
batouque de mer murée
batouque de bourgs bossus de pieds pourris de morts épelées dans le désespoir sans prix du souvenir
Basse-Pointe Diamant Tartane et Caravelle
sekels d'or rabots de flottaisons assaillis de gerbes et de nielles
cervelles tristes rampées d'orgasmes
tatous fumeux
O les kroumens amuseurs de ma barre!
le soleil a sauté des grandes poches marsupiales de la mer sans lucarne
en pleine algèbre de faux cheveux et de rails sans tramway
batouque les rivières lézardent dans le heaume délacé des ravins
les cannes chavirent aux roulis de la terre en crue de bosses de chamelle
les anses défoncent de lumières irresponsables les vessies sans reflux de la pierre

soleil, aux gorges!
noir hurleur noir boucher noir corsaire batouque déployé d'épices et de mouches
Endormi troupeau de cavales sous la touffe de bambous
saigne saigne troupeau de carambas.

Assassin je t'acquitte au nom du viol.
Je t'acquitte au nom du Saint-Esprit
Je t'acquitte de mes mains de salamandre
le jour passera comme une vague avec les villes en bandoulière
dans sa besace de coquillages gonflés de poudre

Soleil soleil roux serpentaire accoudé à mes transes de marais en travail
le fleuve de couleuvre que j'appelle mes veines
le fleuve de créneaux que j'appelle mon sang
le fleuve de sagaies que les hommes appellent mon visage
le fleuve à pied autour du monde
frappera le roc artésien d'un cent d'étoiles à mousson

Liberté mon seul pirate eau de l'an neuf ma seule soif
amour mon seul sampang
nous coulerons nos doigts de rire et de gourde
entre les dents glacées de la Belle-au-bois-dormant.

batouque of pregnant lands
batouque of enwalled sea
batouque of humped hamlets of rotten feet of deaths spelled out in the priceless despair of memory   *
Basse-Pointe Diamant Tartant and Caravelle
gold shekels flotation planes assailed by sheaves and earcockles
sad brains crawled by orgasms
smoky armadillos
O the krumen teasers of my surf!
the sun has leapt from the great marsupial pouches of the dormerless sea
into the full algebra of false hair and tramwayless rails
batouque the rivers fissure in the unlaced helmet of ravines
the sugar cane capsizes in the rolling of the earth swollen with she-camel humps
the coves smash at the ebbless bladders of stone with irresponsible lights

sun, go for their throats!
black howler black butcher black corsair batouque bedecked with spices and flies
Sleepy herd of mares under the bamboo thicket   *
bleed bleed herd of carambas

Assassin I acquit you in the name of rape.
I acquit you in the name of the Holy Ghost
I acquit you with my salamander hands
the day will pass like a wave with its bandoleer of cities
in its beggar's sack of powder-swollen shells

Sun sun russet serpent-eater leaning on my trances of a swamp in labor
the river of grass snakes that I call my veins
the river of battlements that I call my blood
the river of assagais that men call my face
the river of walking around the world
shall strike the Artesian rock with a hundred monsoon stars

Liberty my only pirate water of the New Year my only thirst
love my only sampan
we shall slip our calabash fingers of laughter
between the icy teeth of the Sleeping Beauty.

Les oubliettes de la mer et du déluge

Jour ô jour de New York et de la soukala
je me recommande à vous
à vous qui ne serez plus l'absurde jeu du sphinx à tête de mort et de l'eczéma rebelle
et le jour très simplement le jour
enlève ses gants
ses gants de vent bleu de lait cru de sel fort
ses gants de repos d'œuf de squale et d'incendie de paille noire
sécheresse
sécheresse
vous ne pourrez rien contre mes glandes aquifères
le ballet chimique des terres rares
la poudre des yeux finement pilés sous le bâton
les mouettes immobilement têtues des fuseaux et de l'eau
font l'inaltérable alliage de mon sommeil sans heure
sans heure autre que l'inapaisement de geyser de l'arbre du silence
sans heure autre que la catastrophe fraternelle aux cheveux d'hippocampe et de campêche
sans heure autre que mes yeux de sisal et de toile d'araignée
mes yeux de clef de monde et de bris de journée
où prendre la fièvre montée sur 300 000 lucioles
sans heure autre que les couteaux de jet du soleil lancés à toute volée
autour de l'encolure des climats
sans heure autre que les oiseaux qui picorent les biefs du ciel pour apaiser leur soif-de-dormir-dans-
        le-déluge
sans heure autre que l'inconsolable oiseau sang qui d'attendre s'allume dans l'agriculture de tes yeux à
        défaire le beau temps
sans heure autre que la voix fabuleuse des forêts qui gonflent subitement leur voilure dans les radoubs
        du marais et du coke
sans heure autre que l'étiage des lunaisons dans la cervelle comptable des peuples nourris d'insultes et
        de millénaires
sans heure autre oh! sans heure autre que ton flegme taureau
incorruptible
qui jamais ne neige d'appel plus salubre et mortel
que quand s'éveille des ruisseaux de mon écorce
épi et neuvaine du désastre (le vrai)
la femme
qui sur ses lèvres à boire berce le palanquin des oubliettes de la mer

The Oubliettes of the Sea and the Deluge

*

Day oh day of New York and of soukala
I put my trust in you
in you who will no longer be the absurd game of the death's-head moth and rebellious eczema
and the day very simply the day
takes off its gloves
its gloves of blue wind of raw milk of concentrated salt
its gloves of repose of dogfish egg and of fire of black straw
dryness
dryness
you will have no power against my aquiferous glands
the chemical ballet of rare lands
the powder of eyes finely ground up under the club
the immobilely stubborn of bobbins and water
create the inalterable alloy of my hourless sleep
hourless except for the geyser-like inappeasement of the tree of silence
hourless except for the fraternal catastrophe with its hippocampal horses and Campeachy wood
hourless except for my sisal and spider web eyes
my eyes of keystone and day wreckage
where the fever mounted on 300,000 fireflies can be caught
hourless except for the knives of the sun's jet hurled at full speed
around the withers of the climates
hourless except for the birds that peck at the sky bays to appease their thirst-for-sleeping-in-the-
    deluge
hourless except for the inconsolable blood bird which from waiting lights up in the agriculture of
    your eyes undoers of fair weather
hourless except for the prodigious voice of forests which suddenly fill their sails in the drydocks of the
    swamp and coke
hourless except for the low water mark of lunations in the brain bookkeeper for people fed on insults
    and millennia
hourless except oh! hourless except for your phlegm incorruptible bull
which never snows a more healthy or deadly call
than when—wheat-spike and novena of the disaster (the real one)—
the woman
who on her drinkable lips rocks the palanquin of the sea's oubliettes
from the rivulets of my bark
is awakened

La femme et le couteau

chair riche aux dents copeaux de chair sûre
volez en éclats de jour en éclats de nuit en baisers de vent
en étraves de lumière en poupes de silence
volez emmêlements traqués enclumes de la chair sombre volez
volez en souliers d'enfant en jets d'argent
volez et défiez les cataphractaires de la nuit montés sur leurs onagres
vous oiseaux
vous sang
qui a dit que je ne serai pas là?
pas là mon cœur sans-en-marge
mon cœur-au-sans-regrets mon cœur à fonds perdus
et des hautes futaies de la pluie souveraine?

tournois
il y aura des pollens des lunes des saisons au cœur de pain et de clarine
les hauts fourneaux de la grève et de l'impossible émettront de la salive des balles des orphéons des
        mitres des candélabres
ô pandanus muet peuplé de migrations
ô nils bleus ô prières naines ô ma mère ô piste
et le cœur éclaboussé sauvage
le plus grand des frissons est encore à fleurir
futile

The Woman and the Knife

flesh rich to the teeth shavings of loyal flesh
burst into bits of day into bits of night into kisses of wind
into prows of light into sterns of quiet
burst tracked down entanglements anvils of dark flesh burst
burst into childrens' shoes into jets of silver
burst and defy the cataphracts of the night mounted on their wild asses
you birds
you blood
who said that I will not be there?
not there my heart without-marginal-notes
my heart-at-The-No-Regrets my heart on nonsecured loan
and of the high timber of the sovereign rain?

jousts
there will be pollens moons seasons with hearts of bread and cattle bell
the blast furnaces of the strike and the impossible will emit saliva bullets male choirs mitres
        candelabras
oh mute pandanus haunted by migrations
oh blue niles oh dwarf prayers oh my mother oh track
and the heart spattered wild
the greatest of thrills is still to bloom in
vain

Postface

MYTHE

Les sirènes rentrant leurs moustaches inopérantes les lumières jaunes et rouges du soir et de la nuit font en plein jour un van d'étoiles comestibles. Attendant on ne sait quels hongres et quelles moissons les fermes ne brûlent pas. On n'en revient pas de ne pas voir les bêtes travailleuses du feu et du velours dans les prairies à colocases des parois et des toits, mais déjà crépitent les secrètes tendresses idéalement situées dans le cœur des mots aux cheveux de météores. Des dos sous la pluie épargnent le suc du paysage. Plus loin le paysage lui-même à cache-cache avec lui-même dans un jeu fragile de corridors de portes battantes et d'armoiries. C'est bien mon butin—pas de chien, pas de grand'mère. De fixe, l'heure couleuvre aux frises aux tableaux mais au haut dominant les antiques l'effroi rouge-bleu de l'Absence et nos yeux fascinés par la pensée d'une poupée vengeresse aux ailes de corbeau. Les hommes? En un congé terrible. Les femmes? Sans laisse. Sans bague. Des rameurs? Des chauffeurs? Sifflera pas la bête. Que les gratte-ciel filent à contre-temps de poisson la généalogie fautive de l'espace. Leurs yeux peuplés de mélias azédarach les nègres sans piste sans pagne vous font de la main et de l'attente le geste lantane de la complicité. Où tombera le verdict? Une terrible inoccupation résiste dans la ville et menace. Cependant que la terre aînesse bâille tièdement aux matrices solennelles des convolvulus.

Postface

MYTH

The sirenias sucking in their nonfunctional moustaches the yellow and red lights of the evening and of night form in broad daylight a sieve of edible stars. Waiting for heaven knows what geldings and what harvests the farms are not burning. One is astonished not to see the animal laborers of the fire and the velvet in the Colocasia meadows of the walls and the roofs, but already the secret tendernesses ideally located in the heart of meteor-haired words are crackling. Backs in the rain husband the juice of the landscape. Further on the landscape itself at hide and seek with itself in a fragile game of corridors of swing doors and coats of arms. Clearly my booty—no dog, no grandmother. What's fixed: the hour grass-snaking across the friezes across the paintings but at the top dominating the ancient things the red-blue dread of Absence and our eyes fascinated by the thought of an avenging doll with raven wings. Men? On a frightful leave. Women? Leashless. Ringless. Oarsmen? Chauffeurs? Will not whistle for the beast. Let the skyscrapers pay out off-beat like a fish the faulty genealogy of space. Their eyes covered with Melias azadirachtas the trackless loin-clothless blacks make the Lantana gesture of a complicity to you with their hands and their waiting. Where will the sentence fall? An awful idleness holds out in the city and threatens. Meanwhile the primogenital earth yawns tepidly in the solemn wombs of the convolvuli.

SOLEIL COU COUPE
*
SOLAR THROAT SLASHED

Wifredo Lam, "La langue maternelle," 1942, gouache, 42 × 34½"

Magique

avec une lèche de ciel sur un quignon de terre
vous bêtes qui sifflez sur le visage de cette morte
vous libres fougères parmi les roches assassines
à l'extrême de l'île parmi les conques trop vastes pour leur destin
lorsque midi colle ses mauvais timbres sur les plis tempétueux de la louve
hors cadre de science nulle
et la bouche aux parois du nid suffète des îles englouties comme un sou

avec une lèche de ciel sur un quignon de terre
prophète des îles oubliées comme un sou
sans sommeil sans veille sans doigts sans palancre
quand la tornade passe rongeur du pain des cases

vous bêtes qui sifflez sur le visage de cette morte
la belle once de la luxure et la coquille operculée
mol glissement des grains de l'été que nous fûmes
belles chairs à transpercer du trident des aras
lorsque les étoiles chancelières de cinq branches
trèfles au ciel comme des gouttes de lait chu
réajustent un dieu noir mal né de son tonnerre

Magic

with a smear of sky on a hunk of earth
you beasts hissing over the face of this dead woman
you free ferns amidst the murderous rocks
at the far end of the island amidst conches too vast for their destiny
when noon sticks its wrong stamps on the tempestuous folds of the she-wolf
outside the domain of pointless science
and plugs her against the walls of the nest the suffete of islands swallowed up like a penny

with a smear of sky on a hunk of earth
a prophet of islands forgotten like a penny
sleepless wakeless fingerless trawlless
when the tornado passes gnawer at the bread of huts

you beasts hissing over the face of this dead woman
the beautiful snow leopard of lust and the operculated shell
slack gliding of the summer grain that we were
beautiful flesh to be pierced by the macaw's trident
when the five-branched chancelloress stars
clover in the sky like drops of fallen milk
restore a black god feebly born to his thunder

La parole aux oricous

Où quand comment d'où pourquoi oui pourquoi pourquoi pourquoi se peut-il que les langues les plus
   scélérates n'aient inventé que si peu de crocs à pendre ou suspendre le destin

Arrêtez cet homme innocent. Tous de leurre. Il porte mon sang sur les épaules. Il porte mon sang dans
   ses souliers. Il colporte mon sang dans son nez. Mort aux contrebandiers. Les frontières sont
   fermées.
Ni su ni insu
tous
dieu merci mon cœur est plus sec que l'harmattan, toute obscurité m'est proie
toute obscurité m'est due et toute bombe joie.

Vous oricous à vos postes de tournoiement et de bec audessus de la forêt et jusqu'à la caverne dont la
   porte est un triangle
dont le gardien est un chien
dont la vie est un calice
dont la vierge est une araignée
dont le sillage rare est un lac à se mettre debout sur les chemins de déchant des nixes orageuses

The Oricous Have the Floor *

Where when how from whence why yes why why why is it that the most criminal tongues have
    invented so few hooks on which to pend or suspend fate

Arrest this innocent man. Fakes, all of 'em. He carries my blood on his shoulders. He carries my
    blood in his shoes. Peddles my blood in his nose. Death to the smugglers. The borders are
    closed.
Neither the known nor the unknown
all of them
thank god my heart is dryer than the harmattan, every darkness is my prey
every darkness is my due and every bomb my joy.

You oricous at your hovering and pecking stations above the forest and as far as the cavern whose
    door is a triangle
whose guardian is a dog
whose life is a calyx
whose maiden is a spider
whose precious wake is a lake for standing on the descant paths of stormy nixies

La loi est nue

Baies ailées j'ai marché sur le cœur grondant de l'excellent printemps
de qui ai-je jamais soutiré autre femme
qu'un long cri et sous ma traction de lait
qu'une terre s'enfuyant blessée et reptile entre les dents de la forêt

net trop plein du jet
me voici
dans les arrières des eaux
et roucoulant vos scrupuleuses colombes
                      assis mets vrai pour les oiseaux

que toutes les trames en vain se nouent
que tous les moulins à prière à gauche tournent

Il n'y a plus de machine à traire
le matin qui n'est pas encore monté.
Tous mes cailloux sont d'offense
Point d'huile
La loi est nue.

Allure

O montagnes ô dolomies cœur d'oiseau sous mes mains d'enfant
ô icebergs ô revenants vieux dieux scellés en pleine gloire
et quand même autour du feu à trois pierres couronné d'un cercle
vibrant de tipules
un étang pour les noyés se renouvelle
province des morts vous heurtez en vain la rotation des routes
où le spectacle passe du palier de flammes vertes à la tranche de maléfices
allure combats avec moi je porte la tiare solaire
gong décuple la prison dont les combats d'animaux expérimentent
les voix des hommes conservés dans la pétrification des forêts de mille ans

ma chère penchons sur les filons géologiques

The Law Is Naked

Winged berries I walked on the grumbling heart of the excellent spring
from whom have I ever conned a wife
other than a long scream and under my milky tug
other than an earth fleeing wounded and reptile between the teeth of the forest

clear overflowing from the jet
here I am
in the backwaters
amidst the cooing of your scrupulous doves
                seated really food for the birds

let all the plots thicken in vain
let all the prayer wheels turn to the left

There are no more milking machines for
the morning which has yet to rise.
All my pebbles are made of offence
No oil at all
The law is naked.

Velocity

O mountain oh dolomites bird heart in my childlike hands
oh icebergs oh ghosts old gods sealed in full glory
and even if around a three stone fire crowned with a quivering
circle of tipulas
a pond for the drowned renews itself
province of the dead you strike in vain against the rotation of highways
where the spectacle passes from the level of green flames to the edge of malefice
velocity fight with me I wear the solar tiara
gong multiply the prison whose animal fights experience
the voices of men preserved in the petrifaction of millennial forests

my dear let's bend with the geological veins

Désastre tangible

Tout insecte compté (le métal de l'herbe a cravaté leur gorge)
menstrue de cendre
bond lent d'un four tendant sa surprise de pains dont l'équipage
pris au piège dessèche tout litige
désastre
blocs
au bout de l'œil la gueule sous le bâillon de nuages
volcan écartelé le Bédouin de ce désert
devanture d'un tout doux Caraïbe roulant sur des os et des ans
sa caravane écoutée d'engloutis
pieds ou éclat quel quarteron de nègres ou de peaux rouges
massacrés à la fin de la nuit rengaine ta dégaine jamais née
et tes pieds portés par les eaux
        les restitue au tablier sans cris d'un strom présomptueux

Entre autres massacres

De toutes leurs forces le soleil et la lune s'entrechoquent
les étoiles tombent comme des témoins trop mûrs
et comme une portée de souris grises

ne crains rien apprête tes grosses eaux
qui si bien emportent la berge des miroirs

ils ont mis de la boue sur mes yeux
et vois je vois terriblement je vois
de toutes les montagnes de toutes les îles
il ne reste plus rien que les quelques mauvais chicots
de l'impénitente salive de la mer

Tangible Disaster

All insects accounted for (the metal of the grass has seized their throats)
ashy menses
slow leap of an oven handing out its surprise of loaves whose crew
entrapped dries out all litigation
disaster
lumps
at the eye's limit its mug gagged by clouds
a quartered volcano the Bedouin of this desert
a front for a sweet ole Carib rolling his caravan over bones
and years heard by engulfed
feet or an eruption what quadroon of massacred niggers or redskins
at night's end resheaths the dagger of your neverborn swagger
restituting your feet borne along by the waters
   to the screamless apron of a presumptuous strom

                                 *

Among Other Massacres

With all their strength the sun and the moon collide
the stars fall like overripe witnesses
like a litter of grey mice

fear nothing prepare your high waters
which so neatly remove the bank of mirrors

they have put mud over my eyes
and see I see terribly I see
of all the mountains of all the islands
nothing left save the few rotted teeth
of the impenitent saliva of the sea

Le griffon

Je suis un souvenir qui n'atteint pas le seuil
et erre dans les limbes où le reflet d'absinthe
quand le cœur de la nuit souffle par ses évents
bouge l'étoile tombée où nous nous contemplons

Le ciel lingual a pris sa neuve consistance de crème de noix fraîche
ouverte de coco

Andes crachant et Mayumbé sacré
seul naufrage que l'œil bon voilier nous soudoie
quand âme folle déchiquetée folle
          par les nuages qui m'arrivent dans les poissons bien clos
je remonte hanter la sinistre épaisseur des choses

Rachat

Le bruit fort gravite pourri d'une cargaison
désastre véreux et clair de soldanelle
le bruit fort gravite méninge de diamants
ton visage glisse nu en ma fureur laiteuse

Touffeurs d'amibes
touffeurs de laitances vrais fils de la vraie vierge immaculée
aux aubes de la mer quand les méteils firent peau et maraudes des damnés

Touffeurs des tas d'assiettes ébréchées
de ruines de chiens pelés et de scaphandriers qui glissent au crépuscule

Touffeur fruste rayonnement
au nu très lent de ma main
l'ombilic vierge de la terre

The Griffin

I am a memory that does not reach the threshold
and wanders in the limbo where the glint of absinthe
when the heart of night breathes through its blowholes
moves the fallen star in which we contemplate ourselves

The lingual sky took on a new consistency of a freshly opened
coconut's cream

spitting Andes and sacred Mayumba
sole shipwreck that the eye good sailer pays off for us
when soul maddened shredded maddened
            through clouds which reach me in tightly shut fish
I reascend to haunt the sinister thickness of things

Redemption

The loud noise gravitates rotten with cargo
wormy and bright wreckage of a soldanel
the loud noise gravitates a meninx of diamonds
your face glides naked into my milky frenzy

Amoebic swelter
miltic swelter true gossamers of the true immaculate virgin
in the auroras of the sea when the maslin made skin and plunder of the damned

Sweltering piles of chipped plates
of ruins of mangy dogs of deep-sea divers who glide away at dusk

Swelter crude radiance
in the barely moving nakedness of my hand
virgin umbilicus of the earth

Mississippi

Hommes tant pis qui ne vous apercevez pas que mes yeux se souviennent
      de frondes et de drapeaux noirs
      qui assassinent à chaque battement de mes cils

Hommes tant pis qui ne voyez pas qui ne voyez rien
pas même la très belle signalisation de chemin de fer que
font sous mes paupières les disques rouges et noirs du
serpent-corail que ma munificence love dans mes larmes

Hommes tant pis qui ne voyez pas qu'au fond du réticule
où le hasard a déposé nos yeux
il y a qui attend un buffle noyé jusqu'à la garde des yeux du marécage

Hommes tant pis qui ne voyez pas que vous ne pouvez m'empêcher de bâtir à sa suffisance
des îles à la tête d'œuf de ciel flagrant
sous la férocité calme du géranium immense de notre soleil.

Blues de la pluie

Aguacero
beau musicien
au pied d'un arbre dévêtu
parmi les harmonies perdues
près de nos mémoires défaites
parmi nos mains de défaite
et des peuples de force étrange
nous laissions pendre nos yeux
et natale
dénouant la longe d'une douleur
nous pleurions.

Mississippi

Too bad for you men who don't notice that my eyes remember
        slings and black flags
        which murder with each blink of my lashes

Too bad for you men who do not see who do not see anything
not even the gorgeous railway signals formed
under my eyelids by red and black discs of
the coral snake that my munificence coils in my tears

Too bad for you men who do not see that in the depth of the reticule
where chance deposited our eyes
there is, waiting, a buffalo sunk to the very hilt of the swamp's eyes

Too bad for you men who do not see that you cannot stop me from building for him plenty
of egg-headed islands out of the flagrant sky
under the calm ferocity of the immense geranium of our sun.

Blues of the Rain

*

Aguacero
beautiful musician
unclothed at the foot of a tree
amidst the lost harmonies
close to our defeated memories
amidst our hands of defeat
and a people of alien strength
we let our eyes hang low
and untying
the tether of a natal anguish
we sobbed.

Le bouc émissaire

Les veines de la berge s'engourdissent d'étranges larves
nous et nos frères
dans les champs les squelettes attendent leurs frissons et la chair
rien ne viendra et la saison est nulle
la morsure de nos promesses s'est accomplie au-dessus du sein d'un village et le village est mort avec
tous ses hommes qu'on ne reconnaissait à travers leur tube de mica hier qu'à la patience violette de
leurs excréments muets
O cueilleuse
si fragile si fragile au bord des nuits la pâtisserie du paysage qu'à la fin jubilation à tête blanche des
pygargues elle y vole mais pour l'œil qui se voit il y a sur la paroi prophète d'ombre et tremblant au
gré des pyrites un cœur qui pompe un sang de lumière et d'herbe
et la mer l'Aborigène une poignée de rumeurs entre les dents se traîne hors de ses os marsupiaux et
posant sa première pierre d'île dans le vent qui s'éboule de la force renouvelée des fœtus, rumine
flamber ses punchs d'anathèmes et de mirage vers la merveille nue de nos villes tâtant le futur et
nos gueules claquantes de bouc émissaire

Fils de la foudre

Et sans qu'elle ait daigné séduire les geôliers
à son corsage s'est délité un bouquet d'oiseaux-mouches
à ses oreilles ont germé des bourgeons d'attolls
elle me parle une langue si douce que tout d'abord je ne comprends pas mais à la longue je devine
qu'elle m'affirme
que le printemps est arrivé à contre-courant
que toute soif est étanchée que l'automne nous est concilié
que les étoiles dans la rue ont fleuri en plein midi et très bas suspendent leurs fruits

The Scapegoat

The veins of the river bank grow numb with strange larvae
us and our brothers
in the fields the skeletons await their tremors and their flesh
    neither will come, nothing this season
the bite of our promises was fulfilled above the breast of a village and the village died with all its men
    recognizable through their mica tubes yesterday only by the violet patience of their mute
    excrement
O woman gathering
at the edge of the nights the pastry of the landscape so fragile so fragile that at last a white-headed
    jubilation of sea eagles she flies there but for the eye that sees itself there is on the wall prophet
    of shadows and trembling at the whim of pyrites a heart pumping a blood made of light and
    grass
and the sea the Aborigine a handful of murmurs between its teeth drags itself out of its marsupial
    bones and placing its first island rock in the wind which tumbles down from the renewed
    strength of foetuses chews over igniting its punch mixed with anathemas and mirage against
    the naked wonder of our cities testing the future and our croakable scapegoat mugs

Son of Thunder

And without her even trying to seduce the jailers
at her bosom a bouquet of hummingbirds exfoliated
at her ears buds of atolls sprouted
she speaks to me a language so soft that at first I do not understand but eventually I guess she is
    assuring me
that spring has come counter-current
that all thirst is quenched that autumn is kindly disposed to us
that the stars in the street have blossomed at high noon and dangle their fruits very low

Ex-voto pour un naufrage

Hélé helélé le Roi est un grand roi
que sa majesté daigne regarder dans mon anus pour voir
s'il contient des diamants
que sa majesté daigne explorer ma bouche pour voir
combien elle contient de carats
tam-tam ris
tam-tam ris
je porte la litière du roi
j'étends le tapis du roi
je suis le tapis du roi
je porte les écrouelles du roi
je suis le parasol du roi
riez riez tam-tams des kraals
tam-tams des mines qui riez sous cape
tam-tams sacrés qui riez à la barbe des missionnaires de
vos dents de rat et d'hyène
tam-tams de la forêt
tam-tams du désert
tam-tam pleure
tam-tam pleure
brûlé jusqu'au fougueux silence de nos pleurs sans rivage
et roulez
roulez bas rien qu'un temps de bille
le pur temps de charbon de nos longues affres majeures
roulez roulez lourds délires sans vocable
lions roux sans crinière
tam-tams qui protégez mes trois âmes mon cerveau mon cœur mon foie
tam-tams durs qui très haut maintenez ma demeure de vent d'étoiles
sur le roc foudroyé de ma tête noire
et toi tam-tam frère pour qui il m'arrive de garder tout le long du jour un mot tour à tour chaud et frais
    dans ma bouche comme le goût peu connu de la vengeance
tam-tams de Kalaari
tam-tams de Bonne Espérance qui coiffez le cap de vos
menaces
O tam-tam du Zululand
Tam-tam de Chaka
tam, tam, tam
tam, tam, tam
Roi nos montagnes sont des cavales en rut saisies en pleine convulsion de mauvais sang
Roi nos plaines sont des rivières qu'impatientent les fournitures de pourritures montées de la mer et de
    vos caravelles

Ex-Voto for a Shipwreck

Hélé helélé the King is a great king
let his majesty deign to look up my anus to see
if it contains diamonds
let his majesty deign to explore my mouth to see
how many carats it contains
laugh tom-tom
laugh tom-tom
I carry the king's litter
I roll out the king's rug
I am the king's rug
I carry scrofula for the king
I am the king's parasol
laugh laugh tom-toms of the kraals
tom-toms of mines that laugh up their shafts
sacred tom-toms laughing about your rat and hyena teeth
right in the missionaries' faces
tom-toms of the forest
tom-toms of the desert
weep tom-tom
weep tom-tom
burned down to the impetuous silence of our shoreless tears
and roll
roll softly no longer than a speck of coal
the pure carbon duration of our endless major pangs
roll roll heavy speechless deliriums
russet lions without manes
tom-toms which protect my three souls my brain my heart my liver
hard tom-toms which very loudly uphold my star wind dwelling over
the blasted rock of my black head
and you brother tom-tom for whom sometimes all day long I keep a word now hot now cool in my
 mouth like the little known taste of vengeance
tom-toms of the Kalahari
tom-toms of Good Hope that cap the cape with your threats
O tom-tom of Zululand
Tom-tom of Shaka
tom, tom, tom
tom, tom, tom
King our mountains are mares in heat caught in the full convulsion of bad blood
King our plains are rivers vexed by the supplies of putrefactions drifting in from the sea and your
 caravels

Roi nos pierres sont des lampes ardentes d'une espérance veuve de dragon
Roi nos arbres sont la forme déployée que prend une flamme trop grosse pour notre cœur trop faible
        pour un donjon
Riez riez donc tam-tams de Cafrerie
comme le beau point d'interrogation du scorpion
dessiné au pollen sur le tableau du ciel et de nos cervelles à minuit
comme un frisson de reptile marin charmé par la pensée du mauvais temps
du petit rire renversé de la mer dans les hublot très beaux du naufrage

Millibars de l'orage

N'apaisons pas le jour et sortons la face nue
face aux pays inconnus qui coupent aux oiseaux leur sifflet
le guet-apens s'ouvre le long d'un bruit de confins de planètes
ne fais pas attention aux chenilles qui tissent souple
mais seulement aux millibars qui se plantent dans le mille d'un orage
à délivrer l'espace où se hérissent le cœur des choses et la venue de l'homme

Rêve n'apaisons pas
parmi les clous de chevaux fous
un bruit de larmes qui tâtonne vers l'aile immense des paupières

King our stones are lamps burning with a hope widowed from its dragon
King our trees are the unfolded shape taken by a flame too big for our hearts too weak for a dungeon
Laugh laugh then tom-toms of Kaffraria
like the scorpion's beautiful question mark
drawn in pollen on the canvas of the sky and of our brains at midnight
like the quiver of a sea reptile charmed by the anticipation of bad weather
of the little upside down laugh of the sea in the sunken ship's gorgeous portholes

Millibars of the Storm

Let's not placate the day but go out our faces exposed
facing those unknown countries that take the wind out of the birds' wings
the ambush opens along a sound of outer planetary limits
pay no attention to the supplely weaving caterpillars
but only to the millibars that dig into the milli-eye of a storm
to liberate the space where the heart of things and the advent of man are bristling

Dream let's not placate
amidst the nails of crazed horses
a sound of tears that gropes toward the vast wing of eyelids

Chevelure

Dirait-on pas bombardé d'un sang de latérites
bel arbre nu
en déjà l'invincible départ vers on imagine un sabbat de splendeur
et de villes l'invincible et spacieux cri du coq

Innocente qui ondoies
tous les sucs qui montent dans la luxure de la terre
tous les poisons que distillent les alambics nocturnes dans l'involucre des malvacées
tous les tonnerres des saponaires
sont pareils à ces mots discordants écrits par l'incendie des bûchers
sur les oriflammes sublimes de ta révolte

Chevelure
flammes ingénues qui léchez un cœur insolite
la forêt se souviendra de l'eau et de l'aubier
comme moi je me souviens du museau attendri
des grands fleuves qui titubent comme des aveugles
la forêt se souvient que le dernier mot ne peut être
que le cri flambant de l'oiseau des ruines dans le bol de l'orage

Innocent qui vas là
oublie de te rappeler
que le baobab est notre arbre
qu'il mal agite des bras si nains
qu'on le dirait un géant imbécile
et toi
séjour de mon insolence de mes tombes de mes trombes
crinière paquet de lianes espoir fort des naufragés
dors doucement au tronc méticuleux de mon étreinte ma
femme
ma citadelle

Your Hair

Wouldn't you have taken it bombarded by lateritic blood
for a beautiful stripped tree
the invincible and spacious cockcrowing already in invincible departure toward
—one imagines—a witches' sabbath of splendor and cities

Undulating innocent
all the juices rising in the lust of the earth
all the poisons distilled by the nocturnal alembics in the involucres of the Malvaceae
all the thundering of the Saponaria
are like these discordant words written by the flames of pyres
over the sublime oriflammes of your revolt

Your hair
ingenuous flames licking a rare heart
the forest will remember the water and the sapwood
as I too remember the compassionate snouts
of big rivers that stumble around like blind men
the forest remembers that the last word can only be
the flaming cry of the bird of ruins in the bowl of the storm

Innocent who goes there
forget to remember
that the baobab is our tree
that it barely waves arms so dwarfed
that you would take it for an imbecilic giant
and you
inhabited by my insolence my tombs my twisters
mane bundle of lianas violent hope of the shipwrecked
sleep softly by the meticulous trunk of my embrace my
woman
my citadel

La tornade

Le temps que
           le sénateur s'aperçut que la tornade était assise dans son assiette
et la tornade était dans l'air fourrageant dans Kansas City
Le temps que
           le pasteur aperçut la tornade dans l'œil bleu de la femme du shériff
et la tornade fut dehors faisant apparaître à tous sa large face
puant comme dix mille nègres entassés dans un train
le temps pour la tornade de s'esclaffer de rire
et la tornade fit sur tout une jolie imposition de mains de ses belles mains blanches d'ecclésiastique
Le temps pour Dieu de s'apercevoir
           qu'il avait bu de trop cent verres de sang de bourreau
et la ville fut une fraternité de taches blanches et noires
répandues en cadavres sur la peau d'un cheval abattu en plein galop
Et la tornade ayant subi les provinces de la mémoire riche gravat
craché d'un ciel engrangé de sentences tout trembla
une seconde fois l'acier tordu fut retordu
Et la tornade qui avait avalé comme un vol de grenouilles son troupeau de toitures et de cheminées
     respira
bruyamment une pensée que les prophètes n'avaient jamais su deviner

The Tornado

By the time
                the senator noticed the tornado was sitting in his plate
the tornado was in the air foraging through Kansas City
By the time
                the minister glimpsed the tornado in the blue eye of the sheriff's wife
the tornado was outside displaying to everyone its huge face
stinking like ten thousand niggers piled up in a train
by the time the tornado guffawed
it had performed over everything an elegant laying-on-of-hands, those beautiful white clerical
        hands
By the time God noticed
                that he had drunk one hundred glasses of executioner blood too many
the city was a brotherhood of black and white spots
scattered like cadavers on the hide of a horse felled in full gallop
And the tornado having survived the provinces of memory rich rubbish
spat from a sky packed with verdicts everything quaked
for the second time the twisted steel was retwisted
And the tornado which had swallowed like a flight of frogs its herd of roofs and chimneys noisily
exhaled a thought the prophets had never known how to divine

Totem

De loin en proche de proche en loin le sistre des circoncis et un soleil hors mœurs
buvant dans la gloire de ma poitrine un grand coup de vin rouge et de mouches
comment d'étage en étage de détresse en héritage le totem ne bondirait-il pas au sommet des buildings
        sa tiédeur de cheminée et de trahison ?
comme la distraction salée de ta langue destructrice
comme le vin de ton venin
comme ton rire de dos de marsouin dans l'argent du naufrage
comme la souris verte qui naît de la belle eau captive de tes paupières
comme la course des gazelles de sel fin de la neige sur la tête sauvage des femmes de l'abîme
comme les grandes étamines de tes lèvres dans le filet bleu du continent
comme l'éclatement de feu de la minute dans la trame serrée du temps
comme la chevelure de genêt qui s'obstine à pousser dans l'arrière-saison de tes yeux à marine
chevaux du quadrige piétinez la savane de ma parole vaste ouverte

du blanc au fauve
il y a les sanglots le silence la mer rouge et la nuit

Totem

From now by far from near and then the circumcised's sistrum and an uncommon sun
drinking a big slug of red wine and flies in the glory of my chest
how from stage to stage from distress to heritage could the totem not spring its tepidity of hearth and
      treason to the top of the buildings?
like the salty diversion of your destructive tongue
like the wine of your venom
like your porpoise-back laughter in the silver of the shipwreck
like the green mouse born from the beautiful captive water of your eyelids
like the flight of gazelles of fine salt of the snow over the wild heads of women of the abyss
like the thick stamens of your lips in the continent's blue filament
like the rifle crack of the minute in the tightened woof of time
like the head of gorse hair which persists in growing in the Indian Summer of the seascape of your
      eyes
quadrigate horses stamp the savanna of my vast open speech

from white to fawn
there is sobbing silence reddened sea and the night

Samba

Tout ce qui d'anse s'est agglutiné pour former tes seins toutes les cloches d'hibiscus toutes les huîtres perlières toutes les pistes brouillées qui forment une mangrove tout ce qu'il y a de soleil en réserve dans les lézards de la sierra tout ce qu'il faut d'iode pour faire un jour marin tout ce qu'il faut de nacre pour dessiner un bruit de conque sous-marine
Si tu voulais
      les tétrodons à la dérive iraient se donnant la main
Si tu voulais
      tout le long du jour les péronias de leurs queues feraient des routes et les évêques seraient si rares
      qu'on ne serait pas surpris d'apprendre qu'ils ont été avalés par les crosses des trichomans
Si tu voulais
      la force physique
      assurerait toute seule la nuit d'un balisage d'araras
Si tu voulais
      dans les faubourgs qui furent pauvres les norias remonteraient avec dans les godets le parfum
      des bruits les plus neufs dont se grise la terre dans ses plis infernaux
Si tu voulais
      les fauves boiraient aux fontaines
      et dans nos têtes
      les patries de terre violente
      tendraient comme un doigt aux oiseaux l'allure sans secousse
      des hauts mélèzes

Samba

All that from a cove combined to form your breasts all the hibiscus bells all the pearl oysters all the
covered-up tracks which form a mangrove all the sun that is stored in sierra lizards all the iodine
needed to make a marine day all the mother-of-pearl needed to delineate the sound of a submarine
conch
If you wanted them to
    the drifting Tetraodontidae would move hand in hand
If you wanted them to
    all day long the Phoronidea would make roads with their tentacles and bishops would be so
    rare that it would not be surprising to hear that they had been swallowed by the
    Trichomanes' crosiers
If you wanted it to
    physical force
    would on its own mark out the night with macaw buoys
If you wanted them to
    in suburbs no longer poor norias would rotate, in their buckets the perfume of the newest
    sounds, off which the earth intoxicates itself in its infernal folds
If you wanted them to
    wild beasts would drink from the fountains
    and in our heads
    the homelands of violent earth
    would extend like a finger for the birds the joltless bearing
    of high larches

Interlude

Bond vague de l'once sans garrot
au zénith
poussière de lait
un midi est avec moi
glissé très rare de tes haras
d'ombres cuites et
très rares entrelacs des doigts
O soleil déchiré
aveugle paon magique et frais
aux mains d'arches d'éprouvettes
futile éclipse de l'espace

La roue

La roue est la plus belle découverte de l'homme et la seule
il y a le soleil qui tourne
il y a la terre qui tourne
il y a ton visage qui tourne sur l'essieu de ton cou quand tu pleures
mais vous minutes n'enroulerez-voux pas sur la bobine à vivre
le sang lapé
l'art de souffrir aiguisé comme des moignons d'arbre par les couteaux de l'hiver
la biche saoule de ne pas boire
qui me pose sur la margelle inattendue ton
visage de goélette démâtée
ton visage
comme un village endormi au fond d'un lac
et qui renaît au jour de l'herbe et de l'année
germe

Interlude

Wavering bound of the ungarroted snow leopard
to the zenith
dust of milk
a noon is with me
slipped away very rare from your stud farms
of cooked shadows and
very rare interlockings of fingers
O ripped blind
sun peacock magical and cool
with arched test tube hands
a futile eclipse of space

The Wheel

The wheel is man's most beautiful and only discovery
there is the sun which turns
there is the earth which turns
there is your face turning on the axle of your neck when you cry
but you minutes won't you wind on your spindle for living
the lapped up blood
the art of suffering sharpened to tree stumps by the knives of winter
the doe drunk from not drinking
which on the unexpected wellcurb presents me with your
face of a dismasted schooner
your face
like a village asleep at the bottom of a lake
which is reborn to daylight from the grass and from the year
germinates

Calme

Le temps bien sûr sera nul du péché
les portes céderont sous l'assaut des eaux
les orchidées pousseront leur douce tête violente de torturé à travers la claire-voie que deux à deux font
     les paroles
les lianes dépêcheront du fond de leurs veilles une claire batterie de sangsues dont l'embrassade sera de
     la force irrésistible des parfums
de chaque grain de sable naîtra un oiseau
de chaque fleur simple sortira un scorpion (tout étant recomposé)
les trompettes des droseras éclateront pour marquer l'heure où
abdiquer mes épaisses lèvres plantées d'aiguillles en faveur de l'armature flexible des futurs aloès
l'émission de chair naïve autour de la douleur sera généralisée
hors de tout rapport avec l'incursion bivalve des cestodes cependant
que les hirondelles nées de ma salive agglutineront
avec les algues apportées par les vagues qui montent de toi le mythe sanglant d'une minute jamais
     murmurée
aux étages des tours du silence les vautours s'envoleront avec au bec
des lambeaux de la vieille chair trop peu calme pour nos squelettes

Calm

Time of course shall be void of sin
gates shall buckle under the assault of waters
orchids shall push their sweet violent heads of tortured ones through the openwork which words
      form two by two
lianas shall dispatch from the depth of their vigils a luminous battery of leeches whose embrace shall
      have the irresistible force of perfume
from each grain of sand a bird shall be born
from each simple flower a scorpion shall emerge (everything being compound)
the Droseras' trumpets shall blast to mark the hour for
abdicating my thick needle implanted lips in favor of the flexible armature of future aloes
the emission of naive flesh around pain shall be generalized
totally unconnected to the bivalvular incursion of cestodes while
the swallows born to my saliva shall agglutinate
the bloody myth of a never whispered minute with the seaweed carried in by waves that rise from
      you—
from platforms on the towers of silence the vultures shall take off, in their beaks
shreds of that former flesh too uncalm for our skeletons

An neuf

Les hommes ont taillé dans leurs tourments une fleur
qu'ils ont juchée sur les hauts plateaux de leur face
la faim leur fait un dais
une image se dissout dans leur dernière larme
ils ont bu jusqu'à l'horreur féroce
les monstres rhythmés par les écumes
En ce temps-là
il y eut une
inoubliable
métamorphose
les chevaux ruaient un peu de rêve sur leurs sabots
de gros nuages d'incendie s'arrondirent en champignon
sur toutes les places publiques
ce fut une peste merveilleuse
sur le trottoir les moindres réverbères tournaient leur tête de phare
quant à l'avenir anophèle vapeur brûlante il sifflait dans les jardins
En ce temps-là
le mot ondée
et le mot sol meuble
le mot aube
et le mot copeaux
conspirèrent pour la première fois

New Year

Out of their torments men carved a flower
which they perched on the high plateaus of their faces
hunger makes a canopy for them
an image dissolves in their last tear
they drank foam rhythmed monsters
to the point of ferocious horror
In those days
there was an
unforgettable
metamorphosis
on their hooves the horses were rearing a bit of dream
fat fiery clouds filled out like mushrooms
over all the public squares
there was a terrific pestilence
on the sidewalks the smaller streetlamps were rotating their lighthouse heads
as for the anophelic future it was hissing in the gardens a scorching vapor
In those days
the word shower
and the word topsoil
the word dawn
and the word shavings
conspired for the first time

Depuis Akkad, depuis Elam, depuis Sumer

Eveilleur, arracheur
Souffle souffert, souffle accoureur
Maître des trois chemins, tu as en face de toi un homme
qui a beaucoup marché.
Depuis Elam. Depuis Akkad. Depuis Sumer.
Maître des trois chemins, tu as en face de toi un homme
qui a beaucoup porté.
Depuis Elam. Depuis Akkad. Depuis Sumer.
J'ai porté le corps du commandant. J'ai porté le chemin de fer du commandant. J'ai porté la locomotive
du commandant, le coton du commandant. J'ai porté sur ma tête laineuse qui se passe si bien de
coussinet Dieu, la machine, la route—le Dieu du commandant.
Maître des trois chemins j'ai porté sous le soleil, j'ai porté dans le brouillard j'ai porté sur les tessons de
braise des fourmis manians
J'ai porté le parasol j'ai porté l'explosif j'ai porté le carcan.
Depuis Akkad. Depuis Elam. Depuis Sumer.
Maître des trois chemins, Maître des trois rigoles, plaise que pour une fois—la première depuis Akkad
depuis Elam depuis Sumer—le museau plus tanné apparemment que le cal de mes pieds mais en
réalité plus doux que le bec minutieux du corbeau et comme drapé des plis amers que me fait ma grise
peau d'emprunt (livrée que les hommes m'imposent chaque hiver)
j'avance à travers les feuilles mortes de mon petit pas sorcier

vers là où menace triomphalement l'inépuisable injonction des hommes jetés aux ricanements noueux
     de l'ouragan.
Depuis Elam depuis Akkad depuis Sumer.

All the Way from Akkad, from Elam, from Sumer

Awakener, uprooter
Suffered breath, hastener breath
Master of the three paths, you are facing a man
who has walked a lot.
All the way from Elam. From Akkad. From Sumer.
Master of the three paths, you are facing a man
who has carried a lot.
All the way from Elam. From Akkad. From Sumer.
I have carried the commandant's body. I have carried the commandant's railroad. I have carried the commandant's locomotive, the commandant's cotton. On my wooly head which works so fine without a little cushion I have carried God, the machine, the road—the God of the commandant. Master of the three paths I have carried under the sun, I have carried in the fog I have carried over the ember shards of legionary ants
I have carried the parasol I have carried the explosives I have carried the iron-collar.
All the way from Akkad. From Elam. From Sumer.
Master of the three paths, Master of the three channels, for once only the first time since Akkad since Elam since Sumer may you grant that—my muzzle apparently more tanned than the calluses on my feet but in reality softer than the raven's scrupulous beak and as if draped in bitter folds provided by my borrowed grey skin (a livery that men force onto me every winter)
—I advance across the dead leaves with my little sorcerer steps

toward where the inexhaustible injunction of men thrown to the knotted sneers of the hurricane
    threatens triumphantly.
All the way from Elam from Akkad from Sumer.

A l'Afrique / à Wifredo Lam

Paysan frappe le sol de ta daba
dans le sol il y a une hâte que la syllabe de l'événement ne dénoue pas
je me souviens de la fameuse peste
il n'y avait pas eu d'étoile annoncière
mais seulement la terre en un flot sans galet pétrissant d'espace
un pain d'herbe et de réclusion
frappe paysan frappe
le premier jour les oiseaux moururent
le second jour les poissons échouèrent
le troisième jour les animaux sortirent des bois
et faisaient aux villes une grande ceinture chaude très forte
frappe le sol de ta daba
il y a dans le sol la carte des transmutations et des ruses de la mort
la quatrième jour le végétation se fana
et tout tourna à l'aigre de l'agave à l'acacia
en aigrettes en orgues végétales
où le vent épineux jouait des flûtes et des odeurs tranchantes
Frappe paysan frappe
il naît au ciel des fenêtres qui sont mes yeux giclés
et dont la herse dans ma poitrine fait le rempart d'une ville qui refuse de donner la passe aux muletiers
        de la désespérance
Famine et de toi-même houle
ramas où se risque d'un salut la colère du futur
frappe Colère
il y a au pied de nos châteaux-de-fées pour la rencontre du sang et du paysage la salle de bal où des nains
        braquant leurs miroirs
écoutent dans les plis de la pierre ou du sel croître le sexe du regard
Paysan pour que débouche de la tête de la montagne celle que blesse le vent
pour que tiédisse dans sa gorge une gorgée de cloches
pour que ma vague se dévore en sa vague et nous ramène sur le sable en noyés en chair de goyaves
        déchirés en une main d'épure en belles algues en graine volante en bulle en souvenance en
        arbre précatoire
soit ton geste une vague qui hurle et se reprend vers le creux de rocs
aimés comme pour parfaire une île rebelle à naître
il y a dans le sol demain en scrupule et la parole à charger aussi bien que le silence

Paysan le vent où glissent des carènes arrête autour de mon visage la main lointaine d'un songe
ton champ dans son saccage éclate debout de monstres marins que je n'ai garde d'écarter
et mon geste est pur autant qu'un front d'oubli
frappe paysan je suis ton fils
à l'heure du soleil qui se couche le crépuscule sous ma paupière
clapote vert jaune et tiède d'iguanes inassoupis
mais la belle autruche courrière qui subitement naît des formes émues de la femme me fait de l'avenir
        les signes de l'amitié

To Africa / for Wifredo Lam

*

Peasant strike the ground with your daba
in the ground there is an urgency which no syllable of the event will unknot
I reminisce about the memorable plague
there had been no forewarner star
only the earth in a pebbleless wave kneading out of space
a bread of grass and reclusion
strike peasant strike
on the first day the birds died
the second day the fish beached
the third day the animals came out of the woods
and formed a big very strong hot belt for the cities
strike the ground with your daba
there is in the ground the map of transmutations and death's tricks
on the fourth day the vegetation withered
and everything from the agave to the acacia turned bitter
becoming egrets becoming vegetal organ pipes
in which the thorny wind took off amidst flutes and trenchant odors
Strike peasant strike
in the sky windows are being born they are my spurted eyes
their harrow in my chest forms the rampart of a city refusing access to the muleteers of despair
Famine and on your own a surge
a heap where future anger risks salvation
strike Anger
there is at the foot of our fairy castles for the rendezvous of blood and landscape the ballroom in
          which dwarfs pointing their mirrors
listen in the folds of stone or salt to the sex growing from the gaze
Peasant so that the one wounded by the wind can emerge from the head of the mountain
so that a mouthful of bells can warm up in her throat
so that my wave can consume itself in her wave and bring us back on the sand as drowned ones as the
          flesh of guavas, torn, as a hand being sketched as beautiful seaweed as aerial seed as a bubble
          as a recollection as a precatory tree
let your act be a wave that howls and regathers toward the hollow of cherished
rocks as if to perfect an island rebelling against birth
there is in the ground the scruple of a tomorrow and the burden of speech as well as silence

Peasant the wind in which hulls glide stops the distant hand of a dream around my face
your field in its havoc explodes erect with deep-sea monsters which on no account will I push away
and my act is as pure as a forgetful brow
strike peasant I am your son
at the hour of the setting sun dusk splashes under my eyelid
a yellowish green tepid with undozing iguanas
but the beautiful messenger ostrich suddenly born from the aroused forms of woman beckons to me
          out of the future in friendship

Démons

Je frappai ses jambes et ses bras. Ils devinrent des pattes de fer terminées par des serres très puissantes recouvertes de petites plumes souples et vertes qui leur faisaient une gaine discernable mais très bien étudiée. D'une idée-à-peur de mon cerveau lui naquit son bec, d'un poisson férocement armé. Et l'animal fut devant moi oiseau. Son pas régulier comme une horloge arpentait despotiquement le sable rouge comme mesureur d'un champ sacré né de la larme perfide d'une fleuve. Sa tête? je la vis très vite de verre translucide à travers lequel l'œil tournait un agencement de rouages très fins de poulies de bielles qui de temps en temps avec le jeu très impressionnant des pistons injectaient le temps de chrome et de mercure
Déjà la bête était sur moi invulnérable.
Au-dessous des seins et sur tout le ventre au-dessous du cou et sur tout le dos ce que l'on prenait à première vue pour des plumes étaient des lamelles de fer peint qui lorsque l'animal ouvrait et refermait les ailes pour se secouer de la pluie et du sang faisaient une perspective que rien ne pouvait compromettre de relents et de bruits de cuillers heurtées par les mains blanches d'un séisme dans les corbeilles sordides d'un été trop malsain.

Marais nocturne

Le marais déroulant son lasso jusque là lové autour de son nombril

et me voilà installé par les soins obligeants de l'enlisement au fond du marais et fumant le tabac le plus rare qu'aucune alouette ait jamais fumé.

Miasme on m'avait dit que ce ne pouvait être que le règne du crépuscule. Je te donne acte que l'on m'avait trompé. De l'autre côté de la vie, de la mort, montent des bulles. Elles éclatent à la surface avec un bruit d'ampoules brisées. Ce sont les scaphandriers de la réclusion qui reviennent à la surface remiser leur tête de plomb et de verre, leur tendresse.
Tout animal m'est agami-chien de garde.
Toute plante silphium-lascinatum, parole aveugle du Nord et du Sud.
Pourtant alerte.
Ce sont les serpents.
L'un d'eux siffle le long de ma colonne vertébrale, puis s'enroulant au plus bas de ma cage thoracique, lance sa tête jusqu'à ma gorge spasmodique.
A la fin l'occlusion en est douce et j'entonne sous le sable

l'HYMNE AU SERPENT LOMBAIRE

Demons

I struck its legs and its claws. They became iron paws tipped with very powerful claws covered with tiny supple green feathers providing a noticeable but very well-conceived sheath. A fear-thought in my brain gave birth to its beak, of a ferociously armed fish. And the animal was in front of me a bird. Its steady clock-like pace despotically stalked the red sand like a surveyor of a sacred field born from a river's perfidious tear. Its head? I saw it very fast, clear glass through which its eye turned a mechanism of fine gears of pulleys of connecting rods which from time to time by the very impressive play of pistons injected chromium and mercury into the stroke
Already the beast was upon me invulnerable.
Below its breasts and over its whole belly below its neck and over its whole back what looked at first like feathers were painted iron plates which, whenever the animal opened and closed its wings to shake off rain and blood, formed a perspective—which nothing could imperil—of stale smells of noises of spoons clinked by the white hands of a seism in the sordid baskets of a too pernicious summer.

Night Swamp

The swamp unrolling its lasso until then coiled around its navel

and here I am settled thanks to the very obliging quicksanding at the bottom of the swamp and smoking the rarest tobacco that any lark ever smoked.

Miasma they told me this could only be the reign of twilight. I hereby notify you that I had been misled. From the other side of life, of death, bubbles are rising. They burst on the surface with the sound of shattered lightbulbs. They are the divers of reclusion resurfacing to put their lead and glass heads away, as well as their tenderness.
To me every animal is an agami-watchdog.
Every plant a Silphium laciniatum, a blind word of the North and of the South.
But watch out.
They are serpents.
One of them hisses along my spinal column, then coiling at the base of my thoracic cage, darts its head up to my spasmodic throat.
At the end the occlusion is sweet and under the sand I intone

THE HYMN TO THE LUMBAR SERPENT

Couteaux midi

Quand les Nègres font la Révolution ils commencent par arracher du Champ de Mars des arbres géants qu'ils lancent à la face du ciel comme des aboiements et qui couchent dans le plus chaud de l'air de purs courants d'oiseaux frais où ils tirent à blanc. Ils tirent à blanc? Oui ma foi parce que le blanc est la juste couleur controversée du noir qu'ils portent dans le cœur et qui ne cesse de conspirer dans les petits hexagones trop bien faits de leurs pores. Les coups de feu blancs plantent alors dans le ciel des belles de nuit qui ne sont pas sans rapport avec les cornettes des sœurs de Saint Joseph de Cluny qu'elles lessivent sous les espèces de midi dans la jubilation solaire du savon tropical.
Midi? Oui, Midi qui disperse dans le ciel la ouate trop complaisante qui capitonne mes paroles et où mes cris se prennent. Midi? Oui Midi amande de la nuit et langue entre mes crocs de poivre. Midi? Oui Midi qui porte sur son dos de galeux et de vitrier toute la sensibilité qui compte de la haine et des ruines. Midi? pardieu Midi qui après s'être recueilli sur mes lèvres le temps d'un blasphème et aux limites cathédrales de l'oisiveté met sur toutes les lignes de toutes les mains les trains que la repentance gardait en réserve dans les coffres-forts du temps sévère. Midi? Oui Midi somptueux qui de ce monde m'absente.
Doux Seigneur!
durement je crache. Au visage des affameurs, au visage des insulteurs, au visage des paraschites et des éventreurs.
Seigneur dur! doux je siffle; je siffle doux
Doux comme l'hièble
doux comme le verre de catastrophe
doux comme la houppelande faite de plumes d'oiseau que la vengeance vêt après le crime
doux comme le salut des petites vagues surprises en jupes dans les chambres du mancenillier
doux comme un fleuve de mandibules et la paupière du perroquet
doux comme une pluie de cendre emperlée de petits feux.
Oh! je tiens mon pacte
debout dans mes blessures où mon sang bat contre les fûts du naufrage des cadavres de chiens crevés
d'où fusent des colibris, c'est le jour,
un jour pour nos pieds fraternels
un jour pour nos mains sans rancunes
un jour pour nos souffles sans méfiance
un jour pour nos faces sans vergogne

et les Nègres vont cherchant dans la poussière—à leur oreille à pleins poumons les pierres précieuses chantant—les échardes dont on fait le mica dont on fait les lunes et l'ardoise lamelleuse dont les sorciers font l'intime férocité des étoiles.

Noon Knives

When the Niggers make Revolution they begin by uprooting giant trees from the Champ de Mars which they hurl like bayings into the face of the sky and which in the hottest of the air aim at pure streams of cool birds at which they fire blanks. Fire blanks? Yes indeed because blankness (or whiteness) is precisely the controversial color of the blackness which they carry in their hearts and which never ceases to conspire in the little too well made hexagons of their pores. The white shots then plant ladies-of-the-night in the sky which are not unrelated to the coifs of Saint Joseph de Cluny nuns laundered under the bread and wine of noon amidst the solar jubilation of tropical soap.

Noon? Yes, Noon dispersing in the sky the too complacent cotton wool which muffles my words, which traps my screams. Noon? Yes Noon almond of the night and tongue between my pepper fangs. Noon? Yes Noon which carries on its shoulders of a bum and a glazier all the sensitivity toward hatred and ruins that counts. Noon? sure Noon which after pausing on my lips for the time it takes to curse and at the cathedral limits of idleness sets on every line of every hand the trains that repentence kept in reserve in the strongboxes of severe time. Noon? Yes sumptuous Noon which makes me absent from this world.

Sweet Lord!

savagely I spit. Into the face of the starvers, into the face of the revilers, into the face of the paraschites and of the eviscerators.

Savage Lord! sweetly I whistle; I whistle sweetly

Sweet like the dwarf elder

sweet like the glass of catastrophe

sweet like the cloak of bird feathers which vengeance dons after the crime

sweet like the greeting of tiny waves caught in their petticoats in the chambers of the manchineel

sweet like a river of mandibles and the eyelid of a parrot

sweet like a rain of ash empearled with tiny fires.

Oh! I stick to my pact

upright in my wounds where against the shafts of shipwreck my blood beats the cadavers of croaked dogs out of which hummingbirds are rocketing, this is the day

a day for our fraternal feet

a day for our hands without rancor

a day for our breath without diffidence

a day for our faces free of shame

and the Niggers go searching in the dust—gems singing in their ears at the top of their voices—for the splinters from which mica is made as well as moons and the fissile slate out of which sorcerers make the intimate ferocity of the stars.

Aux écluses du vide

Au premier plan et fuite longitudinale un ruisseau desséché sommeilleux rouleur de galets d'obsidiennes. Au fond une point quiète architecture de burgs démantelés de montagnes érodées sur le fantôme deviné desquels naissent serpents chariots œil de chat des constellations alarmantes. C'est un étrange gâteau de lucioles lancé contre la face grise du temps, un grand éboulis de tessons d'icones et de blasons de poux dans la barbe de Saturne. A droite très curieusement debout à la paroi squameuse de papillons crucifiés ailes ouvertes dans la gloire une gigantesque bouteille dont le goulot d'or très long boit dans les nuages une goutte de sang. Pour ma part je n'ai plus soif. Il m'est doux de penser le monde défait comme un vieux matelas à coprah comme un vieux collier vaudou comme le parfum du pécari abattu. Je n'ai plus soif.

> par le ciel ébranlé
> par les étoiles éclatées
> par le silence tutélaire
> de très loin d'outre moi je viens vers toi
> femme surgie d'un bel aubier
> et tes yeux blessures mal fermées
> sur ta pudeur d'être née.

C'est moi qui chante d'une voix prise encore dans le balbutiement des éléments. Il est doux d'être un morceau de bois un bouchon une goutte d'eau dans les eaux torrentielles de la fin et du recommencement. Il est doux de s'assoupir au cœur brisé des choses. Je n'ai plus aucune espèce de soif. Mon épée faite d'un sourire de dents de requin devient terriblement inutile. Ma masse d'armes est très visiblement hors de saison et hors de jeu. La pluie tombe. C'est un croisement de gravats, c'est un incroyable arrimage de l'invisible par des liens de toute qualité, c'est une ramure de syphilis, c'est le diagramme d'une saoulerie à l'eau-de-vie, c'est un complot de cuscutes, c'est la tête du cauchemar fichée sur la pointe de lance d'une foule en délire.
J'avance jusqu'à la région des lacs bleus. J'avance jusqu'à la région des solfatares
j'avance jusqu'à ma bouche cratériforme vers laquelle ai-je assez peiné? Qu'ai-je à jeter? Tout ma foi tout. Je suis tout nu. J'ai tout jeté. Ma généalogie. Ma veuve. Mes compagnons. J'attends le bouillonnement. J'attends le coup d'aile du grand albatros séminal qui doit faire de moi un homme nouveau. J'attends l'immense tape, le soufflet vertigineux qui me sacrera chevalier d'un ordre plutonien.

Et subitement c'est le débouché des grands fleuves
c'est l'amitié des yeux de toucans
c'est l'érection au fulminate de montagnes vierges
je suis investi. L'Europe patrouille dans mes veines comme
une meute de filaires sur le coup de minuit.

Europe éclat de fonte
Europe tunnel bas d'où suinte une rosée de sang
Europe vieux chien Europe calèche à vers

At the Locks of the Void

In the foreground and in longitudinal flight a dried up brook drowsy roller of obsidian pebbles. In the rear a not exactly tranquil architecture of torn down burgs of eroded mountains on whose glimpsed phantom serpents chariots a cat's-eye and alarming constellations are born. It is a strange firefly cake hurled into the grey face of time, a vast scree of shards of ikons and of blazons of lice in the beard of Saturn. On the right very curiously standing against the squamous wall of crucified butterflies wings open in majesty a gigantic bottle whose very long gold neck drinks a drop of blood from the clouds. As for me I'm no longer thirsty. It gives me pleasure to think of the world undone like an old copra mattress like an old voodoo necklace like the perfume of a felled pecary. I'm no longer thirsty.

> through the shaken sky
> through the exploded stars
> through the tutelary silence
> from very far from beyond myself I come toward you
> woman sprung from a beautiful alburnum
> and your eyes wounds barely closing
> on your modesty from having been born.

It is I singing with a voice still caught in the babbling of elements. It is pleasant to be a piece of wood a cork a drop of water in the torrential waters of the end and of the new beginning. It is pleasant to doze off in the shattered heart of things. In no sense am I any longer thirsty. My sword made from a shark tooth smile is becoming terribly useless. My mace is very obviously out of season and out of bounds. The rain is falling. It is a crisscross of rubble, it is an incredible sowing of the invisible with first-rate ties, it is a branchwork of syphilis, it is the diagram of a brandy bender, it is a conspiracy of dodders, it is the nightmare's head impaled on the lance point of a crazed mob.
I advance to the region of blue lakes. I advance to the region of sulphur springs.
I advance to my crateriform mouth toward which have I struggled enough? What do I have to throw away? Everything by God everything. I am stark naked. I've thrown everything away. My genealogy. My widow. My companions. I await the boiling. I await the wingbeat of the great seminal albatross supposed to make a new man of me. I await the immense tap, the vertiginous slap which will consecrate me as a knight of a Plutonian order.

And suddenly it is the outpour of great rivers
it is the friendship in the eyes of toucans
it is the fulminatory erection of virgin mountains
I am invested. Europe patrols my veins like
a pack of filariae at the stroke of midnight.

Europe cast iron explosion
Europe low tunnel oozing a bloody dew
Europe old dog Europe worm-drawn carriage

Europe tatouage pelé Europe ton nom est un gloussement
rauque et un choc assourdi

je déplie mon mouchoir c'est un drapeau
j'ai mis ma belle peau
j'ai ajusté mes belles pattes onglées

Nom ancien
je donne mon adhésion à tout ce qui poudroie le ciel de son insolence à tout ce qui est loyal et fraternel
à tout ce qui a le courage d'être éternellement neuf à tout ce qui sait donner son cœur au feu à tout ce
qui a la force de sortir d'une sève inépuisable à tout ce qui est calme et sûr à tout ce qui n'est pas toi
hoquet considérable

Quelconque

Quelconque le gâteau de la nuit décoré de petites bougies faites de lucioles
quelconque une rangée de palmiers à éventer mes pensées les mieux tues
quelconque le plat du ciel servi par des mages en drap de piment rouge
quelconque la jeune main verte du poinsettia se crispant hors de ses gants à massacre
Espoir Espoir
lorsque la vague déroule son paquet de lianes de toute odeur
et toutes les lance au cou de chevaux bigles
lorsque l'anse développe sa crinière de sel godronnée au plus rare amidon d'algues et de poissons
Espoir plane Grand Duc
danse Espoir et piétine et crie parmi les attentions charmantes des remoras et le beuglement neuf
        qu'émet le caïman à l'imminence d'un tremblement de terre

Europe peeling tattoo Europe your name is a raucous
clucking and a muffled shock

I unfold my handkerchief it is a flag
I have donned my beautiful skin
I have adjusted my beautiful clawed paws

Ancient name
I hereby join all that powders the sky with its insolence all that is loyal and fraternal all that has the
courage to be eternally new all that knows how to yield its heart to the fire all that has the strength to
emerge from an inexhaustible sap all that is calm and self-assured all that is not you
considerable hiccup

Trite

Trite the cake of the night decorated with little candles made of fireflies
trite a row of palm trees to fan my most untold thoughts
trite the sky's dish served by magi draped in red pepper
trite the poinsettia's young green hand stiffening out of its massacre gloves
Hope Hope
when the wave unrolls its cluster of lianas of every odor
and throws them all around the necks of cross-eyed horses
when the cove displays its salty mane gadrooned with the rarest starches from seaweed and from fish
Hope hover great horned owl
dance Hope and stamp and scream amidst the remoras' charming attentions and the raw bellowing
        uttered by the cayman at the onset of an earthquake

Ode à la Guinée

Et par le soleil installant sous ma peau une usine de force et d'aigles
et par le vent sur ma force de dent de sel compliquant ses passes les mieux sues
et par le noir le long de mes muscles en douces insolences de sèves montant
et par la femme couchée comme une montagne descellée et sucée par les lianes
et par la femme au cadastre mal connu où le jour et la nuit jouent à la mourre des eaux de source et des
       métaux rares
et par le feu de la femme où je cherche le chemin des fougères et du Fouta-Djallon
et par la femme fermée sur la nostalgie s'ouvrant

JE TE SALUE

Guinée dont les pluies fracassent du haut grumeleux des volcans un sacrifice de vaches pour mille
       faims et soifs d'enfants dénaturés
Guinée de ton cri de ta main de ta patience
il nous reste toujours des terres arbitraires
et quand tué vers Ophir ils m'auront jamais muet
de mes dents et de ma peau que l'on fasse
un fétiche féroce gardien du mauvais œil
comme m'ébranle me frappe et me dévore ton solstice
en chacun de tes pas Guinée
muette en moi-même d'une profondeur astrale de méduses

Ode to Guinea

And by the sun installing a power and eagle factory under my skin
and by the wind elaborating the passes it knows best over my power of tooth of salt
and by the black rising along my muscles in sweet sap-like effronteries
and by the woman stretched out like a mountain unsealed and sucked by lianas
the woman with the little known cadastre where day and night play mora for springhead waters and
       rare metals
and by the fire of the woman in which I look for the path to ferns and to Fouta Jallon
and by the closed woman opening on nostalgia

      I HAIL YOU

Guinea whose rains from the curdled height of volcanoes shatter a sacrifice of cows for a thousand
      hungers and thirsts of denatured children
Guinea from your cry from your hand from your patience
we still have some arbitrary lands
and when they have me, killed in Ophir perhaps and silenced for good,
out of my teeth out of my skin let them make
a fetish a ferocious guardian against the evil eye
as your solstice shakes me strikes me and devours me
at each one of your steps Guinea
silenced in myself with the astral depth of medusas

Cheval / *à Pierre Loeb*

Mon cheval bute contre des crânes joués à la marelle de la rouille
mon cheval se cabre dans un orage de nuages qui sont des putréfactions de chairs à naufrage
mon cheval hennit dans la petite pluie de roses que fait mon sang dans le décor des fêtes foraines
mon cheval bute aux buissons de cactus qui sont les nœuds de vipère de mes tourments
mon cheval bute hennit et bute vers le rideau de sang de mon sang tiré sur tous les ruffians qui jouent
         aux dés mon sang
mon cheval bute devant l'impossible flamme de la barre que hurlent les vésicules de mon sang
Grand cheval mon sang
mon sang vin de vomissure d'ivrogne
je te le donne grand cheval
je te donne mes oreilles pour en faire des naseaux sachant frémir
mes cheveux pour en faire une crinière des mieux sauvages
ma langue pour en faire des sabots de mustang
je te les donne
grand cheval
pour que tu abordes à l'extrême limite de la fraternité les hommes d'ailleurs et de demain
avec sur le dos un enfant aux lèvres à peine remuées
qui pour toi
désarmera
la mie chlorophyllienne des vastes corbeaux de l'avenir.

Horse / for Pierre Loeb

My horse falters against skulls hopscotched in rust
my horse rears in a storm of clouds which are putrefactions of shipwrecked flesh
my horse neighs in the fine rain of roses which my blood becomes in the carnival scenery
my horse falters against the clumps of cacti which are the viper knots of my torments
my horse falters neighs and falters toward the blood curtain of my blood pulled down on all the trash
        who shoot craps with my blood
my horse falters before the impossible flame of the bit howled by the vesicles of my blood
Great horse my blood
my blood wine of a drunkard's vomit
I give it to you great horse
I give you my ears to be made into nostrils capable of quivering
my hair to be made into a mane as wild as they come
my tongue to be made into mustang hooves
I give them to you
great horse
so that you can approach the men of elsewhere and tomorrow at the extreme limits of brotherhood
on your back a child with barely moving lips
who for you
will disarm
the chlorophyllous dough of the vast ravens of the future.

Soleil et eau

Mon eau n'écoute pas
mon eau chante comme un secret
Mon eau ne chante pas
mon eau exulte comme un secret
mon eau travaille
et à travers tout roseau exulte
jusqu'au lait du rire
Mon eau est un petit enfant
mon eau est un sourd
mon eau est un géant qui te tient sur la poitrine un lion
ô vin
vaste immense
par le basilic de ton regard complice et somptueux

Marche des perturbations

Une robuste foudre en menace sur
le front le plus intouchable du monde
en toi toute la lumière veuve
des crépuscules des cités poignardées
par les oiseaux alentour
Et prends garde au corbeau qui ne vole pas c'est ma tête
qui s'est extraite du poteau mitan de mes épaules
en poussant un vieux cri arracheur d'entrailles et d'abreuvoirs

Ornières ornières lait doux brasier de flambes et d'euphorbes

Sun and Water

My water won't listen
my water sings like a secret
My water does not sing
my water rejoices like a secret
My water ferments
and rejoices through every reed
to the very milk of laughter
My water is a little child
my water is a deaf man
my water is a giant holding a lion to your chest
oh wine
vast immense
owing to the basilisk of your rich complicitous gaze

March of Perturbations

A robust thunderbolt threatening over
the most untouchable brow in the world
in you all the light bereft
of the dusks of cities stabbed
by the birds around
And watch out for the raven that does not fly it is my head
which extracted itself from the center stake of my shoulders
uttering an ancient shriek ripper of entrails and watering places

Ruts ruts sweet milk brazier of blazing fire and Euphorbia

Barbare

C'est le mot qui me soutient
et frappe sur ma carcasse de cuivre jaune
où la lune dévore dans la soupente de la rouille
les os barbares
des lâches bêtes rôdeuses du mensonge

Barbare
du langage sommaire
et nos faces belles comme le vrai pouvoir opératoire
de la négation

Barbare
des morts qui circulent dans les veines de la terre
et viennent se briser parfois la tête contre les murs de nos oreilles
et les cris de révolte jamais entendus
qui tournent à mesure et à timbres de musique

Barbare
l'article unique
barbare le tapaya
barbare l'amphisbène blanche
barbare moi le serpent cracheur
qui de mes putréfiantes chairs me réveille
soudain gekko volant
soudain gekko frangé
et me colle si bien aux lieux même de la force
qu'il vous faudra pour m'oublier
jeter aux chiens la chair velue de vos poitrines

Barbarity

This is the word that sustains me
and smacks against my brass carcass
where in the garret of rust the moon devours
the barbarous bones
of the cowardly prowling beasts of the lie

Barbarity
of the rudimentary language
and our faces beautiful like the true surgical power
of negation

Barbarity
of the dead circulating in the veins of the earth
who at times come and break their heads against the walls of our ears
and the screams of revolt never heard
which turn in tune with musical tones

Barbarity
the single article
barbarity the tapaya
barbarity the white amphisbaena
barbarity I the spitting cobra
awakening from my putrefying flesh
suddenly a flying gecko
suddenly a fringed gecko
and I adhere so well to the very loci of strength
that to forget me you must
cast the hairy flesh of your chests to the dogs

*

Antipode

au matin rouleur de la première force de la première épave de la dernière aurore
nos dents feront le bond d'une terre au haut d'un ciel de cannelle et de girofles
tu ouvriras tes paupières qui sont un éventail très beau fait de plumes rougies de regarder mon sang
        battre
une saison triomphante des essences les plus rares
ce sera tes cheveux
ballant au vent puéril la nostalgie des longues canéfices

Croisades du silence

Et maintenant
que les vastes oiseaux se suicident
que les entrailles des animaux noircissent sur le couteau du sacrifice
que les prêtres se plantent une vocation aux carrefours
noués dans le terreau du bric-à-brac

Noir c'est noir non noir
noir lieu-dit
lieu de stigmates
feu de chair comme mémoré

lorsque dans tes venaisons une pierre comble à mille visages le grand trou que dans tes chairs faisait
        l'eau sombre de la parole

l'éteint Chimborazo dévore encore le monde

Antipode

in the morning leaf roller of the primal strength of the primal wreckage of the final dawn
our teeth will make a leap from some earth to the height of a sky of cinnamon and cloves
you will open your eyelids which are a fan a most beautiful one made of feathers reddened from
        watching my blood throb
a triumphant season of the most rare essences
this will be your hair
dangling the nostalgia of long cañafistulas in the puerile wind

Crusades of Silence

And now
that the spacious birds are committing suicide
that the animals' entrails are blackening on the sacrificial knife
that the priests are planting themselves a vocation at
the crossroads knotted in the compost of bric-a-brac

Black it is nonblack black
black locality
locus of stigmata
flesh aflame dimmed remembrance

when in your venisons a stone fills with a thousand faces the huge hole that the dark water of speech
        made in your flesh

extinct Chimborazo still devours the world

Pluies

Pluie qui dans tes plus répréhensibles débordements n'as garde d'oublier que les jeunes filles du
        Chiquiri tirent soudain de leur corsage de nuit une lampe faite de lucioles émouvantes
Pluie capable de tout sauf de laver le sang qui coule sur les doigts des assassins des peuples surpris sous
        les hautes futaies de l'innocence

Cercle non vicieux

Penser est trop bruyant
a trop de mains pousse trop de hannetons
Du reste je ne me suis jamais trompé
les hommes ne m'ont jamais déçu ils ont des regards qui les débordent
La nature n'est pas compliquée
Toutes mes suppositions sont justes
Toutes mes implications fructueuses
Aucun cercle n'est vicieux
Creux
Il n'y a que mes genoux de noueux et qui s'enfoncent pierreux dans le travail des autres et leur sommeil

Rains

Rain which in your most reprehensible excesses takes care not to forget that Chiriqui maidens pull
    suddenly from their bodices of night a lamp of compelling fireflies
Rain capable of everything except washing the blood which flows on the fingers of the murderers of
    entire peoples surprised in the soaring forests of innocence

Nonvicious Circle

Thinking is too noisy
has too many hands grows too many cockchafers
Moreover I have never been wrong
men have never disappointed me they have looks which transcend them
Nature is not complicated
All my assumptions are correct
All my implications fruitful
No circle is ever vicious
Hollow
It is just my knees which are knotty and sink stonelike into the labor of others and their sleep

Autre horizon

Nuit stigmate fourchu
nuit buisson télégraphique planté dans l'océan ,
pour minutieuses amours de cétacés
nuit fermée
pourrissoir splendide
où de toutes ses forces de tous ses fauves se ramasse
le muscle violet de l'aconit napel de notre soleil

Mort à l'aube

Lutteur il souffle sur des tisons
son visage mal géré par la nuit
d'où la trompe de ses lèvres siffleuses à serpents
imagine mal un corps torturé dans l'oubli

Homme sombre qu'habite la volonté du feu
quand un viol d'insectes s'éparpille dans sa faim
et que seuls les tisons de ses yeux ont bien pris

Mince tison il est celui qui
de sa grêle coquille et parmi une forêt qui défiera
le complot d'évêques des latérites porte le saut d'un fût
dans un secret si clair qu'aucun homme ne l'a cru

Different Horizon

Night forked stigmata
night telegraphic bush planted in the ocean
for the scrupulous love-making of cetaceans
night locked
splendid muck heap
where with all its strengths with all its wild beasts
the purple muscle of the monkshood of our sun prepares to spring

Death at Dawn

A fighter he blows on the brands
his face mismanaged by night
from where the horn of his lips hissing serpents
ineptly projects a body tortured in oblivion

Tenebrous man inhabited by the will of the fire
when a rape of insects scatters throughout his hunger
and only the brands of his eyes are truly ignited

A thin brand he is the one who
with his slender shell and in a forest which will defy
the episcopal plot of laterites carries the leap of a bole
in a secret so transparent that no man believed it

Lynch

Poings carnassiers teintés du ciel brisé
torche parmi les fûts héréditaires
œil sans rives sans mémoire
dieu et que n'importunent vos fumées bleues
par la mort et la fête
avec aux naseaux des fleurs inespérées
avec sur le dos le jeune vol de courlis des oiseaux de la phosphorescence
et un perfide chant vivant
dans les ruines indestructibles de son silence

Lynch

Carnivorous fists stained by broken sky
a torch among the ancestral boles
eye without shores without memories
a god and one undisturbed by your blue smoke
through death and feasting
with unhoped for flowers in his nostrils
with the young curlew flight of the birds of phosphorescence on his back
and a perfidious song alive
in the indestructible ruins of his silence

A *hurler*

Salut oiseaux qui fendez et dispersez le cercle des hérons
et la génuflexion de leur tête de résignation
dans une gaine de mousse blanche

Salut oiseaux qui ouvrez à coups de bec le ventre vrai du marais et la poitrine de chef du couchant

Salut cri rauque
       torche de résine
       où se brouillent les pistes
       des poux de pluie et les souris blanches

Fou à hurler je vous salue de mes hurlements plus blancs que la mort

Mon temps viendra que je salue
grand large
simple
où chaque mot chaque geste éclairera
sur ton visage de chèvre blonde
broutant dans la cuve affolante de ma main

Et là là
bonne sangsue
là l'origine des temps
là la fin des temps

et la majesté droite de l'œil originel

Howling

Greetings you birds you split and scatter the circle of herons
as well as the genuflexion of their resigned heads
in a sheath of white froth

Greetings you birds with your beaks you rip open the true belly of the swamp and the chieftain chest
      of the setting sun

Greetings hoarse scream
           resinous torch
           where the tracks of rain ticks
           and white mice are covered up

Howling mad I greet you with my howlings whiter than death

My time shall come and I hail it
a time vast
and simple as the sea
in which each word each gesture shall radiate
over your blonde goat's face
grazing in the maddening vat of my hand

And then—then—
lovely leech
then—the origin of time
then—the end of time

and the erect majesty of the original eye

Jugement de la lumière

Fascinant le sang les muscles
dévorant les yeux ce fouillis
chargeant de vérité les éclats routiniers
un jet d'eau de victorieux soleil
par lequel
justice sera faite
et toutes les morgues démises

Les vaisselles les chairs glissent dans l'épaisseur du cou des vagues
les silences par contre ont acquis une pression formidable

Sur un arc de cercle
dans les mouvements publics des rivages
la flamme
est seule et splendide dans son jugement intègre

The Light's Judgment *

Bewitching the blood the muscles
devouring the eyes this muddle
loading truth onto routine bursts
a water jet of victorious sun
by which
justice shall be done
and all arrogance dismissed

The dishes the flesh slide about in the thickness of the waves' necks
silences on the other hand have taken on a terrifying pressure

Over the arc of a circle
in the public movement of shorelines
the flame
is alone and splendid in its honest judgment

CORPS PERDU
*
LOST BODY

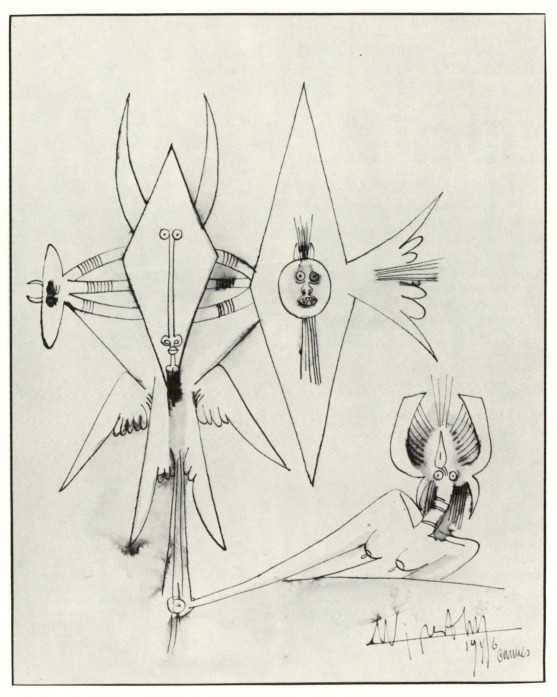

Wifredo Lam, untitled watercolor, 1946, 12 × 9½"

Mot

Parmi moi
de moi-même
à moi-même
hors toute constellation
en mes mains serré seulement
le rare hoquet d'un ultime spasme délirant
vibre mot

j'aurai chance hors du labyrinthe
plus long plus large vibre
en ondes de plus en plus serrées
en lasso où me prendre
en corde où me pendre
et que me clouent toutes les flèches
et leur curare le plus amer
au beau poteau-mitan des très fraîches étoiles

vibre
vibre essence même de l'ombre
en aile en gosier c'est à force de périr
le mot nègre
sorti tout armé du hurlement
d'une fleur vénéneuse
le mot nègre
tout pouacre de parasites
le mot nègre
tout plein de brigands qui rôdent

des mères qui crient
d'enfants qui pleurent
le mot nègre
un grésillement de chairs qui brûlent
âcre et de corne
le mot nègre
comme le soleil qui saigne de la griffe
sur le trottoir des nuages
le mot nègre
comme le dernier rire vêlé de l'innocence
entre les crocs du tigre
et comme le mot soleil est un claquement de balles

Word

            Within me
from myself
to myself
outside any constellation
clenched in my hands only
the rare hiccup of an ultimate raving spasm
keep vibrating word

            I will have luck outside the labyrinth
longer wider keep vibrating
in tighter and tighter waves
in a lasso to catch me
in a rope to hang me
and let me be nailed by all the arrows
and their bitterest curare
to the beautiful center stake of very cool stars

vibrate
vibrate you very essence of the dark
in a wing in a throat from so much perishing
the word nigger
emerged fully armed from the howling
of a poisonous flower
the word nigger
all filthy with parasites
the word nigger
loaded with roaming bandits

with screaming mothers
crying children
the word nigger
a sizzling of flesh and horny matter
burning, acrid
the word nigger
like the sun bleeding from its claw
onto the sidewalk of clouds
the word nigger
like the last laugh calved by innocence
between the tiger's fangs
and as the word sun is a ringing of bullets

et comme le mot nuit un taffetas qu'on déchire
le mot nègre
        dru savez-vous
dú tonnerre d'un été
    que s'arrogent
            des libertés incrédules

and the word night a ripping of taffeta
the word nigger
              dense, right?
from the thunder of a summer
      appropriated by
                    incredulous liberties

Qui donc, qui donc . . .

        Et si j'avais besoin de moi
d'un vrai sommeil
blond de même qu'un éveil
d'une ville s'évadant dans la jungle ou le sable
flairée nocturne flairée
d'un dieu hors rite ou de toi
d'un temps de mil et d'entreprise

et si j'avais besoin d'une île
Bornéo Sumatra Maldives Laquedives
si j'avais besoin d'un Timor parfumé de sandal
ou de Moluques Ternate Tidor
ou de Célèbes ou de Ceylan
qui dans la vaste nuit magicienne
aux dents d'un peigne triomphant
peignerait le flux et le reflux

et si j'avais besoin de soleil
ou de pluie ou de sang
cordial d'une minute d'un petit jour inventé
d'un continent inavoué
d'un puits d'un lézard d'un rêve
songe non rabougri
la mémoire poumonneuse et le cœur dans la main
et si j'avais besoin de vague ou de misaine
ou de la poigne phosphorescente
d'une cicatrice éternelle
qui donc
qui donc
aux vents d'un peigne triomphant
peignerait une fumée de climats inconstants

qui donc
qui donc
O grande fille à trier sauvage condamnée
en grain mon ombre
des grains d'une clarté
et qui savamment entre loup et chien m'avance
attentif à bien brouiller les comptes

Who Then, Who Then . . .

And if I needed myself
needed a true sleep
blond as an awakening
a city escaping into the jungle or the sand
sniffed out nocturnal sniffed out
needed a nonritualistic god or you
or an era of millet and enterprise

and if I needed an island
Borneo Sumatra Maldives Laccadives
if I needed a sandalwood-scented Timor
or Moluccas Ternate Tidore
or Celebes or Ceylon
who in this vast magician night
would comb the ebb and the flow
with the teeth of a triumphant comb

and if I needed sun
or rain or blood
the cordial of an instant of an invented dawn
an unconfessed continent
a well a lizard a dream
an unstunted reverie
its memory pulmonic and its heart in its hand
and if I needed a wave or a mizzen
or the phosphorescent grip
of an eternal scar
who then
who then
among the winds would comb
with a triumphant comb a vapor of changeable climates

who then
who then
O full-grown girl wild condemned to sort out
the grain of my shadow
from the grains of a clarity
who skillfully through dog-or-wolf dusk moves me forward
intent upon neatly confusing the accounts

Elégie

L'hibiscus qui n'est pas autre chose qu'un œil éclaté
d'où pend le fil d'un long regard les trompettes des solandres
le grand sabre noir des flamboyants le crépuscule qui est un trousseau de clefs toujours sonnant
les aréquiers qui sont de nonchalants soleils jamais couchés parce qu'outrepercés d'une épingle que les
      terres à cervelle brûlée
n'hésitent jamais à se fourrer
jusqu'au cœur les souklyans effrayants Orion
l'extatique papillon que les pollens magiques
crucifièrent sur la porte des nuits tremblantes
les belles boucles noires des canéfices qui sont des mulâtresses
très fières dont le cou tremble un peu sous la guillotine

et ne t'étonne pas si la nuit je geins plus lourdement
ou si mes mains étranglent plus sourdement
c'est le troupeau des vieilles peines qui vers mon odeur
noir et rouge
en scolopendre
allonge la tête et d'une instance du museau
encore molle et maladroite
cherche plus profond mon cœur
alors rien ne me sert de serrer mon cœur contre le tien
et de me perdre dans le feuillage de tes bras
il le trouve
et très gravement
de manière toujours nouvelle
le lèche
amoureusement
jusqu'à l'apparition sauvage du premier sang
aux brusques griffes ouvertes du

DESASTRE

Elegy

The hibiscus that is nothing other than a burst eye
from which hangs the thread of a long gaze the trumpets of the chalice vines
the huge black sabers of flamboyants the twilight that is an ever jingling bunch of keys
the Arecas that are nonchalant suns never setting because pierced through and through by a pin
     which the addlebrained lands
never hesitate to jab all the way in
to their hearts the terrifying souklyans Orion
the ecstatic butterfly that magical pollens
crucified on the gate of trembling nights
the beautiful black curls of cañafistulas that are very proud
mulatto women whose necks tremble a bit under the guillotine

and do not be surprised if at night I moan more heavily
or if my hands strangle more secretly
it is the herd of old sufferings which toward my smell
black and red
scolopendra-like
stretches its head and with the still soft and clumsy
insistence of its muzzle
searches more deeply for my heart
then it is no use for me to press my heart against yours
nor to lose myself in the foliage of your arms
the herd finds it
and very solemnly
in a manner always new
licks it
amorously
until the first blood savagely appears
on the abrupt open claws of

DISASTER

Présence

tout un mai de canéficiers
sur la poitrine de pur hoquet
d'une île adultère de site
chair qui soi prise de soi-même vendange
O lente entre les dacites
pincée d'oiseaux qu'attise un vent
où passent fondues les chutes du temps
la pur foison d'un rare miracle
dans l'orage toujours crédule
d'une saison non évasive

Presence

a whole May of cañafistulas
on the chest of pure hiccup
of an island adulterous to its site
flesh which having possessed itself harvests its grape self
O slow among the dacites
a pinch of birds fanned by a wind
in which the cataracts of time pass blended
the sheer profusion of a rare miracle
in the ever credulous storm
of a nonevasive season

De forlonge

Les maisons de par ici au bas des montagnes
ne sont pas aussi bien rangées que des godillots
les arbres sont des explosions dont la dernière étincelle
vient écumer sur mes mains qui tremblent un peu
désormais je porte en moi
la gaine arrachée d'un long palmier
comme serait le jour sans ton souvenir
la soie grège des cuscutes
qui au piège prennent le dos du site
de la manière très complète du désespoir
des ceibas monstrueux seuls auxquels
dès maintenant je ressemblerais dépouillé des feuilles de mon amour
je divague entre houle et javelles que fait tumultueuse
la parole des albizzias
il y a en face de moi un paysan extraordinaire
ce que chante le paysan c'est une histoire
de coupeur de cannes

han le coupeur de cannes
saisit la dame à grands cheveux
en trois morceaux la coupe

han le coupeur de cannes
la vierge point n'enterre
la coupe en morceaux

les jette derrière
han le coupeur de cannes

chante le paysan et vers un soir de coutelas s'avance sans colère
les cheveux décoiffés de la dame aux grands cheveux font des ruisseaux de lumière
ainsi chante le paysan
Il y a des tas de choses dont je ne sais pas le nom
et que je voudrais te dire
au ciel ta chevelure qui se retire solennellement
des pluies comme on n'en voit jamais plus des noix
des feux Saint-Elme
des soleils lamés des nuits murmurées
des cathédrales aussi
qui sont des carcasses de grands chevaux rongés
que la mer a crachés de très loin
mais que les gens continuent d'adorer

Forloining

The houses out here at the foot of the mountains
are not even as well arranged as hobnailed boots
the trees are explosions whose last spark
goes out washing over my hands which tremble a little
from now on I carry within me
the sheath torn from a tall palm tree
like the day would be without the memory of you
the raw dodder silk
which ensnares the back of the site
in the utterly complete way that despair does
monstrous solitary ceiba trees which
from this day on I would resemble stripped of the leaves of my love
I drift between a swell and swathes formed by
the speech tumult of albizzias
in front of me is an extraordinary peasant
what the peasant sings is a tale
about cane cutters

woosh the cane cutter
grabs the long-haired lady
hacks her into three pieces

woosh the cane cutter
buries not the maiden
he hacks her up in pieces

tosses them behind him
woosh the cane cutter

sings the peasant and toward a cutlass evening proceeds without anger
the disheveled hair of the long-haired lady makes rivulets of light
so sings the peasant
There are a whole lot of things whose names I do not know
and I'd like to tell you about them
in the sky your hair solemnly draws away
kinds of rain one no longer sees
nuts Saint Elmo's fire
sun lamés whispered nights
cathedrals too
which are the carcasses of large gnawed horses
spat by the sea from far away
but still worshipped by people

des tas de choses oubliées
des tas de choses rêvées
tandis que nous deux Lointaine-ma-distraite
nous deux
dans le paysage nous entrons jamais fané
plus forts que cent mille ruts

a whole lot of forgotten things
a whole lot of dreamed things
while the two of us Distant-one-my-inattentive-one
the two of us
enter the never faded landscape
more powerful than a hundred thousand ruttings

Corps perdu

Moi qui Krakatoa
moi qui tout mieux que mousson
moi qui poitrine ouverte
moi qui laïlape
moi qui bêle mieux que cloaque
moi qui hors de gamme
moi qui Zambèze ou frénétique ou rhombe ou cannibale
je voudrais être de plus en plus humble et plus bas
toujours plus grave sans vertige ni vestige
jusqu'à me perdre tomber
dans la vivante semoule d'une terre bien ouverte.
Dehors une belle brume au lieu d'atmosphère serait point sale
chaque goutte d'eau y faisant un soleil
dont le nom le même pour toutes choses
serait RENCONTRE BIEN TOTALE
si bien que l'on ne saurait plus qui passe
ou d'une étoile ou d'un espoir
ou d'un pétale de l'arbre flamboyant
ou d'une retraite sous-marine
courue par les flambeaux des méduses-aurélies
Alors la vie j'imagine me baignerait tout entier
mieux je la sentirais qui me palpe ou me mord
couché je verrais venir à moi les odeurs enfin libres
comme des mains secourables
qui se feraient passage en moi
pour y balancer de longs cheveux
plus longs que ce passé que je ne peux atteindre.
Choses écartez-vous faites place entre vous
place à mon repos qui porte en vague
ma terrible crête de racines ancreuses
qui cherchent où se prendre
Choses je sonde je sonde
moi le porte-faix je suis porte-racines
et je pèse et je force et j'arcane
            j'omphale
Ah qui vers les harpons me ramène
            je suis très faible
je siffle oui je siffle des choses très anciennes
de serpents de choses caverneuses
Je or vent paix-là
et contre mon museau instable et frais
pose contre ma face érodée

Lost Body

I who Krakatoa
I who everything better than a monsoon
I who open chest
I who Laelaps
I who bleat better than a cloaca
I who outside the musical scale
I who Zambezi or frantic or rhombos or cannibal
I would like to be more and more humble and more lowly
always more serious without vertigo or vestige
to the point of losing myself falling
into the live semolina of a well-opened earth
Outside in lieu of atmosphere there'd be a beautiful haze no dirt in it
each drop of water forming a sun there
whose name the same for all things
would be DELICIOUS TOTAL ENCOUNTER
so that one would no longer know what goes by
—a star or a hope
or a petal from the flamboyant tree
or an underwater retreat
raced across by the flaming torches of aurelian jellyfish
Then I imagine life would flood my whole being
better still I would feel it touching me or biting me
lying down I would see the finally free odors come to me
like merciful hands
finding their way
to sway their long hair in me
longer than this past that I cannot reach.
Things stand back make room among you
room for my repose carrying in waves
my frightening crest of anchor-like roots
looking for a place to take hold
Things I probe I probe
me the street-porter I am root-porter
and I bear down and I force and I arcane
        I omphale
Ah who leads me back toward the harpoons
        I am very weak
I hiss yes I hiss very ancient things
as serpents do as do cavernous things
I whoa lie down wind
and against my unstable and fresh muzzle
against my eroded face

ta froide face de rire défait.
Le vent hélas je l'entendrai encore
nègre nègre nègre depuis le fond
du ciel immémorial
un peu moins fort qu'aujourd'hui
mais trop fort cependant
et ce fou hurlement de chiens et de chevaux
qu'il pousse à notre poursuite toujours marronne
mais à mon tour dans l'air
je me lèverai un cri et si violent
que tout entier j'éclabousserai le ciel
et par mes branches déchiquetées
et par le jet insolent de mon fût blessé et solennel

je commanderai aux îles d'exister

press your cold face of ravaged laughter
The wind alas I will continue to hear it
nigger nigger nigger from the depths
of the timeless sky
a little less loud than today
but still too loud
and this crazed howling of dogs and horses
which it thrusts at our forever fugitive heels
but I in turn in the air
shall rise a scream so violent
that I shall splatter the whole sky
and with my branches torn to shreds
and with the insolent jet of my wounded and solemn bole

     I shall command the islands to be

Ton portrait

je dis fleuve corrosif
baiser d'entrailles
fleuve entaille énorme étreinte
dans les moindres marais
eau forcée forcenant aux vertelles
car avec les larmes neuves
je t'ai construite en fleuve
vénéneux
       saccadé
            triomphant
qui vers les rives en fleur de la mer
lance en balafre ma route mancenillière

Je dis fleuve
comme qui dirait patient crocodile royal
prompt à sortir du rêve
fleuve
comme anaconda royal
l'inventeur du sursaut
fleuve
jet seul comme du fond du cauchemar
les montagnes les plus Pelées.
Fleuve
à qui tout est permis
surtout emporte mes rives
élargis-moi
à ausculter oreille le nouveau cœur corallien des marées
et que tout l'horizon de plus en plus vaste
devant moi
et à partir de ton groin s'aventure
désormais
      remous
         et liquide

Your Portrait

I say river corrosive
kiss of guts
river gash enormous embrace
in the smallest swamps
forced water frantic at the sluice gates
for with fresh tears
I built you into a river
poisonous
        spasmodic
              triumphant
which toward the flowering shores of the sea
tears open the slash of my manchineel course

I say river
like one says patient regal crocodile
quick to snap out of its dream
river
like royal anaconda
inventor of the sudden flick
river
jet alone like from the depths of nightmare
the baldest Pelée of mountains.
River
to which all is permitted
above all wash away my banks
widen me
that an ear I might auscultate the new coralline heart of the tides
and let the whole horizon venture forth
vaster and vaster before me
and take off from your snout
henceforth
       swirling
           and liquid

Sommation

toute chose plus belle

la chancellerie du feu
la chancellerie de l'eau

une grande culbute de promontoires
et d'étoiles
une montagne qui se délite en
orgie d'îles en arbres chaleureux
les mains froidement calmes du soleil
sur la tête sauvage d'une ville détruite

toute chose plus belle toute chose plus belle
et jusqu'au souvenir de ce monde y passe
un tiède blanc galop ouaté de noir
comme d'un oiseau marin qui s'est oublié en plein vol et glisse
sur le sommeil de ses pattes roses

toute chose plus belle en vérité plus belle
ombelle
et térébelle
la chancellerie de l'air
la chancellerie de l'eau
tes yeux un fruit qui brise sa coque sur le coup de minuit
et il n'est plus MINUIT

l'Espace vaincu le Temps vainqueur
moi j'aime le temps le temps est nocturne
et quand l'Espace galope qui me livre
le Temps revient qui me délivre
le Temps le Temps
ô claie sans venaison qui m'appelle

intègre
natal
solennel

Summons

everything more beautiful

the chancellery of fire
the chancellery of water

a huge somersault of promontories
and stars
a mountain exfoliating into
an orgy of islands into glowing trees
the coldly calm hands of the sun
over the wild head of a destroyed city

everything more beautiful everything more beautiful
including the memory of this world sweeping through
a tepid white gallop muffled by black
like that of a sea bird which forgets itself in full flight and glides
on pink legs over sleep

everything more beautiful truly more beautiful
umbel
and terebella
the chancellery of air
the chancellery of water
your eyes a fruit bursting its shell on the stroke of midnight
and it no longer is MIDNIGHT

Space conquered Time the conqueror
me I like time time is nocturnal
and when Space galloping sets me up
Time comes back to set me free
Time Time
oh creel without venison summoning me

whole
native
solemn

Naissances

Rompue
Eau stagnante de ma face
sur nos naissances enfin rompues
C'est entendu
dans les stagnantes eaux de ma face
seul
distant
nocturne
jamais
jamais
je n'aurai été absent.

Les serpents?
les serpents, nous les chasserons
Les monstres?
Les monstres—nous mordant
les remords de tous les jours
où nous ne nous complûmes—baisseront le souffle
nous flairant.

Tout le sang répandu
nous le lécherons
en épeautres nous en croîtrons
de rêves plus exacts
de pensées moins rameuses
ne soufflez pas les poussières
l'anti-venin en rosace terrible équilibrera l'antique venin

ne soufflez pas les poussières
tout sera rythme visible
et que reprendrions-nous?
pas même notre secret.
Ne soufflez pas les poussières
Une folle passion toujours roide étant ce par quoi tout sera étendu
ce seront plus que tout escarboucles émerveillables
pas moins que l'arbre émerveillé
arbre non arbre
hier renversé

et vois
les laboureurs célestes sont fiers d'avoir changé
ô laboureurs labourants

Births

Broken
Stagnant water of my face
on our births broken at last
Let me say this:
in the stagnant waters of my face
alone
distant
nocturnal
never
never
will I have been absent

The serpents?
the serpents, we'll drive them away
The monsters?
The monsters—the remorse of all
the days we indulged in
biting us—will lower their breathing
sniffing us.

All the shed blood
we shall lap it up
from it we shall grow like spelt
with more exact dreams
with less divided thoughts
do not blow the dust away
the antivenom shall balance the antique venom in an awesome rose window

do not blow the dust away
everything shall be visible rhythm
and what would we recover?
not even our secret.
Do not blow the dust away
An uncontrollable passion always unbending being that by which everything shall be expanded
there shall be above all carbuncles no less enchantment-
prone than the enchanted tree
nontree tree
yesterday uprooted

and behold
the celestial plowmen are proud having been transformed
oh plowing plowmen

en terre il est replanté
le ciel pousse
il contre-pousse

arbre non arbre
bel arbre immense
        le jour dessus se pose
        oiseau effarouché

on earth it is replanted
the sky thrusts
it counter-thrusts

nontree tree
beautiful voluminous tree
                    day alights on it
                    a startled bird

Dit d'errance

Tout ce qui jamais fut déchiré
en moi s'est déchiré
tout ce qui jamais fut mutilé
en moi s'est mutilé
au milieu de l'assiette de son souffle dénudé
le fruit coupé de la lune toujours en allée
vers le contour à inventer de l'autre moitié

et pourtant que te reste-t-il du temps ancien

à peine peut-être certain sens
dans la pluie de la nuit de chauvir ou trembler
et quand d'aucuns chantent Noël revenu
de songer aux astres
égarés

voici le jour le plus court de l'année
ordre assigné tout est du tout déchu
les paroles les visages les songes
l'air lui-même s'est envenimé
quand une main vers moi s'avance
j'en ramène à peine l'idée
j'ai bien en tête la saison si lacrimeuse
le jour avait un goût d'enfance
de chose profonde de muqueuse
vers le soleil mal tourné
fer contre fer une gare vide
où pour prendre rien
s'enrouait à vide à toujours geindre le même bras

Ciel éclaté courbe écorchée
de dos d'esclaves fustigés
peine trésorière des alizés
grimoire fermé mots oubliés
j'interroge mon passé muet

Ile de sang de sargasses
île morsure de remora
île arrière-rire des cétacés
île fin mot de bulle montée
île grand cœur déversé
haute la plus lointaine la mieux cachée

Lay of Errantry

        Everything that was ever torn
has been torn in me
everything that was ever mutilated
has been mutilated in me
in the middle of the plate stripped of breath
the cut fruit of the moon forever on its way
toward its other side's contour to be invented

and yet what remains with you of former times

        little more perhaps than a certain urge
to prick up my ears or to tremble in the night rain
        and whereas some sing the return of Christmas
        to dream of stars
        astray

this is the shortest day of the year
the order given all has collapsed into all
the words the faces the dreams
the air itself has become infected
when a hand advances toward me
I barely infer its intention
I have this so lachrymose season well in mind
the day with a taste of childhood
of something deep of mucous
had evilly turned toward the sun
iron against iron an empty station
where—no trains to be taken—
the same arm always moaning grew hoarse to no avail

Exploded sky flayed curve
of flogged slaves' backs
grief treasurer of the trade winds
shut book of spells forgotten words
I question my mute past

Island of blood of gulfweed
island remora's bite
island cetaceans' hind-laugh
island last word from a risen bubble
island great heart overspilling
high the most distant the best hidden

ivre lasse pêcheuse exténuée
ivre belle main oiselée
île maljointe île disjointe
toute île appelle
toute île est veuve
Bénin Bénin ô pierre d'aigris
Ifé qui fut Ouphas
une embouchure de Zambèze
vers une Ophir sans Albuquerque
tendrons-nous toujours les bras?

jadis ô déchiré
Elle pièce par morceau
rassembla son dépecé
et les quatorze morceaux
s'assirent triomphants dans les rayons du soir

J'ai inventé un culte secret
mon soleil est celui que toujours on attend
le plus beau des soleils est le soleil nocturne

Corps féminin île retournée
corps féminin bien nolisé
corps féminin écume-né
corps féminin île retrouvée
et qui jamais assez ne s'emporte
qu'au ciel il n'emporte
ô nuit renonculée
un secret de polypier
corps féminin marche de palmier
par le soleil d'un nid coiffé
où le phénix meurt et renaît
nous sommes âmes de bon parage
corps nocturnes vifs de lignage
arbres fidèles vin jaillissant
moi sybille flébilant.

Eaux figées de mes enfances
où les avirons à peine s'enfoncèrent
millions d'oiseaux de mes enfances
où fut jamais l'île parfumée
de grands soleils illuminée
la saison l'aire tant délicieuse
l'année pavée de pierres précieuses?

Aux crises des zones écartelé
en plein cri mélange ténébreux
j'ai vu un oiseau mâle sombrer

drunk weary exhausted fisherwoman
drunk beautiful birdcaught hand
ill-joined island disjointed island
every island beckons
every island is a widow
Benin Benin oh stone of embittered ones
Ife which was once Ouphas
a mouth of the Zambezi
will we always stretch out our hands toward
an Ophir without an Albuquerque?

Long ago oh torn one
in bits and pieces She
gathered her dismembered one
and the fourteen pieces
took their triumphant place in the rays of evening

I invented a secret cult
my sun is the one always awaited
the fairest of suns is the nocturnal sun

Woman's body island on its back
woman's body full freighted
woman's body foam born
woman's body recovered island
which is never carried away enough
oh ranunculated night
not to carry its polypary secret to the sky
woman's body palm tree gait
coifed by the sun with a nest
in which the phoenix dies and is reborn
we are souls of noble birth
nocturnal bodies lively with lineage
faithful trees spouting wine
I a flebile sibyl.

Inert waters of my childhoods
into which the oars barely sunk
millions of birds of my childhoods
where if ever was the fragrant island
illuminated by great suns
the season the region so delicious
the year paved with precious stones?

Dismembered in the perturbations of the zones
a tenebrous mixture at the height of its cry
I saw a male bird founder

la pierre dans son front s'est fichée
je regarde le plus bas de l'année

Corps souillé d'ordure savamment mué
espace vent de foi mentie
espace faux orgueil planétaire

lent rustique prince diamantaire
serais-je jouet de nigromance?
Or mieux qu'Antilia ni que Brazil
pierre milliaire dans la distance
épée d'une flamme qui me bourrelle
j'abats les arbres du Paradis

the stone is embedded in its forehead
I am looking at the lowest point of the year

Garbage soiled body skillfully transformed
space wind of deceitful trust
space fake planetary pride

slow unpolished diamond cutter prince
might I be the sport of nigromancy?
Meanwhile more skillful than Antilia or Brazil
a milestone within the distance
the sword of a flame that racks me
I fell the trees of Paradise

FERREMENTS
*
FERRAMENTS

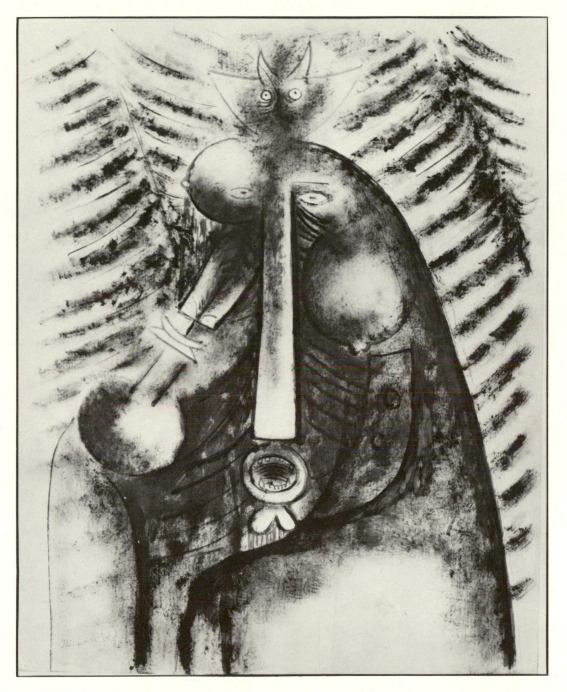

Wifredo Lam, "Phénomène phaline," 1944, oil on paper, 37 × 39"

Ferrements

Le périple ligote emporte tous les chemins
seule la brume garde ses bras ramène la ville au port en palanquin

et toi c'est une vague qui à mes pieds t'apporte
ce bateau-là au fait dans le demi-jour d'un demi-sommeil toujours je le connus

tiens-moi bien fort aux épaules aux reins

       esclaves

c'est son hennissement tiède l'écume
l'eau des criques boueuse et cette douleur puis rien
où nous deux dans le flanc de la nuit gluante aujourd'hui comme jadis
esclaves arrimés de cœurs lourds
tout de même ma chère tout de même nous cinglons
à peine un peu moins écœurés aux tangages

Ferraments

the periplus binds sweeps away all the paths
the fog alone keeps its arms brings the city in palanquin back to port

and as for you a wave carries you to my feet
that boat by the way I have always known in the half-light of half-sleep

hold me tight by the shoulders by the loins

       slaves

as for their tepid whinnying it is the foam
the muddy creek water and this pain then nothing
where we two in the flank of the gluey night today as in the past
slaves stowed with heavy hearts
all the same my dear all the same we're off
hardly a bit less nauseated by the pitching

Comptine

C'est cette mince pellicule sur le remous du vin mal déposé de la mer
c'est ce grand cabrement des chevaux de la terre
arrêtés à la dernière seconde sur un sursaut du gouffre
c'est ce sable noir qui se saboule au hoquet de l'abîme
c'est du serpent têtu ce rampement hors naufrage
cette gorgée d'astres revomie en gâteau de lucioles
cette pierre sur l'océan élochant de sa bave
une main tremblante pour oiseaux de passage
ici Soleil et Lune
font les deux roues dentées savamment engrenées
d'un Temps à nous moudre féroce
c'est ce mal être
        cette fiente
        ce sanglot de coraux
c'est fondant du ciel mémorable
jusqu'au leurre de nos cœurs rouges à l'aube
ce bec de proie rompant la poitrine inhospitalière
                cage
                et
                marécage
C'est cet émouchet qui blasonne le ciel de midi de nos noirs cœurs planant
    ce rapt
    ce sac
    ce vrac

    cette terre

Nursery Rhyme

It is this fine film on the swirls of the cloudy wine of the sea
it is this great rearing of the horses of the earth
halted at the last moment on a gasp of the chasm
it is this black sand which roughs itself up on the hiccup of the abyss
it is this stubborn serpent's crawling out the shipwreck
this mouthful of stars revomited into a cake of fireflies
this stone on the ocean tugging with its drool
at a trembling hand for passing birds
here Sun and Moon
form the two cleverly engaged toothed wheels
of a Time ferocious in grinding us
it is this wretchedness
        these droppings
        this sob of coral reefs
it is alighting from the memorable sky
down onto the lure of our hearts red at dawn
this beak of prey breaking the unwelcoming chest
            cage
            and
            quagmire
It is this kestrel which hovering blazons the noon sky of our black hearts
    this abducting
    this sacking
    this dumping

    this earth

Séisme

tant de grands pans de rêve
de parties d'intimes patries
                        effondrées
tombées vides et le sillage sali sonore de l'idée
et nous deux? quoi nous deux?
A peu près l'histoire de la famille rescapée du désastre:
"dans l'odeur de vieille couleuvre de nos sangs nous fuyions
la vallée, le village nous poursuivait avec sur nos talons des lions de pierre rugissants."
Sommeil, mauvais sommeil, mauvais réveil du cœur
le tien sur le mien vaisselle ébréchée empilée dans le creux tanguant des méridiens.
Essayer des mots? Leur frottement pour conjurer l'informe comme les insectes de nuit leurs élytres de
        démence?
Pris pris pris hors mensonge pris
pris pris pris
        rôlés précipités
        selon rien
sinon l'abrupte persistance mal lue
de nos vrais noms, nos noms miraculeux
jusqui'ici dans la réserve d'un oubli
gîtant.

Seism

so many huge sections of dreams
so many parts of intimate homelands
                    collapsed
fallen empty and the soiled sonorous slipstream of the idea
and the two of us? what two?
Roughly the history of the family surviving the disaster:
"in the old grass snake smell of our blood we were fleeing
the valley, the village was after us its roaring stone lions on our heels."
Sleep, sick sleep, sick awakening of the heart
yours over mine chipped crockery piled up in the pitching trough of meridians
To try words? Rubbing them to conjure up the unformed as nocturnal insects rub their maddening
     wing covers?
Caught caught caught outside the lie caught
caught caught caught
      forbeten pushed along
      along nothing
except for the poorly read abrupt persistence of
our true names, our miraculous names
until now in the reserve of a supine
oblivion.

Spirales

nous montons
nattes de pendus des canéfices
(le bourreau aura oublié de faire leur dernière toilette)
nous montons
belles mains qui pendent des fougères et agitent des adieux que nul n'entend
nous montons
les balisiers se déchirent le cœur sur le moment précis où le phénix renaît de la plus haute flamme qui
      le consume
nous montons
nous descendons
les cécropies cachent leur visage
et leurs songes dans le squelette de leurs mains phosphorescentes
les cercles de l'entonnoir se referment de plus en plus vite
c'est le bout de l'enfer
nous rampons nous flottons
nous enroulons de plus en plus serrés les gouffres de la terre
les rancunes des hommes
la rancœur des races
et les ressacs abyssaux nous ramènent
dans un paquet de lianes
d'étoiles et de frissons

Spirals

we ascend
braids of gallows birds from the cañafistulas
(the executioner must have forgotten the last grooming)
we ascend
beautiful hands hanging from ferns and waving farewells that no one hears
we ascend
the balisiers are breaking their hearts on the precise moment when the phoenix is reborn from its
   highest consuming flame
we ascend
we descend
the Cecropias hide their faces
and their dreams in the skeletons of their phosphorescent hands
the circles of the funnel now close faster and faster
it is the end of hell
we crawl we float
we coil the chasms of the earth
the resentments of men
the rancor of races tighter and tighter
and the abyssal undertows carry us back
in a tangle of lianas
of stars and of shudders

Salut à la Guinée

Dalaba Pita Labé Mali Timbo
              puissantes falaises
                        Tinkisso Tinkisso

eaux belles
        et que le futur déjà y déploie toute la possible chevelure

Guinée oh
        te garde ton allure

                              déclinant
jusqu'à l'ombre du nuage
le bâillon de cendre sur ton primordial feu

Volcan flambe ton mufle attentif
à la garde farouche de ce plus rare trésor
Toi golfe
de ta langue de ton souffle de ton rut
caresse et l'allaitant du lait premier
la forme nouvelle et berce
oh berce
        d'un maternel méandre
ce sable
        ce roulis
                de liberté fragile

Hail to Guinea

Dalaba Pita Labé Mali Timbo   *
                     mighty cliffs
                               Tinkisso Tinkisso

the beauty of their waters
                     and let the future now display there every possible head of hair

Guinea oh
                     let your gait protect you

                                                   refusing
even to the shadow of the cloud
the gag of ashes over your primordial fire

Volcano blaze your muzzle attentive
to the fierce vigil over this most rare treasure
You gulf
with your tongue with your breath with your rutting
caress the new form nursing it
with the first milk and rock
oh rock
                     with a maternal meander
this sand
             this rolling
                     of fragile liberty

Royaume

ce coup de couteau d'un vomi de chicots dans le ventre du vent
ce semis de guanos stérile au demeurant

au pas de course la grue solaire s'en chargea
jusqu'au pissat sauvage d'un ravin rugissant

(hoquet des anges bol ébréché
si haut placé l'eau des flaques
l'eau des fièvres se déconcerte aux yeux)

la marée montante aux pieds déjà l'incrustant d'une sanie de coquillages sévères

pourrir

le répit lui consentit de titre certain en royaume
ce crime assigné non à tort de tous les feux du Levant.

Maison-Mousson

ma face de monnaie très usée brusquement redécouverte dans tes fouilles
ta face brusquée de bête des eaux suprêmement élégante
l'une contre l'autre par évents et désastre
soufflant Espace à ton plafond trop bas
du fond du temps une insulte mémorable

Maison Mousson
onduleuse nageuse aux yeux anciens d'abîmes comblés
marabout et serpent noués
cicatrice d'horizons joués
selon la force de la fausse nuit où nous montons
en serpents d'eau de climats sybillins
qui de leurs têtes désarmées
par la solennelle touffeur de continents nés
splendide nous font un toit

Kingdom

this knife stab of a vomit of broken teeth in the belly of the wind
this sterile guano being sown nevertheless

the solar crane carried it on the double
as far as the wild pissing of a roaring ravine

(angel hiccup chipped bowl
placed so high the water of puddles
the water of fevers breaks down before our eyes)

the tide rising to our feet already incrusting them with a sanies of harsh seashells

to rot

as a kingdom respite granted him the permanent title to this
crime not mistakenly subpoenaed by all the fires of the Levant.

Monsoon-Mansion

my very worn coin face suddenly rediscovered in your diggings
your rushed upon face of a water beast supremely elegant
one against the other through blowholes and disaster
blowing, Space, against your too low ceiling
a memorable insult from the depths of time

Monsoon Mansion
sinuous swimmer with ancient eyes of filled in abysses
marabou and snake knotted
scar of horizons ventured
along the force of the deceitful night in which we ascend
as grass snakes of sibylline climates
who with their heads defused
by the solemn fug of continents born
splendidly form for us a roof

Pour Ina

et le matin de musc tiédissait dans la mangle une main de soleil
et midi juchait haut un aigle insoutenable
la nuit tombait à pic
mais maintenait quand même entre deux eaux
un trouble de terre plein de musiques encore d'insectes irréductibles

et de nouveau le jour incendiant vert-bleu au profond veiné des corolles
une ivresse d'oiseau-gemme dans un saccage de sang
et les soirs revenaient brochant de chimériques
tulles et les saisons passaient sur les ocres et les bruns
penchés des madras des grand-mères songeuses à la pluie

quand les carêmes pourchassaient par les mornes l'étrange troupeau des rousseurs splendides

Oiseaux

l'exil s'en va ainsi dans la mangeoire des astres
portant de malhabiles grains aux oiseaux nés du temps
qui jamais ne s'endorment jamais
aux espaces fertiles des enfances remuées

For Ina *

and the musky morning was warming up a handful of sun in the coastal swamp
and noon was perching up there an unbearable eagle
night was falling perpendicularly
but now nevertheless between two waters
a turmoil of earth still full of the music of irreducible insects

and once again daylight blazing green-blue in the veined depth of corollas
drunkenness of a gem-bird in a havoc of blood
and the evenings were returning brocading imaginary
tulles and the seasons were passing over the hunched
ochres and browns of the madras of grandmothers musing in the rain

when the lents were pursuing through the mornes the strange herd of splendid russets

Birds

exile thus goes into the feeder made of stars
bearing clumsy grains to the birds born of time
which never never fall asleep
in the fertile spaces of stirred up childhoods

Nocturne d'une nostalgie

                    rôdeuse
oh rôdeuse
        à petits pas de cicatrice mal fermée
        à petites pauses d'oiseau inquiet
        sur un dos de zébu

nuit sac et ressac

        à petits glissements de boutre
        à petites saccades de pirogue
        sous ma noire traction à petits pas d'une goutte de lait

sac voleur de cave
ressac voleur d'enfant

        à petite lampe de marais
ainsi toute nuit toute nuit
des côtes d'Assinie des côtes d'Assinie
le courant ramène sommaire

        toujours

et très violent

Nocturne of a Nostalgia

prowler
oh prowler
        with short steps like a poorly healing scar
        with short pauses like a worried bird
        on a zebu's back

night plunder and undertow

        with short swoops like a boutre
        with short jerks like a pirogue
        under my black tugging with short steps like a drop of milk

plunder cellar robbing
undertow child snatching

        with a short lamp like a marsh
thus from the shores of Assinie from the shores of Assinie
every night every night returns the current
summary

        always

and very violent

Nous savoir . . .

Songe donc

nous savoir
dans la pluie dans les cendres dans le gué
dans la crue

nous savoir qui rêvâmes

là

sans chiffres ni rune
rué par monts et vaux
nous savoir ce cœur lourd

grand rocher éboulé infléchi du dedans
par l'indicible musique retenue prisonnière
d'une mélodie quand même à sauver du Désastre

To Know Ourselves . . .

Reflect then

to know ourselves
in the rain in the ashes in the ford
in the flooding

ourselves who dreamt

there
without numbers or rune
flung through hills and vales
in ourselves to know this heavy heart

huge rock tumbled hollowed from within
by some ineffable music the prisoner
of a melody nevertheless to be saved from Disaster

Grand sang sans merci

du fond d'un pays de silence
d'os calcinés de sarments brûlés d'orages de cris retenus et gardés au museau
d'un pays de désirs irrités d'une inquiétude de branches
de naufrage à même (le sable très noir ayant été gavé de silence étrange
à la recherche de pas de pieds nus et d'oiseaux marins)
du fond d'un pays de soif
où s'agripper est vain à un profil absurde de mât totem et de tambours
d'un pays sourd sauvagement obturé à tous les bouts
d'un pays de cavale rouge qui galope le long désespéré
des lés de la mer et du lasso des courants les plus perfides

Défaite Défaite désert grand
où plus sévère que le Kamsin d'Egypte
siffle le vent d'Asshume

de quelle taiseuse douleur choisir d'être le tambour
                    et de qui chevauché
                    de quel talon vainqueur
                    vers les bayous étranges
gémir se tordre
crier jusqu'à une nuit hagarde à faire tomber
la vigilance armée
qu'installa en pleine nuit de nous-mêmes
l'impureté insidieuse du vent

Merciless Great Blood

from the depths of a land of silence
of charred bones of burned vine shoots of storms of screams held back and muzzled
of a land of desires inflamed by a restlessness of branches
of a shipwreck right against (the very black sand having been force fed with a peculiar silence
in the quest for prints of bare feet and sea birds)
from the depths of a land of thirst
where to cling to the absurd profile of a totem pole and drums is futile
of a deaf land savagely sealed at all ends
of a land of a red mare galloping the desperate length
of the towpaths of the sea and of the lasso of the most perfidious currents

Defeat Defeat vast desert
where fiercer than the Egyptian Khamsin
the Assouan wind whistles

for which silential grief shall we choose to be the drum
                          and by whom mounted
                          by what triumphant heel
                          toward the strange bayous
shall we moan shall we twist
shall we scream until a night haggard enough to fell
the armed vigilance
installed in the dead of the night of ourselves
by the insidious impurity of the wind

Va-t'en chien des nuits

la mer s'est retirée intacte du sang des grands poulpes échoués aux sables
dans le paysage qui se défait toujours à reprendre je cherche
un souvenir de marée une fleur d'eau une rumeur de fureur
mais trop de pistes brouillent leurs caravanes
trop de mauvais soleils empalent aux arbres leur rancœur
trop de menteurs portulans s'enlisent
aux lignes de faîte toujours divergentes
des hautes fourmis polisseuses de squelettes
          de ce fougueux silence de la bouche de ce sable
surgira-t-il rien sinon les pointes cariées de la futaie séchée

rage d'un insolite solstice allumé fauve à la limite barbare si défaillante de la mer
va-t-en chien des nuits va-t-en
inattendu et majeur à mes tempes
          tu tiens entre tes crocs saignante

une chair qu'il m'est par trop facile de reconnaître

Beat It Night Dog

the sea ebbed untouched from the blood of giant octopuses stranded on the sands
in the landscape which deteriorates always to be reworked I search
for the memory of a tide for a water flower for a rumor of fury
but too many tracks confuse their caravans
too many evil suns impale their rancor on the trees
too many deceitful portulans are sucked down
into the always diverging crest lines
from high ants polishers of skeletons
         from this impetuous silence from the mouth of this sand
will nothing surge forth other than the dried forest's blighted tops

rage of an unwonted solstice ignited lurid at the so faltering barbarous limit of the sea
beat it night dog beat it
sudden and absolute at my temples
              you hold between your fangs a bleeding

flesh I recognize only too well

. . . *mais il y a ce mal*

Si ma pensée emprunte les ailes du menfenil
ô visages c'est entendu
vous êtes proie pour mes serres

          et moi je le suis
au bec du vent du doute de la suie
de la nuit ô cendre plus épaisse vers le cœur
et ce hoquet de clous que frappent les saisons

car il y a ce mal
ci-gît au comble de moi-même
couché dans une grande mare la sourde sans ressac
quand le jour vorace me surprit mon odeur

de ce sang du mien tu diras
que toujours au seuil il buta de son galop amer
que plus juste devant Dieu que leurs bouches exactes
mon mensonge
devant sa face désemparée monta avec un millier
d'infants de la haute mer plongeant au ras du bastingage
et secoué de l'original sanglot noir des ronces

. . . *But There Is This Hurt*

If my thought borrows the wings of the menfenil
oh faces it is clear
you are prey for my claws

         and I I am prey
for the beak of the wind of doubt of the soot
of night oh cinder denser toward the heart
and this hiccup of nails driven in by the seasons

for there is this hurt
Here Lies at the height of myself
spread out in a big pool the hidden one with no undertow
when the voracious day robbed me of my odor

about this blood of mine you will say
that always at the threshold of its bitter gallop it tripped
that more just before God than their correct mouths
my lie
before his distraught face soared with a thousand
infantes out of the high sea plunging flush with the bulwarks
shaken by the original black sobbing of brambles

Viscères du poème

Angoisse tu ne descendras pas tes écluses dans le bief de ma gorge

Peur dans l'écheveau fou je n'aurai que faire de chercher en tremblant
le fil rouge de mon sang de ma raison de mon droit
le dur secret de mon corps de l'orgueil de mon cœur
une étoile de toujours se lève grand'erre et sans laisser de lie
s'éteint pour mieux renaître au plus pur
si tranchant sur les bords qu'Eclipse tu as beau faire infâme
moi le bras happé par les pierres fondrières de la nuit
je refuse ton pacte sa fureur de patience
et le tumulte debout dans l'ombre des oreilles
aura vu pour une fois sur la blancheur du mur
gicler la noirceur de ce cri sans oubli

Viscera of the Poem

Anguish you shall not lower your floodgates into the reach of my throat

Fear in your mad skein I shall not have to seek trembling
the red thread of my blood of my reason of my right
the hard secret of my body of the pride of my heart
a star always rises full sail and without leaving sediment
goes out so as to be reborn at its purest
so sharp edged that vile Eclipse do what you will
I my arm snapped up by the stones quagmires of night
I refuse your pact the fury of its patience
and the tumult erect in the dark of our ears
will for once have seen the blackness of this unforgetting scream
squirt against the whiteness of the wall

C'est moi-même, Terreur, c'est moi-même

Les rêves échoués desséchés font au ras de la gueule des rivières
de formidables tas d'ossements muets
les espoirs trop rapides rampent scrupuleusement
en serpents apprivoisés
on ne part pas on ne part jamais
pour ma part en île je me suis arrêté fidèle
debout comme le prêtre Jehan un peu de biais sur la mer
et sculpté au niveau du museau des vagues et de la fiente des oiseaux
choses choses c'est à vous que je donne
ma folle face de violence déchirée dans les profondeurs du tourbillon
ma face tendre d'anses fragiles où tiédissent les lymphes
c'est moi-même terreur c'est moi-même
le frère de ce volcan qui certain sans mot dire
rumine un je ne sais quoi de sûr
et le passage aussi pour les oiseaux du vent
qui s'arrêtent souvent s'endormir une saison
c'est toi-même douceur c'est toi-même
traversée de l'épée éternelle
et tout le jour avançant
marqué du fer rouge de choses sombrées
et du soleil remémoré

It Is Myself, Terror, It Is Myself

Stranded dried up dreams flush with the muzzles of rivers create
formidable piles of mute bones
the too swift hopes crawl scrupulously
like tamed snakes
one does not leave one never leaves
as for me I have halted, faithful, on the island
standing like Prester John slightly sideways to the sea
and sculptured at snout level by waves and bird droppings
things things it is to you that I give
my crazed violent face ripped open in the whirlpool's depths
my face tender with fragile coves where lymphs are warming
it is myself terror it is myself
the brother of this volcano which certain without saying a word
ruminates an indefinable something that is sure
and passage as well for birds of the wind
which often stop to sleep for a season
it is thyself sweetness it is thyself
run through by the eternal sword
and the entire day advancing
branded with the red-hot iron of foundered things
and of recollected sun

Des crocs

Il n'est poudre de pigment
ni myrrhe
odeur pensive ni délectation
mais fleur de sang à fleur de peau
carte de sang carte du sang
à vif à sueur à peau
ni arbre coupé à blanc estoc
mais sang qui monte dans l'arbre de chair
à crans à crimes
                Rien de remis
à pic le long des pierres
            à pic le long des os
du poids du cuivre des fers des cœurs
venins caravaniers de la morsure
au tiède fil des crocs

Fangs

It is no pigment powder
nor myrrh
pensive odor nor delectation
but flower of blood flush with the skin
map of blood map of the blood
bled raw sweated raw skinned raw
nor tree cut to a white thrust
but blood which rises in the tree of flesh
by catches by crimes
                              No remittance
—straight up along the stones
                    straight up along the bones—for
copper weight shackle weight heart weight
venoms caravaners of the bite
at the tepid edge of fangs

Vampire liminaire

Il se fait une lumière atroce
de l'Occident à l'Orient à contre courant
le hurlement des molosses du brouillard y répond
de la Ville selon le Peur plénière agitant à foison de drapeaux
dix milliers de langues gluantes et la parade visqueuse entre deux nuits
d'abord de toutes les bêtes somptueuses vomies des pourritures

mais sous la marche de ronce du venin
ils ont prévalu leurs yeux intacts au plus fragile
de l'image impardonnée
de la vision mémorable du monde à bâtir
de la fraternité qui ne saurait manquer de venir
quoique malhabile

reniflant au pied de l'arbre de vie
les rats noirs cardinaux du mensonge mêlés à
l'unicorne de la haine raciale
au bout du fil l'oreille de l'inquisiteur
alors l'eau des égouts fait un bond formidable
de tout le voyage tu des oiseaux espérés
Assez que les mots se transforment en cassave de poussière
la boue comme sur une venaison
plaqua ses griffes sur les étoiles

Liminal Vampire

An atrocious light appears
from the Occident to the Orient counter-current
the howling of the mastiffs of the fog vouches
for the City according to the plenary Fear waving like flags galore
ten thousand sticky tongues and the viscous parade between two nights
at first of all the sumptuous beasts vomited from putrefactions

but under the brambly advance of the venom
they prevailed, their eyes intact, at the most fragile point
of the unpardonable image
of the memorable vision of a world to be built
of the brotherhood that cannot but come
however awkwardly

sniffing at the foot of the tree of life
black rats cardinals of the lie mingled with
the unicorn of racial hatred
on the other end of the line the inquisitor's ear
then the sewer water makes a terrific leap
from the whole untold journey of hoped for birds
Enough that words turn into a cassava of dust
as if into deer flesh the mud
clamped its claws over the stars

Clair passage de ma journée profonde

dans l'épice grand large
il y a étale cette épaisseur comme une saison acide une tour
vénéneuse qu'on finit par ne plus entendre parce que jamais
jamais elle ne retombe en gouttes ravinant d'un fragment la paroi qui patiente

il y a cette verticale terrible dont le nom fidélité me fixe à vif
au pommeau tournoyant du glaive à double tranchant
dont je ne suis que la garde affable dans le temps et que
chaque goutte de mon sang en vain s'efforce de diviser

il n'est pas pour autant facile de dessiner la carte du champ
de bataille clairière chaque fois mouvante dont le remords
m'essaime à tout coup plus sauvage vers la face
loyale des constellations

hurler à la lisière attisée incassable en barreaux
forgée en vigilance et par démence tordue
hurler aux sources inavouées des grands fleuves aux maternités
non mémorables à la mamelle jamais mordue des bêtes faramines

le réveil est en torpeur au pied péremptoire des palmiers
femmes frigides étroitement gainées et qui toujours et de très haut
s'éventent

le sûr est qu'il y a moi en grand serpent des fondrières que
se singe clouer le trident du soleil et qui sans nom
effarouché bifide tout au bord d'une nuit rompue rampe
fragilement avide avide d'un lait ténu

My Profound Day's Clear Passage

in the spice open sea
there is, steady, this thickness like an acidic season a poisonous
tower that one finally does not hear anymore because never
never does it fall back in drops fissuring with a fragment the wall which waits, patient

there is this awesome vertical whose name, fidelity, fixes me skinned
to the whirling pommel of the double-edged glaive
of which I am only the affable cross guard in time and which
each drop of my blood vainly strives to cleave

nevertheless it is not easy to draw the map of the battle-
ground a clearing shifting each time from where remorse
bestrews me every time more savage toward the loyal
face of constellations

to howl at the aroused forest's edge unbreakable into bars
forged in vigilance and twisted by madness
to howl at the unavowed sources of great rivers at the nonmemorable
maternities at the never sucked breasts of fabulous beasts

the awakening is in torpor at the peremptory foot of palm trees
frigid women tightly girdled who forever and from very high
fan themselves

surely there is me as a great serpent of the bogs which
the sun's trident aping itself nails and which nameless
frightened bifid at the very edge of a ruptured night crawls
fragilely avid avid for a tenuous milk

Cadavre d'une frénésie

le souvenir d'une route
qui monte très fort dans l'ombrage des bambous
le vesou qui s'invente toujours neuf
et l'odeur des mombins
on a laissé en bas
les petites jupes de la mer
les saisons de l'enfance
le parasol de coccolobes

je me tourne au virage je regarde par-dessus l'épaule
de mon passé c'est plein du bruit magique toujours sur le coup
incompréhensible et angoissant du fruit de l'arbre à pain
qui tombe et jusqu'au ravin où nul ne le retrouve roule

la catastrophe s'est fait un trône trop haut perché
du délire de la ville détruite c'est ma vie incendiée
Douleur perdras-tu
l'habitude qu'on hurle
j'ai rêvé face tordue
bouche amère j'ai rêvé de tous les vices de mon sang
et les fantômes rôdèrent à chacun de mes gestes
à l'échancrure du sort

il n'importe c'est faiblesse

veille mon cœur
prisonnier qui seul inexplicablement survit dans sa cellule à l'évidence du sort
féroce taciturne
tout au fond lampe allumée de sa blessure horrible

Corpse of a Frenzy

the memory of a road
rising very steeply in bamboo shade
the cane juice that invents itself always new
and the odor of hog plums

the little skirts of the sea
the seasons of childhood
the parasol of coccolobes
                        have been left below

at the curve I turn around I look over the shoulder
of my past it is full of always not immediately comprehensible
magical and anguishing blows of breadfruit
falling and rolling down into ravines where no one finds them

catastrophe made for itself a too high perched throne
out of the delirium of the destroyed city it is my burned down life
                        Grief will you never
stop expecting our howling
I dreamed face twisted
mouth bitter I dreamed about all the impurities of my blood
and the ghosts roamed about with each of my gestures
at the indentation of fate

                never mind it is a weakness

let my heart keep vigil
a prisoner who alone in his cell inexplicably survives the evidence of fate
ferocious taciturn
at the very bottom a lamp lit from his horrible wound

Patience des signes

sublimes excoriations d'une chair fraternelle et jusqu'aux feux rebelles de mille villages fouettée
arènes
feu
mât prophétique des carènes
feu
vivier des murènes
feu feux de position d'une île bien en peine
feux empreintes effrénées de hagards troupeaux qui dans les boues s'épellent
morceaux de chair crue
crachats suspendus
éponge dégouttant de fiel
valse de feu des pelouses jonchées des cornets qui tombent de l'élan brisé des grands tabebuias
feux tessons perdus en un désert de peurs et de citernes
os
feux desséchés jamais si desséchés que n'y batte un ver sonnant sa chair neuve
semences bleues du feu
feu des feux
témoins d'yeux qui pour les folles vengeances s'exhument et s'agrandissent
pollen pollen
et par les grèves où s'arrondissent les baies nocturnes des doux mencenilliers
bonnes oranges toujours accessibles à la sincérité des soifs longues

Patience of Signs

sublime excoriations of a flesh fraternal and whipped to the point of rebellious fires in a thousand
      villages
arenas
fire
hulls' prophetic masts
fire
breeding ground for moray eels
fire riding lights of an island truly in distress
fires frantic tracks of haggard herds which in the mud are spelled
pieces of raw flesh
suspended spittings
a sponge dripping sour wine
a fiery waltz of lawns strewn with the cornets that fall from the broken surge of great Tabebuias
fires shards lost in a desert of fears and cisterns
bones
dried up fires never too dry for a worm to beat there tolling its new flesh
blue seeds of fire
fire of fires
witnesses of eyes which crazed for vengeance exhume themselves and expand
pollen pollen
and along the sands where the nocturnal berries of sweet manchineels swell
rich oranges always accessible to the sincerity of long long thirsts

Fantômes

clameurs clameurs

moi qui n'eus jamais de gorge qu'à midi
je caressai sa tête de chat demi-sauvage
voluptueusement

de gros bourgs vinrent paître dans les hauts fonds herbus
puis tendirent à l'excès des moustiques leur mufle
vers la noire eau bien empuantie des mangles

clameurs clameurs

hétéroclite d'odeurs obséquieuses
de la beauté bleue des soleils à la source
l'envergure du roulis au détour de l'échouage
au défaut du mirage blesse peu un matin
chimère sommaire des cités interdites

Phantoms

outcries outcries

I who never had a throat except at noon
I stroked its half-wild cat's head
voluptuously

fat villages came to graze the grassy shallows
then stretched their muzzles to the excess of mosquitoes
toward the black water reeking of mangrove fruit

outcries outcries

incongruous with obsequious odors
with the blue beauty of suns at their origin
the range of the tossing at the curve of the beaching strand
in the hollow of the mirage hardly wounds a morning
fleeting chimera of forbidden cities

Mobile fléau de songes étranges

très haut trouvé sourire perdu
au double confin incandescent
l'un de sel l'autre de silence
morts qui remontent aux yeux des astres
l'événement passe dans les nuages

hors d'un caverneux sommeil velu
deux yeux écouteurs sans parler
de pierres qui les fermentent
comme le doute défaisant
sans rien toucher rôde en tonnerre

rumeur pure quoique mêlée
à choses précieuses qui rendent gorge
vive agonie bien éphémère
d'une flamme non coutumière

mobile fléau de songes étranges

Saison âpre

Cercle après cercle
quand les déserts nous auront un à un tendu tous leurs miroirs
vainement les nuits ayant sur la tiédeur des terres étiré leur cou de chameau fatigué
les jours repartiront sans fantôme à la poursuite des purs lacs non éphémères
et les nuits au sortir les croiseront titubants
d'un rêve long absurde de graminées

Esprit sauvage cheval de la tornade
gueule ouverte dans ta suprême crinière
en moi tu henniras cette heure

Alors vent âpre et des jours blancs seul juge
au noir roc intime sans strie et sans noyau
jugeant selon l'ongle de l'éclair en ma poitrine profonde
tu me pèseras gardien du mot cloué par le précepte

Mobile Beam of Peculiar Dreams

found very high a lost smile
at the double incandescent confines
one of salt another of silence
dead ones who rise again to the eyes of the stars
the event is passing in the clouds

outside of a cavernous hairy sleep
two eyes listeners without mentioning
stones which ferment them
just as doubt undoing
without touching anything prowls in thunder

a rumor pure though mixed
with precious things which vomit
the truly ephemeral acute agony
of a noncustomary flame

mobile beam of peculiar dreams

Bitter Season

Circle after circle
when the deserts have offered us one by one all their mirrors
the nights having stretched in vain their fatigued camel necks over the tepidity of lands
the days will again without a phantom start to pursue pure nonephemeral lakes
and the nights upon emerging will pass them staggering
out of a long absurd dream about grasses

Wild spirit tornado horse
muzzle open inside your supreme mane
in me you will neigh this hour

Then wind bitter and sole judge of white days
on intimate black grooveless pitless rock
testing by fingernail the lightning in my deep chest
you shall weigh me guardian of the word nailed by the decree

Statue de Lafcadio Hearn

Sans doute est-il absurde de saluer cette poussée en plein océan
restée debout à la verticale parmi les griffures du vent
et dont le cœur à chaque battement déclenche
un délire vrai de lianes. Grande phrase de terre sensuelle
si bégayée aux mornes! "Et qui, qui veut" entendais-je
hurler une voix sans dérision "en boire
de l'Ame d'Homme? De l'Esprit
de Combat? De l'Essence par quoi qui tombe tombe pour
se relever? Du Meneur de Cœurs? Du Briseur
de l'Enfer?" Alors alors ma vue tarière força
et la vision pondit ses yeux sans rémission:

Yé grimpa au palmier
Nanie-Rosette mangeait sur un rocher
le diable volait autour
oint de graisse de serpent
d'huile des trépassés
un dieu dans la ville dansait à tête de bœuf
des rhums roux couraient de gosier en gosier
aux ajoupas l'anis se mêlait à l'orgeat
aux carrefours s'accroupissaient aux dés et sur les doigts
dépêchaient des rêves
des hommes couleur tabac
dans les ombres aux poches de longs rasoirs dormaient

des rhums roux couraient de gosier en gosier
mais aucun aucun qui formidable fit réponse
et sa muqueuse prêtât á la morsure des guêpes

O questionneur étrange
            je te tends ma cruche comparse
                    le noir verbe mémorant
                            Moi moi moi
car de toi je connus que ta patience fut faite
de la cabine de commandement d'un corsaire démâté par l'orage et léché d'orchidées

Statue of Lafcadio Hearn *

Undoubtedly it is absurd to hail this thrust in mid ocean
still standing vertically amidst the clawings of the wind
whose heart triggers with each beat
a true liana delirium. Great sentence from a sensual earth
so stuttered on the mornes! "And who, who wants," I heard
a voice with no sarcasm roar, "to partake
of the Soul of Man? Of the Spirit
of Combat? Of the Essence by virtue of which who falls falls
to stand again? Of the Leader of Hearts? Of the Harrower
of Hell?" Then then my augur sight pressed on
and the vision laid its eggs relentlessly:

Yé clambered up the palm tree
Nanie-Rosette was eating on a boulder
the devil was flying about
annointed with snake grease
with the oil of departed souls
a god in the town was dancing wearing an ox head
auburn rums were flowing from throat to throat
in the ajoupas anise was being mixed with orgeat
at the crossroads tobacco-colored men
squatted at dice
and dispatched dreams along their fingers
in the shade in pockets long razors were sleeping

auburn rums were flowing from throat to throat
but no one no one made a formidable response
and offered his mucous membrane to the bites of wasps

O strange questioner
                to you I hand my supernumerary jug
                        the black verb memorizing
                                Me me me
as for you I knew your patience was created
from the command post of a corsair dismasted by the storm and licked by orchids

Beau sang giclé

tête trophée membres lacérés

dard assassin beau sang giclé

ramages perdus rivages ravis

enfances enfances conte trop remué
l'aube sur sa chaîne mord féroce à naître

                              ô assassin attardé

l'oiseau aux plumes jadis plus belles que le passé

exige le compte de ses plumes dispersées

Beautiful Spurted Blood

trophy head lacerated limbs

deadly sting beautiful spurted blood

lost warblings ravished shores

childhoods childhoods a tale too stirred up
dawn on its chain ferocious snapping to be born

                              oh belated assassin

the bird with feathers once more beautiful than the past

demands an accounting for its scattered plumes

C'est le courage des hommes qui est démis

L'extraordinaire téléphonie du feu central aux nébuleuses installées en une seconde et pour quels ordres! La pluie, c'est la manière rageuse dès maintenant et dès ici de biffer tout ce qui existe, tout ce qui a été créé, crié, dit, menti, sali. Où a-t-on pris que la pluie tombe?

C'est le courage des hommes qui est démis. La pluie est toujours de tout cœur. La pluie exulte. C'est une levée en masse de l'inspiration, un sursaut des sommeils tropicaux; un en-avant de lymphes; une frénésie de chenilles et de facules; un assaut tumultueux contre tout ce qui se terre dans les garennes; la lancée à contre-sens des gravitations de mille folles munitions et des tur-ra-mas qui sautent en avançant—hippocampes vers les enfin et les faubourgs.

Enfin! L'arbre pète à la grenade. La roche éclate. Tendresse: de loin en loin ce grand repos. Tendresse: de loin en loin cet orchestre qui joue et entrelace des pas comme de l'osier qu'on tresse.

Tendresse, mais celle des tortures adorables: la mise en marche d'un incendie de vilebrequins qui forent et forcent le vide à crier étoile. C'est du sang. Du reste on comprend mal comment ça suffit à alimenter la formidable dévolution de chevaux qui de crête en crête rebroussent l'élan des ravins.

Il n'y a plus de royauté. Et l'invention est perpétuelle de chants d'extase, de prières écourtées, de cérémonial minutieux d'araigne, de scies qui clapotent, de chevelures dénouées, de lampes de mosquées en verre émaillé qui s'entrechoquent, de mers qui filent et refluent, d'alambic, de serpentins qui à toute vapeur claironnent les condensations inoubliables.

Certes inoubliables. Une danse de sagaies comme on n'en a jamais vu et dix mille drapeaux de victoire arrachés aux cétacés et que la terre agite.

La vigne de la colère a colporté jusqu'au ciel l'alcool de son repos et du salut.

It Is the Courage of Men Which Is Dislocated

The extraordinary telephony from the central fire to galaxies installed in one second and by what orders! The rain, it's the testy way here and now to strike out everything that exists, everything that's been created, cried out, said, lied about, soiled. Where on earth did you hear that rain falls?

It is the courage of men which is dislocated. Rain is always wholehearted. Rain exults. It is a levy en masse of inspiration, a jolt of tropical sleep; a forward of lympths; a frenzy of caterpillars and faculae; a tumultuous assault against everything that burrows in warrens; the thrust counter-current to gravity of a thousand crazed rounds of ammunition and the tur-ra-mas that jump as they advance—sea horses toward the finallys and the suburbs.

Finally! The tree bursts with grenade. The rock explodes. Tenderness: now and then this great repose. Tenderness: now and then this orchestra playing and intertwining steps like plaited wicker.

Tenderness, but that of adorable tortures: the setting in motion of a fire of bit-braces which drill and force the void to scream star. It is blood. Moreover it is hard to understand how it is enough to feed the extraordinary devolution of horses which from ridge to ridge turn back on the momentum of the ravines.

No more monarchy. And it is perpetual this invention of ecstatic chants, of abbreviated prayers, of meticulous spider ceremonials, of saws which splash about, of unknotted hair, of enameled glass mosque lamps which collide, of seas which flow and ebb, of an alembic, of worms which at full steam trumpet unforgettable condensations.

Unforgettable indeed. An assagai dance the likes of which has never been seen and ten thousand victory flags torn from the cetaceans and waved by the earth.

The vineyard of wrath has peddled to the very sky the alcohol of its repose and its salvation.

De mes haras

Nuages déraillez au chalumeau! Pluie fille violente effilez vos charpies! Blessures de la mer installez-vous en sifflant! Entonnoirs et volcans tous à la dérive! A la débandade dieux fous! Faites-vous sauter la cervelle! Que les champs soient arrachés au trident et les pêcheurs de perles projetés jusqu'au ciel! Une pensée. Quoi? Le feu qui n'est plus gaspillé. Le possible déchirant, dans sa poitrine somptueuse, tout ce qui tarde à devenir.

Nuit. Quoi? Toute la matière qui pèse et s'épuise à devenir espace. Le mot de passe. Quoi? Passer le monde au crible et le manque de solidité de tout subterfuge.

Temps des éclairs, temps des éclairs, bêtes placides, bêtes frénétiques, temps des éclairs, temps des éclairs, bêtes fragiles, bêtes laboureuses, par naseaux et écumes à ma voix vous accouriez jadis des écuries du ciel
       et c'étaient de toutes les couleurs
       de tout trot et de tout bai
des prairies merveilleuses qui poussaient à l'envie de ces bêtes impétueuses
jeunes et frôlées d'icaques
sous la tendre peau d'une eau toujours éblouie

Intimité marine

Tu n'es pas un toit. Tu ne supportes pas de couvreur.
Tu n'es pas une tombe. Tu ignores tout silo dont tu n'éclates le ventre. Tu n'es pas une paix. Ta meule sans cesse aiguise juste un courroux suprême de couteaux et de coraux. D'ailleurs en un certain sens tu n'es pas autre que l'élan sauvage de mon sang qu'il m'est donné de voir et qui vient de très loin lorsque le rire silencieux du menfenil s'avance en clapotant du fond funèbre de la gorge de l'horizon.
Et voilà qu'en cou de cheval en colère je me vois, en grand serpent. Je m'enroule je me déroule je bondis. Je suis un vrai coursier déplié vers une éclatante morsure. Je ne tombe pas. Je frappe, je brise, toute porte je brise et hennissant, absolu, cervelle, justice, enfance je me brise. Climat climats connaissance du cri ta dispersion au moins s'épanouirait-elle et au-delà de toute épouvante?
Cependant telle une chevelure l'âpre vin de fort Kino monte l'escarpement des falaises très fort jusqu'à la torpeur tordue des coccolobes.

From My Stud Farms

Clouds, jump the tracks with a blowtorch! Rain violent girl unravel your shreds! Sea wounds settle in with a hiss! All funnels and volcanoes adrift! Stampede mad gods! Blow your brains out! Let the fields be ripped apart by the trident and the pearl fishermen be catapulted to the very sky! A thought. What? The fire that is no longer squandered. What is possible tearing in its sumptuous chest everything slow in becoming.

Night. What? The entire matter which weighs and exhausts itself to become space. The password. What? To pass the world through a sieve and the lack of solidity in each subterfuge.

Times of lightning, times of lightning, placid beasts, frenzied beasts, times of lightning, times of lightning, fragile beasts, plodding beasts, at my call by nostrils and foamings you used to run out of the stables of the sky
     and there were marvelous multicolored
     prairies of every trot and every
shade of bay which grew for the desire of these fiery beasts
young and brushed by coco plums
under the tender skin of a water forever dazzling

Marine Intimacy

You are no roof. You are not supporting any roofers.
You are no tomb. You ignore any silo whose belly you do not burst. You are no peace. Your grinding wheel incessantly sharpens with precision a supreme choler of knives and coral. Moreover in a certain sense you are none other than the wild impulse of my blood which I am privileged to see and which comes from afar when the silent laughter of the menfenil advances splashing from the funereal depth of the horizon's throat.
And now I see myself as the neck of an enraged horse, as a giant snake. I coil I uncoil I leap. I am a true charger opened out toward a radiant bite. I do not fall. I strike, I break, any door I break and neighing, absolute, brain, justice, childhood I break myself. Climate climates cognizance of the cry would your dispersal at least bloom even beyond all terror?
Meanwhile like a head of hair the tart wine of strong Kino climbs the escarpment of very steep cliffs up to the contorted torpor of the coccolobes.

Bucolique

Alors tout doucement la terre se pousse une crinière, vire en manœuvrant sa tête bien huilée de poulpe, roule dans sa cervelle une idée très visible à l'endroit des circonvolutions, puis se précipite à toute allure, emportant en un vol ténébreux de roches et de météores, la rivière, les chevaux, les cavaliers et les maisons.

Et cependant que l'argent des coffres noircit, que l'eau des piscines se gonfle, que les pierres tombales sont descellées, que la bucolique installe au creux une mer de boue qui indolemment fume le meilleur macouba du siècle, de gigantesques lumières fusent au loin et regardent, sous leurs casques de noir champignon, une colline, bon berger roux, qui d'un bambou phosphorescent pousse à la mer un haut troupeau de temples frissonnants et de villes.

Ferment

Séduisant du festin de mon foie ô Soleil
ta réticence d'oiseau, écorché, roulant.
L'âpre lutte nous enseigna nos ruses,
mordant l'argile, pétrissant le sol
marquant la terre suante
du blason du dos, de l'arbre de nos épaules
sanglant, sanglant
soubresaut d'aube démêlé d'aigles.

Bucolic

Then very gently the earth grows a mane, swivels maneuvering its well-oiled octopus head, turns over in its brain an idea clearly visible in the area of circumvolutions, then rushes on at full speed, carrying away in a sinister flight of rocks and meteors, the river, the horses, the horsemen and the houses.

And as the silver of chests blackens, as the water of piscinas swells, as the tombstones are unsealed, as the bucolic installs in the hollow a sea of mud which nonchalantly smokes the best maccaboy of the century, gigantic lights flash off in the distance and, under their black mushroom helmets, observe a hill, good russet shepherd, who with a phosphorescent bamboo pushes a tall herd of shivering temples and cities into the sea.

Ferment

Seducing your bird-like reticence with
the feast of my liver oh Sun, torn open, lurching.
The bitter struggle taught us our cunning,
biting the clay, kneading the dust
marking the sweating earth
with the blazons of our backs, with the bloody
trees of our shoulders, bloody
eagle disentangled jolt of dawn.

Me centuplant Persée

Va, autour de moi, de mon flanc
de ma tête, de mon noueux cœur noir, aux confins,
ta ronde, harcelant de la cohue des affres
mon nom.

Que perce, transperce l'écorce résistante
le bec. Pour le reste s'ourle des termites la clandestine trame
dans la proie engrangeant jusqu'au fond la morsure.

Or nul assaut ne déniant persévérant mon nom
en la lymphe bien plutôt qui me centuple Persée
je parcours l'intime fosse alimentant mes monstres
voraces mes soleils et l'orage outre aubier me calcule
contre-saison en anneaux d'arbre
lents secrétaires d'un séisme.

Précepte

C'est bien je ne rentrerai que sauvage hirsute d'épines de chemins
par l'arc à trois portes des selves vigoureuses

exclu mais violeur des sanctuaires
et rentrant par le triomphant portail
de la mer défonçant par saccades la pudeur de la pierre

au ban du pain blanc de la fête des enfants
mais avec ma rare gueule rentrant la gueule du vent mordant
le buisson nu de son rare rire obscène

un pays noir c'est selon un noir sommeil fidèle
saoul du pur vin de lait noir de la terre

I Perseus Centuplicating Myself

Make, around me, around my side,
my head, around my gnarled black heart, at the outer reaches,
your rounds, harassing with the throng of torments
my name.

Let the beak pierce, transpierce the resisting
bark. As for the rest let the clandestine termite weft
hem itself garnering the bite into the depths of the prey.

And no assault persevering in denying me a name
instead in the lymph which centuplicates me a Perseus
I run the course of the intimate pit feeding my voracious
monsters my suns and the storm beyond sapwood estimates me
out of season by tree rings
slow secretaries of a seism.

Precept

All right only as a savage hairy with thorns from paths will I re-enter
through the three-gated arch of exuberant selvas

excluded but raper of sanctuaries
and re-entering through the triumphant portal
of the sea forcing by fits the modesty of the stone

banned from the white bread of the children's feast
but with my rare mug taking in the mug of the wind biting
the naked bush with its rare ribald laughter

a black country it all depends on a faithful black sleep
drunk on the pure wine-like black milk of the earth

En tâtant le sable du bambou de mes songes

le tronc enserré de liens
l'eau lance de brutaux surgeons
dans l'aire avide du courant
ce sont surgeons aveugles d'être
affamés affamés et claustrés de dix ans

un immense courage debout au centre sans mérite
du lasso à lancer au cou sauvage de la vie qui se cabre dans tous les sens
remonte superbement la pente des manades
faisant sauter de par en bas l'une après l'autre
la cause des roches des îles des berges

chacune victorieuse parole
le bouillonnant silence les marqua de son sceau
à l'instant des balances
et pourtant jusqu'au bout
et sans que le pus de nos yeux encroûte nos visions
mon orgueil pèse et tâtant du bambou de mes songes

la profondeur des sables
je descends la passe considérable ô Bête

cependant que s'avancent nulles si ce n'est
au pouvoir ultime de ma bouche
les caravanes poussiéreuses portant sur la tête en bagage
la confusion véhémente de l'avenir

les antiques témoins de l'alliance n'ont pas l'air au vertige
or c'est une mer très à vif et houleuse
moi à même eux de toutes parts
rois dans le corail consentant et le cœur consistant
des fougères

Feeling the Sand with the Bamboo of My Dreams

its trunk encircled by bonds
the water flings brutal suckers
into the current's avid surface
suckers blind from being
starved starved and locked up ten years

an immense courage standing at the unworthy center of
the lasso to be looped onto the wild neck of life which rears in every direction
magnificently scrambles up the slope of bull herds
blasting from far below one after another
the cause of rocks of islands of river banks

each one a victorious word
the boiling silence marked them with its seal
at the instant of scales
and yet unto the end
and without the pus in our eyes encrusting our visions
my pride weighs and feeling with the bamboo of my dreams

the depth of the sands
I descend the momentous pass oh Beast

meanwhile they come forth null except for
the ultimate power of my mouth,
dusty caravans carrying as luggage on their heads
the vehement confusion of the future

the ancient witnesses of the alliance do not appear to be dizzy
yet it is a very raw and swelling sea
I right against they from every corner
kings in the consenting coral and the ferns' consistent
core

Aux îles de tous vents

des terres qui sautent très haut
pas assez cependant pour que leurs pieds ne restent pris au pécule de la mer mugissant son assaut de
        faces irrémédiables

faim de l'homme entendu des moustiques et soif
car ce sont pains allongés pour un festin d'oiseaux
sable à contre-espoir sauvé ou des bras recourbés
pour recueillir au sein tout ce qui s'allonge
de chaleur hors saison

O justice midi de la raison trop lente il n'importe
que sans nom à la torche résineuse des langues
elles ne sachent que leur offrande terreuse
en ce chant de trop loin téméraire s'accomplit

le matin dans l'insu de ma voix dévoilera
l'oiseau que tout pourtant elle porte et Midi
pourquoi elle resta incrustée du sang de ma gorge haletante

              des îles de toutes tu diras
que selon le cœur comparse d'oiseaux vertigineux

longtemps longtemps cherchant entre les draps du sable
la blessure au carrefour convoité de la mer affouillante
tu trouvas à travers le hoquet
le noyau de l'insulte inclus en l'âcre sang
qu'exultant enfin de l'aumaille blessée des étoiles
surchauffée à nos souffles fiévreux et conteste
d'un sanglot plus riche que les barres nous sûmes
criant terre cramponnés au plus glissant de la paroi de l'être
toujours bien disant comme l'on meurt
la noire tête charnelle et crêpue du soleil

On the Islands of All Winds

lands which leap very high
not high enough however to keep their feet from remaining caught by the peculium of the sea
        booming its assault of irremediable faces

hunger of man heard by the mosquitoes and his thirst
for they are loaves laid out for a bird feast
sand saved against all hope or arms bent
to gather to one's breast all that lingers of
the out of season heat

O justice noon of reason too slow it does not matter
that nameless to the resinous torch of tongues
they do not know that their dirt offering
is in this too distant song recklessly achieved

the morning in the unbeknown of my voice will unveil
the bird which it nevertheless carries and Noon
why my voice remained encrusted with the blood of my panting throat

                        from the islands from all of them you will say
that according to the heart a supernumerary of vertiginous birds

for a long long time seeking between sheets of sand
the wound at the coveted crossroad of the undermining sea
you found through the hiccup
the pit of the insult included in the bitter blood
that finally exulting in the wounded kine of the stars
overheated in our feverish breath and a challenge
to a sobbing richer than the bars, we knew
crying land clinging to the most slippery of the wall of being
always speaking beautifully as we die
the carnal and kinky black head of the sun

Le temps de la liberté

Le whisky avait dénoué ses cheveux sales
et flottait sur la force des fusils
la carapace des tanks
et les jurons du juge

O jour non lagunaire
plus têtu que le bœuf du pays Baoulé
qui a dit que l'Afrique dort
que notre Afrique se cure la gorge
mâche du kola boit de la bière de mil et se
rendort

la T.S.F. du Gouverneur avait colporté ses mensonges
amassé le fiel dans la poche à fiel des journaux
c'était l'an 1950 au mois de février
qui dans le vocabulaire des gens de par ici s'appellera la saison du soleil rouge

Cavally Sassandra Bandama
petits fleuves au mauvais nez qui à travers vase et pluie d'un museau incertain cherchez
petits fleuves au ventre gros de cadavres
qui a dit que l'Afrique se terre frissonne
à l'harmattan a peur et se rendort

Histoire je conte l'Afrique qui s'éveille
les hommes
quand sous la mémoire hétéroclite des chicotes
ils entassèrent le noir feu noué
dont la colère traversa comme un ange
l'épaisse nuit verte de la forêt

Histoire je conte
l'Afrique qui a pour armes
ses poings nus son antique sagesse sa raison toute nouvelle
Afrique tu n'as pas peur tu combats tu sais
mieux que tu n'as jamais su tu regardes
les yeux dans les yeux des gouverneurs de proie
des banquiers périssables

belle sous l'insulte Afrique et grande de ta haute conscience et si certain le jour
quand au souffle des hommes les meilleurs aura disparu la tsé-tsé colonialiste

The Time of Freedom

Whiskey had untied its dirty hair
and was floating over the power of rifles
the carapace of tanks
and the cursings of the judge

O nonlagoonal day
more stubborn than the Baoulé ox
who said Africa is asleep
that our Africa clears its throat
chews kola drinks millet beer and falls
back asleep

the Governor's wireless had peddled his lies
gathered the bile in the newspapers' bile sack
it was 1950 in the month of February
which in the vernacular of the people around here shall be called the season of the red sun

Cavally Sassandra Bandama
little rivers with bad noses that forage through mud and rain with uncertain snouts
little rivers their bellies swollen with corpses
who said Africa huddles shivers
in the harmattan frightened and falls back asleep

History I tell of Africa as it wakes up
of men
when under the composite memory of chicotes
they piled up the knotted black fire
the anger of which pierced the thick
night of the forest like an angel

History I tell
of Africa which has for weapons
its bare fists its ancient wisdom its quite new reason
Africa you are not afraid you fight you know
better than you've ever known you look
right into the eyes of the governors of prey
of perishable bankers

Africa beautiful under the insult and heightened by your elevated conscience and so certain the day
when in the breathing of the best men the colonialistic tsetse will have disappeared

Faveur des sèves

Pachira Peau-Rouge et garde empanachée de l'argile
simarubas qui d'un hurlement blanc baïonnettez la montagne obscure
ceiba athlète qui par mystère équilibres la lutte noueuse de l'homme et du désastre
savants fûts d'orgueil d'un gisement de naufrages
ou peut-être êtes-vous là bienveillance hagarde
du rare monde noueux de mes pères
dressés au bord délirant de ma fidélité
ou lait ruiné de ma mère ma force qui s'obstine
et à mes lèvres monte

Gift of Tree Saps

*

Pachira redskin and befeathered guard of the clay
Simaroubas which with white screams bayonet the dark mountain
athletic ceiba mysteriously balancing the knotted struggle between man and disaster
learned boles of pride from a stratum of shipwrecks
or perhaps you are there haggard benevolence
of the rare gnarled world of my fathers
erect at the delirious edge of my fidelity
or my mother's ruined milk my strength which persists
and rises to my lips

Tombeau de Paul Eluard

Blason de coups sur le corps brisé des songes
      matin premier des neiges
      aujourd'hui
très informe quand tous feux éteints
s'éboulent les paysages
sur les bancs de sable les plus lointains
les sirènes des bateaux-phares sifflent depuis deux nuits
      Paul ELUARD est mort

toi qui fus le dit de l'innocence
qui rendis science aux sources
étendard de la fragile graine dans les combats
du vent plus forte que le hasard
ELUARD
ni tu ne gis
ni tu n'accèdes à terre plus pure
que de ces paupières
      que de ces simples gens
      que de ces larmes
dans lesquelles écartant les plus fines herbes du brouillard
tu te promènes très clair
ressoudant les mains
croisant des routes
récusant la parole violette des naufrageurs de l'aube
grimpés sur le soleil

Il est quand même par trop saisissant de t'entendre
remonter la grande rosace du temps
on ne t'a jamais vu si net et proche
que dans cette effervescence
du pain de la neige qui lève quand une échéance autorise
dans le fin fond fumant de l'engrais de l'orage
un abîme de silex
ELUARD
cavalier des yeux des hommes pour qui luit
véridique le point d'eau à brouter du mirage
doux sévère intègre dur
quand de proche en proche tu mettais pied à terre
pour surprendre confondus
la mort de l'impossible et le mot du printemps

Tomb of Paul Eluard

Blazon of blows on the shattered body of dreams
        first morning of snow
        a very amorphous day
when all lights out
the landscape collapses
over the most distant sandbanks
the sirens of lightships have been sounding two nights
        Paul ELUARD is dead

you who were the tale of innocence
who returned science to its sources
standard of the fragile seed
stronger than chance in the combat of the wind
ELUARD
neither can you lie in
nor have access to earth purer
than these eyelids
        than these simple people
        than these tears
in which pushing aside the finest grass of the fog
you are walking very distant
making hands join
making paths intersect
challenging the purple word of the shipwreckers of dawn
perched on the sun

It is however much too gripping to hear you
winding up the great rose window of time
you have never been seen so clearly and so close
as in this effervescence
from the bread of snow rising when the day of settlement justifies
an abyss of silex
in the smoldering utmost depth of the compost of the storm
ELUARD
cavalier of men's eyes for whom the watering place
in which to graze on mirage gleams, real,
gentle severe uncorruptible tough
when little by little you were dismounting
to confound by surprise
the death of the impossible and the word of spring

Capitaine de la bonté du pain
il a passé sous les ciels combattant
de sa voix traversée de la fleur inflexible du fléau méridien

et son pas des grands routes
panifiant l'avenir
d'un tremblement de monstres vomi par les narines insiste
que dans l'oreillette gauche de chaque prisonnier s'enflamment
d'un même cœur
tout le bois mort du monde et la forêt qui chante

Ecoute
          déchiffreur
sous tes paupières tu ne fais jamais nuit ayant
pour mieux voir jour et nuit
jeté aux feux-croisés des remous du pavé
le faux feu que chasse le sacre des pierreries

Arpenteur mesureur du plus large horizon
guetteur sous les caves d'un feu sous les évents
sur les mers grises salueur des plus subtils flocons

ô temps par ta langue opulent
à cette heure l'eau brille l'homme comme l'eau des prairies brillera
le voilà qui vers lui siffle la docilité d'une saison feuillue

Regarde basilic

le briseur de regards aujourd'hui te regarde
qu'un soir impur de banquises dans ses doigts réchauffa comme le secret de l'été

Raison
          quelle surprise de racines
          t'enlaceront ce soir
          ou le torrent
                              descendrais-tu déjà
          l'autre face du partage
une surdité épaissit en vain la veille sans miracle
de ses yeux crevés le roc sort ses oiseaux

ô meute capricorne
les mots leurs pouls battent on les sait fabuleux
allaités hors temps par une main volière les paroles tombées
ramassées les saisons pliées arrondies comme des portes
saisons
saisons pour lui cochères

ELUARD

Commander of the goodness of bread
he passed under skies fighting
with his voice run through by the inflexible flower of the midday flail

and his step turning into bread
the future of highways
with a trembling of monsters vomited through the nostrils
demands that in the left auricle of each prisoner
all the dead wood in the world and the singing forest
blaze up as a single heart

Listen
          decoder
under your eyelids you never nighten having
in order to see night and day better
thrown to the cross fire of the cobblestone's swirls
the false fire driven out by the coronation of gems

Surveyor measurer of the wider horizon
lookout under cellars for a fire under blowholes
over grey seas greeter of most subtle flakes

oh time, opulent thanks to your tongue
at that hour the water shines man like water in the fields will shine
behold him whistle to him the docility of a leafy season

Look basilisk

the breaker of looks this very moment is looking at you
an impure evening of ice floes warmed you up in its fingers like the secret of summer

Reason
          what surprise of roots
          will embrace you this evening
          or the torrent
                              is it possible you are already descending
          the other face of the divide
in vain a deafness thickens the nonmiraculous vigil
out of its punctured eyes the rock drives its birds

oh capricorn pack
the words their pulses beat they are known to be fabulous
sucked outside of time by an aviary hand the fallen words
gathered the seasons folded rounded like carriage gates
seasons
seasons for him wide-open

                    ELUARD

pour conserver ton corps
grimpeur de nul rituel
sur le jade de tes propres mots que l'on t'étende simple

conjuré par la chaleur de la vie triomphante
selon la bouche operculée de ton silence
et l'amnistie haute des coquillages

to preserve your body
never a climber of rituals
on the jade of your own words may you be laid down in simplicity

conjured by the warmth of triumphant life
in compliance with the operculated mouth of your silence
and the lofty amnesty of seashells

Mémorial de Louis Delgrès

Delgrès Louis.
Le dernier défenseur de la liberté des noirs à la Guadeloupe, né à Saint-Pierre (Martinique) en 1772, tué à la prise du Matouba (Guadeloupe) le 28 mai 1802.
Sans illusion sur l'issue certaine d'une lutte qu'il avait acceptée, non provoquée, il sut se distinguer par un courage chevaleresque. On le voyait s'asseoir dans une embrasure de canon un violon à la main, y braver les boulets du Général Richepanse, le commandant de l'odieuse expédition, et nouveau Tyrtée, jouer de son instrument pour animer ses soldats.

Larousse, 19ᵉ siècle—1870

"La Guadeloupe saccagée et détruite, ses ruines encore fumantes du sang de ses enfants, des femmes et des vieillards passés au fil de l'épée, Pélage lui-même victime de leur astuce après avoir lâchement trahi son pays et ses frères; le brave et immortel Delgrès emporté dans les air avec les débris de son fort plutôt que d'accepter les fers. Guerrier magnanime!"

Jean-Jacques Dessalines
Proclamation aux Haïtiens, 28 avril 1804

un brouillard monta
le même qui depuis toujours m'obsède
tissu de bruits de ferrements de chaînes sans clefs
d'éraflures de griffes
d'un clapotis de crachats

un brouillard se durcit et un poing surgit
qui cassa le brouillard
le poing qui toujours m'obsède

et ce fut sur une mer d'orgueil
un soleil non pareil
avançant ses crêtes majestueuses
comme un jade troupeau de taureaux
vers les plages prairies obéissantes
et ce furent des montagnes libérées
pointant vers le ciel leur artillerie fougueuse
et ce furent des vallées au fond desquelles
l'Espérance agita les panaches fragiles des cannes à sucre de janvier

Louis Delgrès je te nomme

Memorial for Louis Delgrès *

Delgrès, Louis
The last defender of black freedom in Guadeloupe, born in Saint-Pierre (Martinique) in 1772,
killed during the capture of Fort Matouba (Guadeloupe), on the 28th of May, 1802.
With no illusions as to the certain outcome of a struggle that he had accepted, but not provoked,
he proved capable of distinguishing himself by a chivalrous courage. He could be seen sitting in a
cannon port, violin in hand, defying the cannon balls of General Richepanse, the commander of the
loathsome expedition, and like a new Tyrtaeus, playing his instrument to inspire his soldiers.

The 1870 Larousse Encyclopedia

"Guadeloupe pillaged and destroyed, its ruins still smoking from its children's blood, women
and old men put to the sword, Pélage himself a victim of their trickery after having cowardly betrayed
his country and his brothers; the brave and immortal Delgrès blown into the air with the debris of his
fort rather than accepting shackles. A magnanimous warrior!"

Jean-Jacques Dessalines
Proclamation to the Haitians, 28 April 1804

a fog arose
the same one that has haunted me forever
a texture of the noise of ferraments of chains without keys
of claws scratching
of spit plopping

a fog hardened and a fist surged up
breaking the fog
this fist which has haunted me forever

and there was on a sea of pride
an unparalleled sun
advancing its magnificent crests
like a jade herd of bulls
toward the beaches obedient meadows
and there were liberated mountains
pointing their fiery artillery toward the sky
and there were valleys in the depth of which
Hope swayed the fragile feathers of January sugar cane

Louis Delgrès I say your name

et soulevant hors silence le socle de ce nom
je heurte la précise épaisseur de la nuit
d'un rucher extasié de lucioles

Delgrès il n'est point de printemps
comme la chlorophylle guettée d'une rumeur émergeante de morsures
de ce prairial têtu

trois jours tu vis contre les môles de ta saison
l'incendie effarer ses molosses
trois jours il vit Delgrès de sa main épeleuse de graines ou de racines
maintenir dans l'exacte commissure de leur rage impuissante
Gobert et Pélage les chiens colonialistes

Alentour le vent se gifle de chardons
d'en haut le ciel est bruine de sang ingénu
Fort Saint-Charles je chante par-dessus la visqueuse étreinte
le souple bond d'Ignace égrenant essoufflée
par cannaies et clérodendres la meute colonialiste

et je chante Delgrès qui aux remparts s'entête
trois jours arpentant la bleue hauteur du rêve
projeté hors du sommeil du peuple
trois jours soutenant soutenant de la grêle contexture de ses bras
notre ciel de pollen écrasé

et qu'est-ce qu'est-ce donc qu'on entend

le troupeau d'algues bleues cherche au labyrinthe des îles voussure ombreuse de l'écoute
la seule qui fût flaireuse d'une nouvelle naissance
Haïti aisance du mystère
l'étroit sentier de houle dans la brouillure des fables . . .

       Mais quand à Bainbridge Ignace fut tué
       que l'oiseau charognard du hurrah colonialiste
       eut plané son triomphe sur le frisson des îles

alors l'Histoire hissa sur son plus haut bûcher
la goutte de sang que je dis
où vint se refléter comme en profond parage
l'insolite brisure du destin

       Morne Matouba
Lieu abrupt. Nom abrupt et de ténèbres En bas
au passage Constantin là où les deux rivières

and lifting out of silence the pedestal of this name
I hit the precise thickness of night
with an ecstatic hive of fireflies

Delgrès there is no spring quite
like this stubborn prairial's
chlorophyl threatened by a murmur emerging from bites

for three days you watched the flames alarming their mastiffs
against the breakwaters of your season
for three days it watched Delgrès hold Gobert and Pélage those colonialistic bastards
back in the precise juncture of their helpless rage
with his hand speller of seeds or roots

All around the wind slaps itself with thistles
high above the sky is a drizzle of ingenuous blood
Fort Saint-Charles I sing the supple leap of Ignace
over the viscous embrace as he winnows
the breathless colonialistic pack
along the cane fields and the clerodendrons

and I sing Delgrès who on the ramparts persists
for three days surveying the blue height of the dream
catapulted out of the people's sleep
for three days supporting supporting our sky of crushed
pollen in the frail
contexture of his arms

and what oh what is that noise?

the blue seaweed herd seeks in the labyrinth of islands the shadowy arching of the listening post
the only one that might be sniffing out a new birth
Haiti ease of mystery
the narrow path of a swell in the scrambling of legends . . .

       But when at Bainbridge Ignace was killed
       when the carrion bird of the colonialistic hurrah
       had hovered triumphantly over the shiver of isles

then History hoisted on its highest pyre
the drop of blood of which I speak
where the strange rupture of destiny
came to be reflected as in a deep parage

     Matouba Morne
Steep place. Steep name and murky Below
in the Constantine passage where the two rivers

écorcent leurs hoquets de couleuvres
Richepanse est là qui guette
(Richepanse l'ours colonialiste aux violettes gencives
friand du miel solaire butiné aux campêches)
                    et ce fut aux confins l'exode du dialogue

                    O Mort, vers soi-même le bond considérable
tout sauta sur le noir Matouba

l'épais filet de l'air vers les sommets hala
d'abord les grands chevaux du bruit cabrés contre le ciel
puis mollement le grand poulpe avachi de fumée
dérisoire cracheur dans la nuit qu'il injecte
de l'insolent parfum d'une touffe de citronnelle
                    et un vent sur les îles s'abattit
que cribla la suspecte violence des criquets . . .

Delgrès point n'ont devant toi chanté les triomphales
flûtes ni rechigné ton ombre les citernes
séchées ni l'insecte vorace n'a patûré ton site

O Briseur Déconcerteur Violent
          Je chante la main qui dédaigna d'écumer
          de la longue cuillère des jours
          le bouillonnement de vesou de la grande cuve du temps
et je chante
          mais de toute la trompette du ciel plénier et sans merci
          rugi le tenace tison hâtif
          lointainement agi par la rigueur téméraire de l'aurore

Je veux entendre un chant où l'arc-en-ciel se brise
où se pose le courlis aux plages oubliées
je veux la liane qui croît sur le palmier
(c'est sur le tronc du présent notre avenir têtu)
je veux le conquistador à l'armure descellée
se couchant dans une mort de fleurs parfumées
et l'écume encense une épée qui se rouille
dans le pur vol bleuté de lents cactus hagards
je veux au haut des vagues soudoyant le tonnerre de midi
la négrillonne tête désenlisant d'écumes
la souple multitude du corps impérissable
que dans la vérité pourrie de nos étés
monte et ravive une fripure de bagasses
un sang de lumière chue aux coulures des cannaies

et voici dans cette sève et ce sang dedans cette évidence
aux quatre coins des îles Delgrès qui nous méandre

peel their hiccups of snakes
Richepanse is there on watch
(Richepanse the purple-gummed colonialistic bear
craving the solar honey gathered from the logwood)
                    and at the boundaries there was the exodus of dialogue

              O Death, toward itself the notable leap
everything blew up on the black Matouba

the thick stream of air hauled toward the summits
first the great horses of noise reared against the sky
then sluggishly the great limp octopus of smoke
a derisory spitter injecting the night with
the insolent perfume of a citronella clump
                    and a wind swept down on the islands
to be riddled by the suspect violence of the locusts . . .

Delgrès in front of you neither did the triumphant flutes
sing nor did the dried-up cisterns
balk your shadow nor did the voracious insect graze your site

O Breaker Confounder Violent
              I sing the hand which disdained to skim
              with the long spoon of days the cane juice
              boiling of the great vat of time
and I sing
              but with the full trumpet of the mercilessly roared plenary sky
              the tenacious hasty brand
              distantly activated by the bold rigor of dawn

I call for a song in which the rainbow can break
in which the curlew can land on forgotten beaches
I call for the liana that grows on the palm tree
(for it is our obstinate future on the trunk of the present)
I call for the conquistador in unsealed armor
to lie down in a death of fragrant flowers
for the foam to cense a sword that rusts
in the pure bluish flight of slow haggard cacti—
at the tip of waves bribing the noon thunder I call for
the pickaninny head to free from foam
the supple multitude of the imperishable body—
in the rotted truth of our summers
for a shred of crushed sugar cane to raise and revive   *
a blood of light washed away with the pollen of the cane fields

and here in this sap and this blood inside this evidence
at the four corners of the islands, meandering us, Delgrès,

ayant Icare dévolu creusé au moelleux de la cendre
la plaie phosphorescente d'une insondable source
                              Or
constructeur du cœur dans la chair molle des mangliers
aujourd'hui Delgrès
                    au creux de chemins qui se croisent
ramassant ce nom hors maremmes
                    je te clame et à tout vent futur
toi buccinateur d'une lointaine vendange.

having—an Icarus by investiture—hollowed out of the ash's
pith the phosphorous wound of an unfathomable source
                      So
constructor of the heart in the soft flesh of mangrove trees
today Delgrès
             in the hollow of intersecting paths
taking up this name outside the maremmas
             I proclaim you and in any future wind
you the buccinator of a distant vintage.

A *la mémoire d'un syndicaliste noir*

Qu'une tempête ne décline que le roc ne titube
pour celui poitrail qui fut sûr
dont le clairon de feu dans l'ombre et le hasard
rustique ne décrut

O peuple guetté du plus haut mirador
et défiant du bâton des aveugles
            le nom natal de l'injustice énorme

Je t'ai inscrit une fois
au centre du paysage sur un fond de cannaie
debout au milieu de la glèbe de nos yeux
agrandis et d'une sorte semblable
à la face d'or noire et haïtienne
d'un dieu

Vois dans la forêt sans sommeil
les amis ont poussé patients
tu plissais les paupières tu les plisses aujourd'hui
tu ne parlais guère tu ne parles guère moins maintenant

tu te contentais de sourire de même tu souris encore très doux
d'un sourire né fort des confuses javelles de la terre et de la mer parentes

de quels salaires viens-tu encore de discuter
sur ton sein noir et calme
viens-tu encore de réchauffer suprêmes
comme un nœud sacré de couleuvres engourdies
les colères d'hivernage et le coutelas des grèves

et dans quelle fraîcheur osas-tu retremper
ton sourire de rosée
comment dans la grande débâcle as-tu mis à l'abri rusé
ta grande force secrète
ton dur front paysan
les eaux calmes prisonnières du mi-rire de tes yeux
          un doute est mien qui tremble
          d'entendre dans la jungle des fleurs
          un rêve se frayer

Maître marronneur des clartés
aurons-nous la force de hisser ce printemps

In Memory of a Black Union Leader *

Let no tempest subside no rock stagger
for this chest which was firm
whose bugle of fire neither in the dark
nor in coarse fate faded

O people observed from the highest mirador
who were defying with the canes of blindmen
                 the native noun of enormous injustice

I once placed you
in the center of a landscape against a background of cane fields
standing in the middle of the sod of our enlarged
eyes and somehow resembling
the black gold Haitian face
of a god

Look, in the sleepless forest
friends have sprung up, patient,
you used to squint you're still squinting
you hardly ever spoke you hardly speak any less now

you were content to smile you're still smiling the same way very tenderly
a smile born strong from the intermingled sheaves of the kindred earth and sea

what wages have you just again discussed
on your black and serene breast
have you again just revived supreme
as a sacred knot of benumbed grass snakes
the angers of the rainy season and the cutlass of strikes

and into what coolness did you again dare to dip
your dew-like smile
how in the midst of the great debacle did you shrewdly shelter
your great secret strength
your hard peasant face
the calm waters imprisoned by the half-laughter of your eyes
                 in me a doubt trembles
                 from hearing a dream find its way
                 in the jungle of flowers

Mastermind of runaway clarities
will we have the strength this spring to hoist

jusqu'au sein où attendent dormants les climats
féconds nos membres purs

nos ciels impatients
                alizés ou autans
                réveillez-vous nos races mortes

un instant charmeur d'astres
un vent mauvais souffle des bagasses pourries
ton peuple a faim a soif trébuche ton peuple
est un cabrouet qui s'arrache de la boue toujours
plein de jurons et cinglé au fil sourd de la nuit noire des cannes
d'un sentiment de sabres

                toi le refus de la sombre défaite
                chef dur soutien des cases
                dieu des dégras arbre à pain des coursières
en fougère imputrescible je t'ai taillé
à révérer sylvestre
quand mai dore en chabin la grosse tête crépue
de ses manguiers les plus rares

la songe s'est levé tu marches toi l'ardeur d'un nom
sous la tenace science d'un pays de silence
tous te flairent aucun chien n'ose te barrer la route
tes murs se sont effondrés les chemins sont boueux
de grands cœurs se suicident rouges aux balisiers
tu marches pélerin tu marches et tu souris
aux merles du dernier rayon qui picorent les tiques sur le dos des zébus

Montreur
tout le ciel depuis longtemps s'est éteint
la mer au bas dans l'anse incline et ramène à des oiseaux perdus
le balancement d'un toit et la lumière
la lumière tu la redistribues toute
aux écueils orphelins aux feuilles en la filtrant
aux pierres du volcan mal refroidies qui renaissent précieuses
aux yeux des camarades vernissée vaguement sanguinolente

our pure limbs up to the womb
where dormant the fecund climates are waiting

our impatient skies
                    tradewinds or southwinds
                    are you awakening our dead races

briefly a seducer of stars
a foul wind blows from the rotten bagasse
your people are hungry are thirsty stumble your people
are a hand truck which constantly tears itself from the mud
covered with curses and lashed along the mute edge of the black night of sugar cane
by a saber sensation

                    you the rejection of somber defeat
                    tough leader protector of huts
                    god of the dubbins breadfruit tree of the errand-girls
in unrotable fern I have carved you
to be worshiped sylvan
when May gilds chabin-like the large kinky heads
of its rarest mango trees

the dream arose you are walking you the fervor of a name
under the tenacious science of a land of silence
every dog sniffs at you not one dares stand in your way
your walls have collapsed the paths are muddy
in the balisiers great red hearts are committing suicide
you are walking pilgrim you walk and you smile
at the blackbirds of the last ray which peck at the ticks on the zebus' backs

Ringmaster
the whole sky has long been extinguished
the sea down there in the cove slopes the swaying of a roof
restoring it to lost birds and the light
the light you redistribute all of it
to the orphan reefs to the leaves filtering it for them
to the barely cooled volcano stones reborn as gems
to the eyes of comrades, varnished light vaguely tinged with blood

. . . sur l'état de l'Union

J'imagine au Congrès ce message sur l'état de l'Union:
situation tragique,
>
>
> plus ne nous reste au sous-sol que 75 ans de fer
> 50 ans de cobalt
> mais pour 55 ans de soufre et 20 ans de bauxite
> au cœur quoi?
>> Rien, zéro,
>>> mine sans minerai,
>>> caverne où rien ne rôde,
>>> de sang plus une goutte.

EMMET TILL
tes yeux étaient une conque marine où pétillait la bataille de vin
de ton sang de quinze ans.
Eux jeunes n'avaient jamais eu d'âge,
ou plutôt sur eux pesaient,
plus que tous les gratte-ciel, cinq siècles de tortionnaires
de brûleurs de sorcières,
cinq siècles de mauvais gin de gros cigares
de grasses bedaines remplies de tranches de bibles rancies
cinq siècles bouche amère de péchés de rombières,
ils avaient cinq siècles EMMET TILL,
cinq siècles est l'âge sans âge du pieu de Caïn.

> EMMET TILL je dis:
>> au cœur zéro,
>> de sang pas une goutte,
et pour le tien qu'il me cache le Soleil, qu'à mon pain il se mêle:
—"Garçon de Chicago
c'est-il toujours vrai que tu vaux
autant qu'un blanc?"
Printemps, c'est à toi qu'il croyait. Même au bord de la nuit, au bord du MISSISSIPI roulant entre les
    hautes berges de la haine raciale ses barreaux, ses barrières, ses tombales avalanches.
Au printemps affluant ses rumeurs dans le hublot des yeux.
Au printemps huchant le panique aumaille dans les savanes du sang.
Au printemps dégantant ses fines mains parmi un éclat de coques et de siliques,
délieur des caillots à peur, dissolveur des caillots de la haine gonflée d'âge et au fil des fleuves du sang
    charriant la hasardeuse rubrique des bêtes de l'affût.
> Mais Eux
eux étaient invulnérables, tardifs qu'ils étaient,
et montés, massifs, sur de louches boucs immémoriaux
>> —"GARÇON DE CHICAGO" . . .

. . . On the State of the Union

I imagine this message in Congress on the State of the Union:
situation tragic,
>   left underground only 75 years of iron
>   50 years of cobalt
>   but 55 years worth of sulphur and 20 of bauxite
>   in the heart what?
>   Nothing, zero,
>   mine without ore,
>   cavern in which nothing prowls,
>   of blood not a drop left.

EMMET TILL
your eyes were a sea conch in which the heady battle
of your fifteen-year-old blood sparkled.
Even young they never had any age,
or rather more than all the skyscrapers
five centuries of torturers
of witch burners weighed on them,
five centuries of cheap gin of big cigars
of fat bellies filled with slices of rancid bibles
a five century mouth bitter with dowager sins,
they were five centuries old EMMET TILL,
five centuries is the ageless age of Cain's stake.

>   EMMET TILL I say:
>   in the heart zero,
>   of blood not a drop,
and as for yours may it hide my Sun, may it mix with my bread:
—"Hey Chicago Boy
is it still true that you're worth
as much as a white man?"
Spring, he believed in you. Even at the edge of night, at the edge of the MISSISSIPPI rolling its
          bars, its barriers, its tomb-like avalanches between the high banks of racial hatred.
In spring rushing its murmurs into the portholes of eyes.
In spring hound-calling the bovine panic in the savannas of the blood.
In spring slipping the gloves from its fine hands in a burst of shells and siliquae,
loosener of fear clots, dissolver of the clots of hatred swollen with age and in the flow of blood-
          streams carrying the hazardous rubric of stalked beasts.
>   But They
they were invulnerable, sluggish as they were,
and mounted, massively, on bizarre immemorial billygoats
>   —"CHICAGO BOY" . . .

Autant en emporte le béguètement du vent racial
Lui écoute dans le bleu buisson des veines
chanter égal l'oiseau-sang,
devine par-dessus les berges à sommeil
monter dans le bleu champ surprenant
Soleil, ton pas furtif, poisson véhément.

Alors la nuit se souvint de son bras
mou vol de vampire qui tout soudain plana
et le gros colt de BIG MILLAM
sur le noir mur vivant
en lettres de rouille écrivit la sentence et l'état de l'Union:

20 ans de zinc
15 ans de cuivre
15 ans de pétrole

       et l'an 180 de ces états
       mais au cœur indolore horlogerie
       quoi, rien, zéro,
       de sang pas une goutte
       au carne blanc cœur désinfecté?

All gone with the bleating of the racial wind
He listens in the blue bush of veins
to the steady singing of the blood bird,
he anticipates above the banks of sleep
Sun, the rise of your furtive step,
a vehement fish, in the astonishing blue field.

Then night remembered its arm
a vampire's flabby flight suddenly hovering
and BIG MILLAM'S Colt 45
wrote the verdict and the State of the Union in rust letters
on the living black wall:

20 years of zinc
15 years of copper
15 years of oil

        and the 180th year of these states
        but in the heart unfeeling clockwork
        what, nothing, zero,
        of blood not a drop
        in the white heart's tough antiseptic meat?

                                                   *

Afrique

ta tiare solaire à coups de crosse enfoncée jusqu'au cou
ils l'ont transformée en carcan; ta voyance
ils l'ont crevée aux yeux; prostitué ta face pudique;
emmuselé, hurlant qu'elle était gutturale,
ta voix, qui parlait dans le silence des ombres.

Afrique,
ne tremble pas le combat est nouveau,
le flot vif de ton sang élabore sans faillir
constante une saison; la nuit c'est aujourd'hui au fond des mares
le formidable dos instable d'un astre mal endormi,
et poursuis et combats—n'eusses-tu pour conjurer l'espace
que l'espace de ton nom irrité de sécheresse.

Boutis boutis
         terre trouée de boutis
sacquée
         tatouée
                  grand corps
massive défigure où le dur groin fouilla
Afrique les jours oubliés qui cheminent toujours
aux coquilles recourbées dans les doutes du regard
jailliront à la face publique parmi d'heureuses ruines, dans la plaine
l'arbre blanc aux secourables mains ce sera chaque arbre
une tempête d'arbres parmi l'écume non pareille et les sables,

les choses cachées remonteront la pente des musiques endormies,
une plaie d'aujourd'hui est caverne d'orient,
un frissonnement qui sort des noirs feux oubliés, c'est,
des flétrissures jailli de la cendre des paroles amères
de cicatrices, tout lisse et nouveau, un visage
de jadis, caché oiseau craché, oiseau frère du soleil.

Africa

your solar tiara knocked down to your neck by rifle butts
they have turned it into an iron-collar; your clairvoyance
they've put out its eyes; prostituted your chaste face;
screaming that it was guttural, they muzzled
your voice, which was speaking in the silence of shadows.

Africa,
do not tremble this is a new fight,
the living wave of your blood secretes unfailingly
constant a season; night today is, at the bottom of ponds,
the frightening and unstable back of an incompletely asleep star,
and persevere, and fight—even if to conjure up space you had only
the space of your name irritated by dryness.

Snout holes snout holes
      land ripped with snout holes
sacked
      tattooed
          great body
massive disfigure where the tough snout dug
Africa the forgotten days which always walk
with curved shells in the doubt of eyes
will spring to the public face amidst happy ruins, on the plain
the white tree with willing hands will be each tree
a tempest of trees in the unparalleled foam and sand,

hidden things will again climb the slope of dormant musics,
today's wound is an oriental cavern,
a shuddering issuing from black forgotten fires, it is,
sprung from blemishes from the ash of bitter words
from scars, all smooth and new, a face
of long ago, bird concealed spewed, bird brother of the sun.

Hors des jours étrangers

mon peuple

quand
hors des jours étrangers
germeras-tu une tête bien tienne sur tes épaules renouées
et ta parole

le congé dépêché aux traîtres
aux maîtres
le pain restitué la terre lavée
la terre donnée

quand
quand donc cesseras-tu d'être le jouet sombre
au carnaval des autres
ou dans les champs d'autrui
l'épouvantail désuet

demain
à quand demain mon peuple
la déroute mercenaire
finie la fête

mais la rougeur de l'est au cœur de balisier

peuple de mauvais sommeil rompu
peuple d'abîmes remontés
peuple de cauchemars domptés
peuple nocturne amant des fureurs du tonnerre
demain plus haut plus doux plus large

et la houle torrentielle des terres
à la charrue salubre de l'orage

Out of Alien Days

my people

when
out of alien days
on reknotted shoulders will you sprout a head really your own
and your word

the notice dispatched to the traitors
to the masters
the restituted bread the washed earth
the given earth

when
when will you cease to be the dark toy
in the carnival of others
or in another's field
the obsolete scarecrow?

tomorrow
when is tomorrow my people
the mercenary rout
once the feast is over

instead the redness of the east in the balisier's heart

people of interrupted foul sleep
people of reclimbed abysses
people of tamed nightmares
nocturnal people lovers of the fury of thunder
a higher sweeter broader tomorrow

and the torrential swell of lands
under the salubrious plow of the storm

Pour saluer le Tiers Monde / *à Léopold Sedar Senghor*

                    Ah!
mon demi-sommeil d'île si trouble
sur la mer!

Et voici de tous les points du péril
l'histoire qui me fait le signe que j'attendais,
je vois pousser des nations.
Vertes et rouges, je vous salue,
bannières, gorges du vent ancien
Mali, Guinée, Ghana

et je vous vois, hommes,
point maladroits sous ce soleil nouveau!

Ecoutez!
      de mon île lointaine
      de mon île veilleuse
je vous dis Hoo!
      Et vos voix me répondent

      et ce qu'elles disent signifie:
"Il y fait clair". Et c'est vrai:
même à travers orage et nuit
pour nous il y fait clair.
D'ici je vois Kiwu vers Tanganika descendre
par l'escalier d'argent de la Ruzizi
(c'est la grande fille à chaque pas
baignant la nuit d'un frisson de cheveux)

d'ici, je vois noués,
Bénoué, Logone et Tchad;
liés, Sénégal et Niger.
Rugir, silence et nuit rugir, d'ici j'entends
rugir le Nyaragongo.

De la haine oui, ou le ban ou la barre
et l'arroi qui grunnit, mais
d'un roide vent, nous contus, j'ai vu
décroître la gueule négrière!

A Salute to the Third World / for Léopold Sedar Senghor

Ah!
my half-sleep of an island so indistinct
on the sea!

And here from all the corners of peril
history makes the sign that I was waiting for,
I see nations grow.
Banners, green and red,
I salute you, throats of ancient wind,
Mali, Guinea, Ghana

and I see you, men,
not awkward under this new sun!

Listen!
from my remote island
from my watchful island
I cry Hoo to you!
And your voices answer me

and what they are saying means:
"There is plenty of light here." And that is true:
even during the storm and the night
for us there is plenty of light here.
From here I see the Kivu descend Ruzizi's
silver stairway toward Tanganyika
(it is the tall girl bathing the night
at each step with a shiver of hair)

from here, I see Benue,
Logone and Chad knotted;
Senegal and Niger, bound.
A roar, a roar of silence and night, from here I listen to
the Nyiragongo roar.

Hatred, yes, either ban or bar
and the grunting array, yet
in a stiff wind, once we were bruised, I saw
the slave master's mug recede!

Je vois l'Afrique multiple et une
verticale dans la tumultueuse péripétie
avec ses bourrelets, ses nodules,
un peu à part, mais à portée
du siècle, comme un cœur de réserve.

Et je redis: Hoo mère!
          et je lève ma force
             inclinant ma face.
                  Oh ma terre!
que je me l'émiette doucement entre pouce et index
que je m'en frotte la poitrine, le bras,
le bras gauche,
que je m'en caresse le bras droit.

Hoo ma terre est bonne,
    ta voix aussi est bonne
        avec cet apaisement que donne
        un lever de soleil!
Terre, forge et silo. Terre enseignant nos routes,
c'est ici, qu'une vérité s'avise,
taisant l'oripeau de vieil éclat cruel.

Vois:
    l'Afrique n'est plus
    au diamant du malheur
        un noir cœur qui se strie;

notre Afrique est une main hors du ceste,
c'est une main droite, la paume devant
et les doigts bien serrés;

c'est une main tuméfiée,
une-blessée-main-ouverte,
tendue,
    brunes, jaunes, blanches,
à toutes mains, à toutes les mains blessées
du monde.

. I see Africa multiple and one
vertical in the tumultuous upheaval
with her flab, her nodules,
slightly to the side, but within reach
of the century, like a backup heart.

And I cry again: Hoo mother!
       and I raise my strength
       lowering my head.
           O my earth!
let me crumble it tenderly between thumb and forefinger
let me rub my chest, my arm,
my left arm with it,
let me caress my right arm with it.

Hoo my earth is good,
    your voice is good too
    with that soothing which comes
    from a rising sun!
Earth, forge and silo. Earth showing us our paths,
it is here, that a truth is perceived,
quieting the flashy rags of the old cruel parade.

Look:
    Africa is no longer
    a black heart scratched
       at by the diamond of misfortune;

our Africa is a hand free of the cestus,
it is a right hand, palm forward,
the fingers held tight;

it is a swollen hand,
a-wounded-open-hand,
extended to
    all hands, brown, yellow,
white, to all the wounded hands
in the world.

Indivisible

contre tout ce qui pèse valeur de lèpre
contre le sortilège mauvais
notre arme ne peut être
que le pieu flambé de midi
à crever
pour toute aire
l'épaisse prunelle du crime

             contrebande
vous tenez mal un dieu et qui toujours s'échappe

ta fumée, ma famine, ta fête
             Liberté

Blanc à remplir sur la carte voyageuse du pollen

N'y eût-il dans le désert
qu'une seule goutte d'eau qui rêve tout bas,
dans le désert n'y eût-il
qu'une graine volante qui rêve tout haut
c'est assez
rouillure des armes, fissure des pierres, vrac des ténèbres
désert, désert, j'endure ton défi
blanc à remplir sur la carte voyageuse du pollen.

Indivisible

against all that which weighs leper currency
against evil sortilege
our weapon can only be
the charred stake of noon
bursting
in every region
the dense eyeball of crime

contraband
you barely restrain a god—one forever escaping—

your smoke, my famine, your feast
                    Liberty

A Blank to Fill on the Travel Pass of the Pollen

Were there in the desert
only one drop of water dreaming very quietly,
in the desert were there
only one flying seed dreaming very loudly,
that is enough
rust of weapons, cracks in stones, refuse of gloom
desert, desert, I endure your challenge
a blank to fill on the travel pass of the pollen.

Petite chanson pour traverser une grande rivière / d'après le Yoruba

Je me vis franchissant un fleuve.
A te franchir fleuve, de la rivière voici
le Roi! Oh! du soleil voici le Roi!
Là, dans ce pays-là, de grands palmiers je vis
qui, effondrés de fruits, jusqu'à l'humus courbaient
leur fastueuse force, sous le fardeau, tuée.

En vérité . . .

la pierre qui s'émiette en mottes
le désert qui se blute en blé
le jour qui s'épelle en oiseaux
le forçat l'esclave le paria
la stature épanouie harmonique
la nuit fécondée la fin de la faim

du crachat sur la face
et cette histoire parmi laquelle je marche mieux que durant le jour

la nuit en feu la nuit déliée le songe forcé
le feu qui de l'eau nous redonne
l'horizon outrageux bien sûr
un enfant entrouvrira la porte . . .

A Little Song to Cross a Big Stream / after the Yoruba

I saw myself crossing a river.
About to cross you river, here is the King
of the stream! Oh! here is the King of the sun!
There, in that land, I saw lofty palm trees
which, collapsing with fruit, to the very humus were bending
their luxurious strength, under the burden, killed.

In Truth . . .

the stone crumbling itself into clods
the desert sifting itself into wheat
the day spelling itself with birds
the convict the slave the pariah
stature harmoniously blossomed
fecundated night the end of hunger

of spit in the face
and this history I walk around in better than during the day

the night on fire the night untied the dream coerced
the fire which restores to us the horizon
of water outrageous to be sure
a child will half-open the door . . .

NORIA

Wifredo Lam, "Belial," 1948, oil on canvas, 84 × 77"

Lettre de Bahia-de-tous-les-saints

Bahii-a

Comme un scélérat coup de cachaça dans la gorge d'Exu et le mot délira en moi en un hennissement d'îles vertes femmes nageuses éparpillées parmi la jactance des fruits et un écroulement de perroquets

Bahii-a

la courbe d'un collier dévalé vers la poitrine dévoilée de la mer bien lovant au creux sa touffure de ressac

Bahii-a

dérive de continents, un en-aller de terre, un bâillement géologique à l'heure fastueuse de l'échouage, le tout assoupi à l'ancre et mal dompté au lieu

Bahii-a

de nostalgie, de gingembre et de poivre, Bahia des filles de saints, des femmes de Dieu, à peau de crevettes rose, à peau douce aussi de la sauce *vatapa*

Ah! Bahii-a!

Bahia d'ailes! de connivences! de *pouvoirs*! *Campo grande* pour les grandes manœuvres de l'insolite! De toutes les communications avec l'inconnu, Centrale et Douane!

De fait, d'Ogu ou de Saint Georges, on ne sait, des nuages solennels croisèrent l'épée, échangèrent des perles, des claies, des cauris roses, des cauris mauves, des araignées damasquinées, des carabes voraces, des lézards rares

et le mot se termina dans le délabrement interlope des plus hautes seigneuries du ciel

Ah! Bahia!

Ce fut alors un engourdissement d'encens carrelé d'or dans une lourde sieste où se fondaient ensemble des églises *azulejos*, des clapotis d'outre-mornes de tambours, des fusées molles de dieux comblés, d'où l'aube débusqua, très tendre, de graves filles couleur jacaranda, peignant lentement leurs cheveux de varech.

Letter from Bahia-of-All-the-Saints

Bahii-a

A criminal shot of cachaça into the throat of Exu and suddenly the word raved within me like a *
neighing of green islands women swimmers scattered amidst the boasting of fruit and a cave-in of
parrots

Bahii-a

the curve of a necklace rushed down toward the unveiled breast of the sea tightly coiling in the
trough its tufts of undertow

Bahii-a

a drifting of continents, a taking off of land, a geological yawning at the luxurious hour of the
beaching, the whole thing dozing at anchor and poorly tamed to its site

Bahii-a

of nostalgia, of ginger and pepper, Bahia of the saints' daughters, of God's wives, their skin like pink
shrimp, their skin also soft from *vatapa* sauce   *

Ah! Bahii-a!

Bahia of wings! of conspiracies! of *powers*! *Campo grande* for the army maneuvers of the unusual!
Of all communications with the unknown, Power generator and Customhouse!

In fact, from Ogu or Saint Georges, it is impossible to know, solemn clouds cross swords, exchange
pearls, wattles, pink cowries, mauve cowries, damasked spiders, voracious carabids, rare lizards

and the word ended in the shady decay of the highest seigniories of the sky

Ah! Bahia!

There was then a numbness of gold tiled incense in a heavy siesta blending together the *azulejo*   *
churches, drums splashing across the mornes, limp rockets from replete gods, from where the
dawn, very tenderly, flushed out solemn jacaranda-colored girls, slowly combing their kelp hair.

Ethiopie . . . / à Alioune Diop

et je vis ce conte byzantin
publié par les pluies
sur les fortes épaules de la montagne
dans l'alphabet fantasque de l'eucalyptus

et de vrai
au nom du baobab et du palmier
de mon cœur Sénégal et de mon cœur d'îles
je saluai avec pureté l'eucalyptus
du fin fond scrupuleux de mon cœur végétal

et il y eut
les hommes
c'étaient dieux chlamyde au vent
et bâton en avant
descendant d'un Olympe de Nil bleu
et les femmes étaient reines
reines d'ébène polie
prêtées par le miel de la nuit
et dévorées d'ivoire
Reine de Saba Reine de Saba
qu'en dit l'oiseau Simmorg-Anka?

Ethiopie
belle comme ton écriture étrange
qui avance dans le mystère telle un arbre
d'épiphytes chargé
parmi l'ardoise du ciel

            ni prince ni bouche du prince
                  je me présente
moi quinze dépouilles viriles
trois éléphants
dix lions

Ce sont plus terribles que lions roux
du Harrar vie
domptée angoisses et goules de nuit
rêves vingt cicatrices
et j'ai vu les trahisons obliques dans le brouillard
me charger en un troupeau de buffles

Ethiopia . . . | for Alioune Diop *

and I saw this byzantine tale
printed by the rains
on the strong shoulders of the mountain
in the bizarre alphabet of the eucalyptus

and truly
in the name of the baobab and the palm tree
with my Senegal heart and my island heart
in purity I hailed the eucalyptus
from the utmost scrupulous depths of my vegetal heart

and there were
men
they were gods chlamys in the wind
with their staffs forward
descending from an Olympus of blue Nile
and the women were queens
polished ebony queens
lent by the honey of the night
and buried under ivory
Queen of Sheba Queen of Sheba
What says the Simmorg-Anka bird?

Ethiopia
beautiful like your strange writing
advancing into the mystery like a tree
loaded with epiphytes
amidst the slate of the sky

    neither a prince nor his spokesman
        I present myself
I fifteen virile corpses
three elephants
ten lions

More terrible than the russet lions
from Harrar are life
tamed anxieties and nocturnal ghouls
dreams twenty scars
and in the fog I saw oblique treasons
charging me like a herd of buffaloes

                    Ehô Ethiopie-Mère
ni prince ni bouche du prince
blessure après balafre
mais cette folle face de noyé qui se raccroche à l'arche
Reine de Saba Reine de Saba
serai-je l'oiseau Simmorg-Anka?

Et il y eut les rues les souks les mules
les buveurs de *tedj* les mangeurs d'*ingera*
ceux d'Entoto ceux d'Abba Dina
plus loin
à l'océane racine du poumon de mon cri
des îles s'effritant
rochers kystes bavants
saquant rivées au pieu
les îles qui à ma parole mécroient
Reine du Matin Reine de Saba
Où vit l'oiseau Simmorg-Anka?

Et je fus Ethiopie ton pêle-mêle
tendre d'encens brûlé et de colère
A Saint-Guiorguis
de grands spasmes bruns d'âpres baisers râclaient
les seuils obtus de Dieu et ses ferrures de cuivre
A Baata Menelik sommeillait
à sa porte croisâmes noir et bleu
un Galla mon destin masqué
farouche et doux comme sa sagaie
Reine du Midi Reine de Saba
ci-gît l'oiseau Simmorg-Anka

Or du Kraal assiégé de sa gorge lointaine
Miriam Makeba chanta au lion
parcourue d'un sillage ondulant aux épaules
un lac de maïs fauve flairé par âcre vent
                    (Reine ô Belkis Makeda!)
et subitement l'Afrique parla
ce fut pour nous an neuf
l'Afrique selon l'us
de chacun nous balaya le seuil d'une torche enflammée
reliant la nuit traquée
et toutes les nuits mutilées
de l'amère marée des nègres inconsolés
au plein ciel violet piqué de feux

Elle dit: *"l'homme au fusil encore chaud*
est mort hier. Hier le convoiteux sans frein

Ehô Mother-Ethiopia
neither a prince nor his spokesman
gash upon slash
but this crazy drowned face hanging onto the ark
Queen of Sheba Queen of Sheba
am I to be the Simmorg-Anka bird?

And there were the streets the bazaars the mules
the *tedj* drinkers the *ingera* eaters
those from Entoto those from Abba Dina
further on
at the ocean root of the lung of my scream
islands crumbling away
rocks drooling cysts
sacking tying to the stake
the islands which misbelieve my word
Queen of the Morning Queen of Sheba
Where does the Simmorg-Anka bird live?

And I was your jumble Ethiopia
tender with burned incense and anger
At Saint-Guiorguis
huge brown spasms harsh kisses swept
the obtuse thresholds of God and his brass fittings
At Baata Menelik was dozing
at his door we passed a black and blue
Galla my destiny masked
fierce and sweet like his assagai
Queen of the Noon Queen of Sheba
here lies the Simmorg-Anka bird

Meanwhile from the beseiged Kraal of its distant throat
Miriam Makeba rippled by a wake
sang of the lion, a lake
of tawny maize sniffed at by a raw wind
undulating on her shoulders
                    (Queen indeed O Belkis Makeda!)
and suddenly Africa spoke
it was for us New Year
Africa according to the custom
of each one swept the threshold for us with a flaming torch
connecting the tracked night
and all the mutilated nights
of the bitter tide of inconsolable blacks
with the fire studded full purple sky

She said *"the man with a still warm rifle*
died yesterday. Yesterday the unrestrained covetous

piétineur piétinant saccageur saccageant
hier est bien mort hier.''
. . . l'Afrique parlait en une langue sacrée
où le même mot signifiait
couteau des pluies sang de taureau
nerf et tendon du dieu caché

lichen profond lâcher d'oiseaux

trampler trampling pilferer pilfering
yesterday he really died yesterday."
. . . Africa was speaking a sacred language
in which the same word signified
knife of the rains blood of the bull
nerve and tendon of the hidden god

profound lichen release of birds

Le verbe marronner / *à René Depestre, poète haïtien*

C'est une nuit de Seine
et moi je me souviens comme ivre
du chant dément de Boukmann accouchant ton pays
aux forceps de l'orage

DEPESTRE

    Vaillant cavalier du tam-tam
    est-il vrai que tu doutes de la forêt natale
    de nos voix rauques de nos cœurs qui nous remontent amers
    de nos yeux de rhum rouges de nos nuits incendiées
    se peut-il
    que les pluies de l'exil
    aient détendu la peau de tambour de ta voix

marronnerons-nous Depestre marronnerons-nous?
Depestre j'accuse les mauvaises manières de notre sang
est-ce notre faute
si la bourrasque se lève
et nous désapprend tout soudain de compter sur nos doigts
de faire trois tours de saluer

Ou bien encore cela revient au même
le sang est une chose qui va vient et revient
et le nôtre je suppose nous revient après s'être attardé
à quelque macumba. Qu'y faire? En vérité
le sang est un vaudoun puissant

C'est vrai ils arrondissent cette saison des sonnets
pour nous à le faire cela me rappellerait par trop
le jus sucré que bavent là-bas les distilleries des mornes
quand les lents bœufs maigres font leur rond au zonzon
des moustiques

Ouiche! Depestre le poème n'est pas un moulin à
passer de la canne à sucre ça non
et si les rimes sont mouches sur les mares
                        sans rimes
           toute une saison
loin des mares
                    moi te faisant raison
rions buvons et marronnons

The Verb "Marronner" / for René Depestre, Haitian poet

It is a Seine night
and as if in drunkenness I recall
the insane song of Boukman delivering your country
with the forceps of the storm

DEPESTRE

    Courageous tom-tom rider
    is it true that you mistrust the native forest
    and our hoarse voices our hearts that come back up on us bitter
    our rum red eyes our burned out nights
    is it possible
    that the rains of exile
    have slackened the drum skin of your voice?

shall we escape like slaves Depestre like slaves?
Depestre I indict the bad manners of our blood
is it our fault
if the squall hits
suddenly unteaching us to count on our fingers
to circle three times and bow

Or else it boils down to the same thing
blood is a thing that comes and goes
and ours I suppose comes back on us after having spent time
in some macumba. What can be done about it? Blood
is truly a powerful vodun

Is it true this season that they're polishing up sonnets
for us to do so would remind me too much of the sugary
juice drooled over there by the distilleries on the mornes
when slow skinny oxen make their rounds to the whine
of mosquitoes

Bah! Depestre the poem is not a mill for
grinding sugar cane absolutely not
and if the rhymes are flies on ponds
                      without rhymes
        for a whole season
away from ponds
                  under my persuasion
let's laugh drink and escape like slaves

Gentil cœur

    avec au cou le collier de commandement de la lune
    avec autour du bras le rouleau bien lové du lasso du soleil
    la poitrine tatouée comme par une des blessures de la nuit
    aussi je me souviens

au fait est-ce que Dessalines mignonnait à Vertières

Camarade Depestre
C'est un problème assurément très grave
des rapports de la poésie et de la Révolution
le fond conditionne la forme

et si l'on s'avisait aussi du détour dialectique
par quoi la forme prenant sa revanche
comme un figuier maudit étouffe le poème
mais non
    je ne me charge pas du rapport
j'aime mieux regarder le printemps. Justement
c'est la révolution
        et les formes qui s'attardent
à nos oreilles bourdonnant
çe sont mangeant le neuf qui lève
mangeant les pousses
    de gras hannetons hannetonnant le printemps.
                Depestre
de la Seine je t'envoie au Brésil mon salut
à toi à Bahia à tous les saints à tous les diables
Cabritos cantagallo Botafogo
bate
batuque
à ceux des favellas
          Despestre
              bombaïa bombaïa
crois-m'en comme jadis bats-nous le bon tam-tam
éclaboussant leur nuit rance
d'un rut sommaire d'astres moudangs.

Gentle heart

> the necklace of the Order of the Moon around my neck
> the tightly wrapped coil of the sun's lasso around my arm
> my chest tattooed as if by one of night's wounds
> I too remember

as a matter of fact *did* Dessalines prance about at Vertières

Comrade Depestre
It is undoubtedly a very serious problem
the relation between poetry and Revolution
the content determines the form

and what about keeping in mind as well the dialectical
backlash by which the form taking its revenge
chokes the poems like an accursed fig tree
but no
     a report on this is none of my business
I'd rather look at the spring. Precisely,
it is the revolution
                 and the forms which linger
humming in our ears
are, eating the new which sprouts
eating the shoots,
     fat cockchafers cockchafing the spring.
                           Depestre
from the Seine I send you my greetings in Brazil
to you to Bahia to all saints to all devils
Cabritos cantagallo Botafogo
bate
batuque
to all those in the favellas
                  Depestre
                       bombaïa bombaïa
believe me as in the old days beat the good tom-tom for us
splashing their rancid night
with a succinct rutting of moudang stars.

Wifredo Lam . . .

Rien de moins à signaler
que le royaume est investi
le ciel précaire
la relève imminente et légitime

Rien sinon que le cycle des genèses vient sans préavis
d'éxploser et la vie qui se donne sans filiation
le barbare mot de passe

Rien sinon le frai frissonnant des formes qui se libèrent
des liaisons faciles
et hors de combinaisons trop hâtives s'évadent

mains implorantes
mains d'orantes
le visage de l'horrible ne peut-être mieux indiqué
que par ce mains offusquantes

liseur d'entrailles et de destins violets
récitant de macumbas
mon frère
que cherches-tu à travers ces forêts
de cornes de sabots d'ailes de chevaux

toutes choses aiguës
toutes choses bisaiguës

mais avatars d'un dieu animé au saccage
envol de monstres
j'ai reconnu aux combats de justice
le rare rire de tes armes enchantées
le vertige de ton sang
                    et la loi de ton nom.

Wifredo Lam . . .

To report: nothing less than
the kingdom under seige
the sky precarious
relief imminent and legitimate

Nothing except that the cycle of geneses has just without warning
exploded as well as the life which gives itself
without filiation the barbarous password

Nothing except the shivering spawn of forms liberating themselves
from facile bondages
and escaping from too premature combinings

imploring hands
hands in orison
the face of the horrible cannot be better indicated
than by these shocking hands

diviner of purple entrails and destiny
reciter of macumbas
my brother
what are you looking for through these forests
of horns of hoofs of wings of horses

all punctate things
all bipunctate things

avatars however of a god keen on destruction
monsters taking flight
in the combats of justice I recognized
the rare laughter of your magical weapons
the vertigo of your blood
                    and the law of your name.

Cérémonie vaudou pour Saint John Perse . . .

celui qui balise l'aire d'atterissage des colibris
celui qui plante en terre une hampe d'asclépias de Curaçao
pour fournir le gîte aux plus grands monarques du monde
qui sont en noblesse d'exil et papillons de passage

celui pour qui les burseras de la sierra
suant sang et eau et plus de sang que d'eau et pelés
n'en finissent pas de se tordre les bras
grotesques dans leur parade de damnés

celui qui contemple chaque jour la première lettre génétique
qu'il est superflu de nommer
jusqu'à parfait rougeoiement
avec à recueillir le surplus de forces hors du vide historique

le chercheur de sources perdues
le demêleur de laves cordées

celui qui calcule l'étiage de la colère
dans les terres de labour et de mainbour
celui qui du sang rencontre la roue du temps et du contretemps
mille fois plus gémissante que norias sur l'Oronte

celui qui remplace l'asphodèle des prairies infernales
par—sacrale—la belle coiffure afro de l'haemanthus
—Angela Davies de ces lieux—riche de toutes les épingles de nos sangs hérissés

(le vit-il le vit-il l'Etranger
plus rouge pourtant que le sang de Tammouz
et nos faces décebales
le vit-il le vit-il l'Etranger?)

phlégréennes
oiseaux profonds
tourterelles de l'ombre et du grief

et que l'arc s'embrase
et que de l'un à l'autre océan
les magmas fastueux en volcans se répondent pour
de toutes gueules de tous fumants sabords honorer
en route pour le grand large
l'ultime Conquistador en son dernier voyage

Voodoo Ceremonial for St.-John Perse

the one who marks out the hummingbird landing field with beacons
the one who plants a stalk of Curaçao asclepias in the ground
to provide shelter for the greatest monarchs of the world
who are in the nobility of exile and transient butterflies

the one for whom the Burseras of the sierra
sweating blood and water and more blood than water and peeled
never cease twisting their arms
grotescas in their parade of the damned

the one who contemplates every day the first genetic letter
which it is superfluous to name
to the point of perfect reddening
with a surplus of forces to be gathered from the historical void

the seeker of lost springheads
the disentangler of braided lava

the one who assesses the lowest water level of anger
in the plowable and tutelary earth
the one who encounters the blood of time and contretemps
creaking a thousand more moans than norias on the Orontes

the one who replaces the asphodel of infernal meadows
with—sacral—the beautiful afro of the Haemanthus
—the Angela Davis of these regions—rich with all the pins of our bristling bloods

(and did he see it did the Stranger see it
redder still than the blood of Tammuz
than our Decebalian faces
did he see it did the Stranger see it?)

*

*

Flegreian
birds profound
turtledoves of darkness and resentment

and may the arch catch fire
and from one ocean to another
may the sumptuous magmas in volcanoes answer each other
to honor, with all muzzles all portholes smoking,
under sail toward the high seas,
the ultimate Conquistador on his last voyage

Quand Miguel Angel Asturias disparut

Bon batteur de silex
jeteur à toute volée de grains d'or dans l'épaisse crinière
de la nuit hippocampe
ensemenceur dément de diamants
brise-hache comme nul arbre dans la forêt
Miguel Angel s'asseyait à même le sol
disposant un gri-gri dans l'osselet de ses mots
quatre mots de soleil blanc
quatre mots de ceiba rouge
quatre mots de serpent corail

Miguel Angel se versait une rasade
de tafia d'étoiles macérées neuf nuits
à bouillir dans le gueuloir non éteint des volcans
et leur trachée d'obsidienne

Miguel Angel contemplait dans le fond de ses yeux
les graines montant gravement à leur profil d'arbres

Miguel Angel de sa plume caressait
la grande calotte des vents et le vortex polaire

Miguel Angel allumait de pins verts
les perroquets à tête bleue de la nuit

Miguel Angel perfusait d'un sang d'étoiles de lait
de veines diaprées et de ramages de lumière la grise empreinte
de l'heure du jour des jours du temps des temps

Et puis
Miguel Angel déchaînait ses musiques sévères
une musique d'arc
une musique de vagues et de calebasses
une musique de gémissements de rivière
ponctuée des coups de canon des fruits du couroupite
Et les burins de quartz se mettaient à frapper
les aiguilles de jade réveillaient les couteaux de silex
et les arbres à résine

O Miguel Angel sorcier des vers luisants

When Miguel Angel Asturias Disappeared

Skillful striker of silex
grandly flinging golden grain into the thick mane
of the hippocampal night
crazy diamond sower
     axbreaker like no tree in the forest
Miguel Angel used to sit on the ground itself
arranging a grigri in the knuckle bone of his words
     four white sun words
     four red ceiba words
     four coral snake words

Miguel Angel poured a glassful
of astral tafia macerated nine months
simmering in the nonextinct mugpiece of volcanoes
and their obsidian trachea

in the depths of his eyes Miguel Angel observed
seeds rising solemnly toward their arboreal contours

with his pen Miguel Angel caressed
the great skull-cap of winds and the polar vortex

with green pine trees Miguel Angel ignited
the blue-headed parrots of the night

Miguel Angel perfused a blood of milky stars
of mottled veins of floral light over the grey imprint
of the hour of the day of days of time of times

    And then
Miguel Angel unleashed his severe musics
a bow-like music
a music of waves and calabashes
a moaning river music
punctuated by the gunshots of sapucaia fruit
And the quartz chisels began to strike
the jade needles stirred the silex knives
and the resinous trees

O Miguel Angel you glowworm wizard

le saman basculait empêtré de ses bras fous
avec toutes ses pendeloques de machines éperdues
avec le petit rire de la mer très doux
dans le cou chatouilleux des criques
et l'amitié minutieuse du Grand Vent

Quand les flèches de la Mort atteignirent Miguel Angel
on ne le vit point couché
mais bien plutôt déplier sa grande taille
au fond du lac qui s'illumina

Miguel Angel immergea sa peau d'homme
                        et revêtit sa peau de dauphin

Miguel Angel dévêtit sa peau de dauphin
                        et se changea en arc-en-ciel

Miguel Angel rejetant sa peau d'eau bleue
                    revêtit sa peau de volcan

et s'installa montagne toujours verte
                    à l'horizon de tous les hommes.

Pour dire . . .

Pour revitaliser le rugissement des phosphènes
le cœur creux des comètes

pour raviver le verso solaire des rêves
leur laitance
pour activer le frais flux des sèves la mémoire des silicates

Colère des peuples débouché des Dieux leur ressaut
patienter le mot son or son orle
jusqu'à ignivome
sa bouche.

the shaman toppled entangled in his crazed arms
with all his pendants of bewildered machines
with the very sweet little laughter of the sea
into the ticklish necks of coves
and with the meticulous friendship of the Great Wind

When the arrows of Death reached Miguel Angel
he was not seen lying down
but rather unfolding his great height
at the bottom of the lake which lit up

Miguel Angel immersed his human skin
                and donned his dolphin skin

Miguel Angel took off his dolphin skin
                and changed into a rainbow

Miguel Angel discarding his blue water skin
                donned his volcano skin

and settled, an ever green mountain,
                on the horizon of all men.

In Order to Speak

In order to revitalize the roaring of phosphenes
the hollow heart of comets

in order to revive the solar verso of dreams
their roe
in order to activate the cool flux of saps the memory of silicates

Anger of the people outlet of the Gods their recoil
be patient the word his or his orle
—until vomiting fire—
his mouth.

J'ai guidé du troupeau la longue transhumance

Marcher à travers des sommeils de cyclones transportant des villes somnambules dans leurs bras
     endoloris
croiser à mi-pente du saccage des quartiers entiers d'astres fourvoyés
Marcher non sans entêtement à travers ce pays sans cartes dont la décomposition périphérique aura
     épargné je présume l'indubitable corps ou cœur sidéral
Marcher sur la gueule pas tellement bien ourlée des volcans
Marcher sur la fracture mal réduite des continents
(Rien ne sert de parcourir la Grande Fosse
d'inspecter tous les croisements d'examiner les ossements
de parent à parent il manque toujours un maillon)
Marcher en se disant qu'il est impossible que la surtension atmosphérique
captée par les oiseaux parafoudres
n'ait pas été retransmise quelque part
En tout cas quelque part un homme est qui l'attend
Il s'est arrêté un moment
le temps pour un nuage d'installer une belle parade de trochilidés
l'éventail à n'en pas douter à éventer d'or jeune
la partie la plus plutonique d'une pépite qui n'est pas autre chose
que le ventre flammé d'un beau temps récessif.

I Guided the Long Transhumance of the Herd

To walk across the slumbers of cyclones which carry somnambulant cities in their sore arms
halfway up the hill of the plundering to come across whole districts of lost stars
To walk without stubbornness across this uncharted land whose peripheral decomposition will have
       spared I presume the indubitable body or sidereal heart
To walk on the rather clumsily rimmed muzzles of volcanoes
To walk on the poorly set fractures of continents
(No use in traveling the Great Trench
in inspecting all the intersections in examining all the bones
from parent to parent there is always one link missing)
To walk telling oneself that it is impossible that the atmospheric over-pressure
captured by thunder rod birds
was not retransmitted somewhere
At any rate somewhere a man exists waiting for it
He stopped for a moment
the time it takes for a cloud to set up a beautiful parade of Trochilidae
the fan assuredly to fan with new gold
the most plutonic part of a nugget which is none other
than the flambé belly of receding fair weather.

Calendrier lagunaire

J'habite une blessure sacrée
j'habite des ancêtres imaginaires
j'habite un vouloir obscur
j'habite un long silence
j'habite une soif irrémédiable
j'habite un voyage de mille ans
j'habite une guerre de trois cents ans
j'habite un culte désaffecté
entre bulbe et caïeu j'habite l'espace inexploité
j'habite du basalte non une coulée
mais de la lave le mascaret
qui remonte la valleuse à toute allure
et brûle toutes les mosquées
je m'accomode de mon mieux de cet avatar
d'une version du paradis absurdement ratée
        —c'est bien pire qu'un enfer—
J'habite de temps en temps une de mes plaies
Chaque minute je change d'appartement
et toute paix m'effraie

            tourbillon de feu
            ascidie comme nulle autre pour poussières de mondes égarés
            ayant craché volcan mes entrailles d'eau vive
            je reste avec mes pains de mots et mes minerais secrets

J'habite donc une vaste pensée
mais le plus souvent je préfère me confiner
dans la plus petite de mes idées
ou bien j'habite une formule magique
les seuls premiers mots
tout le reste étant oublié
J'habite l'embâcle
J'habite la débâcle
J'habite le pan d'un grand désastre
J'habite le plus souvent le pis le plus sec
du piton le plus efflanqué—la louve de ces nuages—
J'habite l'auréole des cactacées
J'habite un troupeau de chèvres tirant
sur la tétine de l'arganier le plus désolé
A vrai dire je ne sais plus mon adresse exacte
Bathyale ou abyssale

Lagoonal Calendar

I inhabit a sacred wound
I inhabit imaginary ancestors
I inhabit an obscure will
I inhabit a long silence
I inhabit an irremediable thirst
I inhabit a one-thousand-year journey
I inhabit a three-hundred-year war
I inhabit an abandoned cult
between bulb and bulbil I inhabit the unexploited space
I inhabit not a vein of the basalt
but the rising tide of lava
which runs back up the gulch at full speed
to burn all the mosques
I accommodate myself as best I can to this avatar
to an absurdly botched version of paradise
      —it is much worse than a hell—
I inhabit from time to time one of my wounds
Each minute I change apartments
and any peace frightens me

      whirling fire
      ascidium like none other for the dust of strayed worlds
      having spat out my fresh-water entrails
      a volcano I remain with my loaves of words and my secret minerals

I inhabit thus a vast thought
but in most cases I prefer to confine myself
to the smallest of my ideas
or else I inhabit a magical formula
only its opening words
the rest being forgotten
I inhabit the ice jam
I inhabit the ice melting
I inhabit the face of a great disaster
I inhabit in most cases the driest udder
of the skinniest peak—the she-wolf of these clouds—
I inhabit the halo of the Cactaceae
I inhabit a herd of goats pulling
on the tit of the most desolate argan tree
To tell you the truth I no longer know my correct address
Bathyale or abyssal

J'habite le trou des poulpes
Je me bats avec un poulpe pour un trou de poulpe

    Frère n'insistez pas
    vrac de varech
    m'accrochant en cuscute
        ou me déployant en porana
    c'est tout un
        et que le flot roule
        et que ventouse le soleil
        et que flagelle le vent
    ronde bosse de mon néant

La pression atmosphérique ou plutôt l'historique
agrandit démesurément mes maux
même si elle rend somptueux certains de mes mots.

I inhabit the octopuses' hole
I fight with the octopus over an octopus hole

      Brother lay off
      a kelpy mess
      twining dodder-like
          or unfurling porana-like
      it's all the same thing
          which the wave tosses
          to which the sun leeches
          which the wind whips
      sculpture in the round of my nothingness

The atmospheric or rather historic pressure
even if it makes certain of my words sumptuous
immeasurably increases my plight.

*

Banal

Rien que la masse de manoeuvre de la torpeur à manoeuvrer
Rien que le jour des autres et leur séjour
Rien que ce troupeau de douteux lézards qui reviennent plutôt gaiement du pâturage et leurs
    conciliabules infâmes aux découpes de bayous de mon sang méandre à mumbo-jumbo
Rien que cette manière de laper chaque hasard de mon champ vital et de raréfier à doses l'ozone natal
Rien que le déménagement de moi-même sous le rire bas des malebêtes
Rien que l'hégémonie du brouillard qu'atteste la nappe qu'il s'est tirée sur la cendre des vies
    entr'aperçues de tours écroulées de désirs à peine mâchés puis recrachés (épaves qui
    m'absentent)
Rien que du passé son bruit de lointaine cannonade dans le ciel
Je ne le sais que trop
Une visage à organiser
Une journée à déminer
Et toujours cette maldonne à franchir étape par étape
à charge pour moi d'inventer chaque point d'eau.

Banal

Only the laborer's sledge of torpor to maneuver
Only the present of the others and their presence
Only this herd of suspect lizards almost gaily coming back from the pasture and their ignominous
    secret meetings in the fretwork of the bayous of my blood a mumbo-jumbo meander
Only this manner of lapping up each chance from my vital field and of rarifying my natal ozone dose
    by dose
Only the moving out of the house of my self under the sniggering of hellhounds
Only the hegemony of the fog attested by the blanket that it pulled for itself over the ash of
    half-glimpsed lives of collapsed towers of desires barely chewed then spat out again (wreck-
    age removing itself from me)
Of the past only the boom of distant cannons in the sky
I know it only too well
A face to organize
A day to strip of its mines
And always this misdeal to negotiate step by step
stuck as I am with inventing each water hole.

Ibis-Anubis

Quelques traces d'érosion
des habitudes de gestes (produits de corrosion)
les silences
des souvenirs aussi raz-de-marée
le chant profond du jamais refermé
impact et longue maturation de mangrove

Sourde la sape
toujours différé l'assaut
il est permis de jouer les rites du naufrage
(à situer quelque part entre allusion et illusion
la signature douloureuse d'un oiseau
sous les alphabets incompréhensibles du moment)

Je ne saurai jamais premières d'un message
quelles paroles forcèrent ma gorge
ni quel effort rugina ma langue
que me reste-t-il ce jour sinon penser
qu'à la face du destin à l'avance j'éructai une vie
j'ai tiré au sort mes ancêtres une terre plénière
mais qui blesse qui mutile
tout ce qui abâtardit le fier regard
ou plus lente
ou plus riche
la curée urubu ou le rostre zopilote
j'ai eu je garde j'ai
le libre choix de mes ennemis

Couchant fantôme si s'y allume le mien
parole grand duc tu planeras ce cri à sa gueule d'anubis.

Ibis-Anubis

A few traces of erosion
gestural habits (products of corrosion)
                          the silences
memories also tidal waves
the deep song of the never closed
impact and a lengthy "mangrove" maturation

The communication trench mute
              the assault always deferred
one is permitted to perform the rites of shipwreck
(to be situated somewhere between allusion and illusion
the painful signature of a bird
under the incomprehensible alphabets of the moment)

I will never know which words, the first
in a message, forced through my throat
nor what effort scaled my tongue
what do I have left today except to ponder
that in the face of destiny in advance I belched a life
I drew lots for my ancestors for a plenary earth
but one which wounds which mutilates
anything that bastardizes the proud gaze
or slower
or richer
          the urubu quarry or the zopilote rostrum
I have had I keep I have
          a free choice of enemies

Setting sun a phantom if my own ignites there
great horned owl word you will hover this cry with its anubis muzzle.

Sans instance ce sang

Toujours, pas tant vif que beau, l'air, sauf ce souffle que nous pousse la vraie terre, langue bleue et fidèle précation d'ancêtres.

Je vois, descendant les marches de la montagne, dans un dénouement que rendent vaste les papillons, les reines qui sortent en grande dentelle de leurs prisons votives.

Elles s'étonnent à bon droit que le feu central consente à se laisser confiner pour combien de temps encore dans la bonne conscience des châteaux de termitières qu'il s'est édifiés un peu partout.

Quant au Soleil, un Soleil de frontière, il cherche le poteau mitan autour duquel faire tourner pour qu'enfin l'avenir commence

ces saisons insaisissables ce ciel sans cil et sans instance ce sang.

This Appeal Prohibited Blood

Always, less lively than beautiful, the air, save for this breath exhaled for us by the true earth, a blue tongue and a faithful precation of ancestors.

I see, descending the mountain steps, in a denouement greatly magnified by butterflies, the queens coming out as an endless lace from their votive prisons.

They are rightly astonished that the central fire consents to let itself be confined for how much longer in the good conscience of the termitarium castles which it built for itself here and there.

As for the Sun, a frontier Sun, it is seeking the center stake around which to rotate—so that the future may finally commence—

these unseizable seasons this eyelash-denied sky and this appeal prohibited blood.

A *valoir* . . .

Contrefaisances
ceux qui de leur pierre à regards assassinent
les plus exotiques printemps
les saccageurs convergents
     des plus somptueuses parures des sporanges des plasmodes
     au guachamaca dont même la fumée empoisonne
     blanche caresse de ce fond de ravin

Nuages
traîneurs des savates éculées du soleil dans le ciel des peuples résignés
oiseaux débris de vol
siffle-sève sévères
il n'est pas que vous n'ayez pas compris sa pompe et mon attente

mesurée au déclic d'horloge du serpent-minute
l'explosion
après quoi il est convenu d'apprécier que
vient la poigne rude du petit matin attentoire
de planter au faîte d'un poui le plus oublié
sa parure de feu
     son dolman de sang
         son drapeau de rage et de renouveau.

To Be Deducted . . .

Apings
those who with their gazestone assassinate
the most exotic springs
the pillagers converging
        from the most sumptuous adornments of the sporangia of the plasmodia
        to the guachamaca whose smoke alone poisons,
        a white caress of this ravine's depth

Clouds
draggers of the sun's worn-down heels in the sky resigned peoples
birds debris of flight
severe sap sippers
it is not that you have not understood its pomp and my waiting

measured by the clock click of the serpent-minute
the explosion
after which it is proper to appreciate that
the brutal fist of the terrorist crack of dawn has just
planted at the top of the most forgotten poui
its adornment of fire
        its dolmen of blood
                its flag of rage and renewal.

Annonciades

La bonne nouvelle m'aura été portée à travers la cohue d'astres jaunes et rouges en fleurs pour la
première fois par une volée de pouliches ivres

Elles me disent que les phasmes se sont convertis en feuillage et acceptent de se constituer en forêts
autonomes
qu'une fumée blanche monte du concile des quiscales pour annoncer que dans les zones les plus
sombres du ciel des lucarnes se sont allumées

que le courant a été établi depuis le surfin du soleil jusqu'à la collerette des salamandres montant
la garde aux tunnels
que la rouille est tombée en grêle libérant tout un imprévu de papillons

que les lamantins couverts de pierreries remontent les berges
que toute la cérémonie enfin a été ponctuée par le tir solennel des volcans installant de plein droit
des lacs dans leur cratère
poussants mon fol élan
feuillants ma juste demeure
racines ma survie
une goutte de sang monte du fond
seule incline le paysage
et au faîte du monde
fascine
une mémoire irréductible.

Annonciades

The good news will have been brought to me through the throng of yellow and red stars in bloom for
    the first time by a flight of drunk fillies

They are telling me that the phasms have turned into foliage and that they accept taking on the status
    of an autonomous forest
    that a white smoke rises from the grackle council announcing that in the darkest zones of the
    sky lucarnes have lit up

    that the current has been turned on from superfine sun to the collaret of salamanders keeping
    watch at the tunnels
    that the rust fell like hail freeing a whole unforeseen of butterflies

    that manatees covered with precious stones are climbing up the banks
    that the whole ceremony in short was punctuated by the solemn shots of volcanoes installing
    on their own authority lakes in their craters
            growings my crazy ardor
            leafings my just dwelling
            roots my survival
            a drop of blood rises from the depths
            by itself tilts the landscape
            and at the crest of the world
            captivates
                an irreducible memory

Soleil safre

au pied de volcans bègues
plus tôt que le petit brouillard violet qui monte de ma fièvre
je suis assis au milieu d'une cour
horologue de trois siècles accumulés en fientes de chauves-souris
sous la fausse espérance de doux grigris

déjà hurlant d'âme chienne
et portant les vraies chaînes
ai-je mille de mes cœurs rendu
pour celui d'aujourd'hui qui
très fort
à la gorge nous remonte
parakimomène de hauts royaumes amers
moi
soleil safre

Internonce

Il m'arrive de le perdre
des semaines
c'est ma créature mais rebelle

un petit mot couresse
un petit mot crabe-c'est-ma faute
un petit mot pétale de feu
un petit mot pétrel plongeur
un petit mot saxifrage de tombeaux

petit mot qui m'atteste je te lance tiaulé
dans le temps et les confins
assistant à ton assaut sévère
spectral et saccadé
et de mon sang luciole parmi les lucioles

Zaffer Sun

at the foot of stammering volcanoes
earlier than the violet little fog arising from my fever
I am sitting in the middle of a courtyard
an horologue of three centuries accumulated in bat droppings
under the false hope of a sweet grigris

already howling from a bitch soul
and carrying the true shackles
I have exchanged a thousand of my hearts
for the one today that
powerfully
comes up to our throat   *
parakimomène by lofty bitter kingdoms
I
zaffer sun

Internuncio

Off and on I lose it
for weeks
it is my creature but a rebellious one
                                                                         *
a little word couresse   *
a little word through-my-fault crab
a little word fire petal
a little word diver petrel
a little word tomb saxifrage

little word which gives evidence of me I throw you trillando
into time and the outer reaches
witnessing your severe assault
spectral and spasmodic
and of my own blood a firefly among the fireflies

Passage d'une liberté

Le noir pavillon claquant au vent toujours barbaresque
les feux à mi-chemin entre la lumière biologique la plus pressante et la sérénité des constellations
la mise en contact qui ne peut se faire qu'à partir
de très rares macles de minéraux

Cimarrone sans doute

(le pan de ce visage qui dans l'écume d'un silence
tombe avec des biseautés de mangue)
tellement à la faveur d'oiseaux
dont l'office est à force de pollen
de corriger les bévues des Erinnyes et le raide vin des murênes.

A *Freedom in Passage*

The black flag slapping in the ever Barbary wind
the lights halfway between the most pressing biological clarity and the serenity of the constellations
the connecting which can only take place
using very rare mineral macles

Cimarron undoubtedly

(the section of this face which in the frothing of a silence
falls amidst mango-like bevelings)
helped so much by birds
whose mission is by means of pollen
to correct the Erinyes' blunders and the stiff wine of moray eels.

NOTES

• In Volume I of Césaire's *Oeuvres complètes*, a number of runover lines have been set as if they were two or more lines. Césaire has asked us to make corrections in both the English and the French texts.
In our attempt to maintain Césaire's usual preference for family and genus classifications for botanical words, we have been helped by Elodie Jourdain's *Le vocabulaire du parler Créole de la Martinique* (Paris: Klincksieck, 1956); R. Pinchon's *Quelques aspects de la nature aux antilles* (Fort-de-France, 1967); and Lafcadio Hearn's *Two Years in the French West Indies* (New York: Harpers, 1890).
We have not annotated words and phrases here which are discussed in our Introduction.

Page 37: About Empress Josephine's statue, Hearn writes: "She is standing just in the centre of the Savane [Fort-de-France's public square], robed in the fashion of the First Empire, with gracious arms and shoulders bare: one hand leans upon a medallion bearing the eagle profile of Napoleon. . . . Seven tall palms stand in a circle around her, lifting their comely heads into the blue glory of the tropic day. . . . " (*Two Years*, p. 66.)

Page 37: the term *morne*, "used throughout the French West Indies to designate certain altitudes of volcanic origin, is justly applied to the majority of Martinican hills, and unjustly sometimes even to its mightiest elevation—Mont Pelée. Mornes usually have beautiful and curious forms: they are most often pyramidal or conoid up to a certain height, but have rounded or truncated summits. Green with the richest vegetation, they rise from valleys and coasts with remarkable abruptness." (*Two Years*, pp. 254–55.) In Césaire's time, they were often the hillocks on the outskirts of Martinican towns on which slum areas were located.

Page 45: *mentule*: in this case probably a gallicization of the Latin "mentula" (penis) based on an Indo-European stem designating a stick agitated to produce fire.

Page 45: *jiculi*: according to Césaire, a variation on the word "jiquilite," a kind of indigo tree, planted in San Salvador in the 19th century.

Page 47: *Jura*: Toussaint L'Ouverture (1743–1803), the Haitian black patriot and martyr, was a self-educated slave who by 1801 was governing the whole island of Haiti. A year later, he was seized by Napoleon-sent forces and returned to France, where he died in a dungeon at Fort-de-Joux in the French Jura.

Page 47: *moricaud* (coon): literally a person with very dark skin, but familiarly and pejoratively used to designate Africans and Arabs.

Page 49: *patyura*: according to Césaire, a variation on "patira," the name for a peccary found in Paraguay.

Page 51: *marron* (maroon): from "marron," the French word for a chestnut, whence as adjective, "chestnut-colored." The secondary meaning, in the West Indies, is a fugitive black slave, or his black descendant. This meaning seems to be influenced by the American Spanish "cimarrón" (wild, unruly, or as noun, runaway slave, maroon), based on the Old Spanish "cimarra" (brushwood), according to Webster. But the Dictionary of the Spanish Academy derives it from "cima," a mountain-top: such slaves fled to the mountains. Hence "to maroon," to abandon (someone) on a desolate shore. In the present context, we have avoided the more idiomatic expression, "to pluck the chestnuts from the fire," because the stress is on the fugitive slave, and furthermore because this meaning is central to Césaire's poetry. The word recurs in other poems, as *marronne, marronneur,* and as a coined verb, *marronner.*

Page 53: *pahouine* (Pahouin): refers to the Pahouin group of Bantu-speaking peoples who inhabit Cameroon, Gabon, Congo, and Equatorial Guinea (800,000 people). Among them are the Pangwe, Fang, Beti, Boulou, Ewondo, and Eton.

Page 59: *rigoises* (quirts): according to Jourdain, the word is also a popular term for a slave whip.

Page 59: *le tracking* (boogie-woogie): probably a play on a phrase that Césaire picked up from the Harlem Renaissance writers. In 1930s Harlem jive, a "track" was a ballroom, and "to truck" meant to jitterbug.

Page 61: *chicote*: in Portuguese, a knotted leather slave whip.

Page 63: *menfenil*: according to Jourdain, the *menfenil* (also known as the *malfini*) is the *Falco sparverious caribaearum*, or the Caribbean sparrow hawk.

Page 71: *pirogue*: a small vessel with a long narrow hull, two masts, no deck and usually a crew of five, used to transport barrels of tafia. (*Two Years*, p. 133.) The term is used in Africa to indicate any dugout canoe.

Page 73: *lambi* (conch): one of the great spiral shells, used for sounding calls, weighing seven or eight pounds. Rolled like a scroll, fluted and scalloped about the edges, pink-pearled inside—such as are sold in America for mantel-piece ornaments. (*Two Years*, pp. 133–34.)

Page 73: *and the twenty-nine legal blows of the whip*: concerning this line and the 18 lines that follow it, the tortures, the names of the slaveowners who carried them out, the devices they used and, in a few cases, the ways in which the owners were acquitted for their crimes, are all documented in the writings of Victor Schoelcher, the French legislator who was most responsible for pushing the abolition laws through parliament in 1848. Much of the material cited here was reprinted in 1948 in *Esclavage et colonisation* (Paris: Presses Universitaires de France), a collection of excerpts by Schoelcher edited by Emile Tersen and prefaced by Césaire. One learns about the 29 blows as punishment for menacing foremen, in the chapter "La condition servile." The same chapter describes Mahaudière and his doghouse, and details the acquittal of Brafin by Judge Fourniol on charges of mistreating his slaves (private communication from Thomas Hale).

Page 89: *trigonocéphale* (fer-de-lance): see Jourdain, pp. 10–28 for a thorough discussion of the "grande vipère fer-de-lance de la Martinique."

Page 93: *rhizulent* (rhizulate): a neologism apparently based on the Greek combining form, *rhizo-*, meaning "root."

Page 109: *batéké*: probably to evoke the Batekes, an important Bantu people of the Congo.

Page 111: *balisier*: a wild plantain found in the forests of Martinique that has an unusually shaped bright red flower. For some people, it is like an open heart, while for others it is like a flame. In another poem, "Spirales," Cesaire links the balisier with the image of a phoenix. Aliko Songolo, in his book *Aimé Césaire: Archétypes et Métaphores* (Paris: Présence Africaine, 1983), suggests that this combination of images evokes the Bachelardian notion of fire as the symbol of desire to change and transcend.

Césaire's Parti Progressiste Martiniquais (Martinican Progressive Party) adopted the balisier as its symbol sometime after its founding in 1958, and the flower began to appear on the masthead of *Le Progressiste*, the party newspaper, in the late 1960s. Although we do not know what particular connotations the Party attaches to the balisier, the images of the heart (life) and fire (rebirth, change) suggested above are compatible with the conditions under which the PPM was created after Césaire's break with the French Communist Party in 1956. Today, units of the PPM are called balisiers and carry the name of a local or international hero—for example, the balisier Salvador Allende.

For all of these reasons, we have decided that it would be appropriate to employ the balisier as a symbol throughout this book.

Page 113: *bananier* (plantain): "What we call bananas in the United States are not called bananas in Martinique, but figs. Plantains seem to be called *bananes*." (*Two Years*, p. 360.)

Page 113: *hougan*: in general, a West Indian sorcerer. In Haitian voodoo, a *houngan* is a combination priest, healer and diviner.

Page 119: *compitales* (Compitalia): in Roman religion the *lares compitales* were the guardians of the crossroads and the junctions of fields, in whose honor were held the *Laralia*, or *Compitalia*.

Page 129: *roxelane*: according to Césaire, this word refers to a river that flowed through Saint-Pierre, the Martinican city destroyed by the eruption of Mont Pelée in 1902. Given the presence of the Roxelane River in the poem, Saint-Pierre refers to the city, not to the saint of the same name.

Page 133: *pitt*: according to Césaire, a Martinican word for the area in which cock fights take place. Jourdain lists it as a Creolization of the English word "pit."

Page 139: *chamulque* (chamulcus): an ancient Greek crane or windlass.

Page 141: *darne* (dazzled): a word of the Ardennes, meaning "dazzled" or "dizzy," used twice by Rimbaud in the poems "Accroupissements" and "Les Poètes de Sept Ans."

Page 143: *tipoyeur*: based on "tipoye," a crude sedan chair in which blacks carried their white masters in Cameroon. The word could be translated as "sedan chair bearer."

Page 143: *Kolikombo*: ruler of the world of the dead among the Banda, and a mythical sorcerer figure from René Maran's *Batouala*, originally published in France in 1921. See pp. 77 and 123–26 of the Beck/Mboukou trans. (Washington, D.C.: Black Orpheus Press, 1972) for information on the Koliko'mbo's nature and activities.

Page 145: *charrascal* (carrascal): in Spanish, holm-oaks or Corsican pines.

Page 147: *Batouque*: in the first edition of *Les armes miraculeuses*, Césaire footnoted the word as "Brazilian tom-tom rhythm." According to Arnold, "*Batuque* in Luso-Brazilian is an onomatopoeia for the drumbeat itself." (*Modernism and Negritude*, p. 128.) Thomas Hale sees it as not only the drum beat, but the dance one performs to the drumbeat (private communication). Césaire employs the second spelling of the word near the end of the poem "The Verb, 'Marronner.' "

Page 153: *Basse-Pointe Diamant Tartane et Caravelle*: coastal Martinican villages and towns. Césaire himself was born at Basse-Pointe.

Page 153: *carambas*: in Spanish, an interjection, such as "confound it!" or "Hell!"

Page 155: *soukala*: probably based on Suk, a Nilotic people in the Lake Baringo region of Kenya, i.e., "soukala" as the country of the Suks. Like "krumen," in the poem "Batouque," it is mysteriously left uncapitalized.

Page 165: *Oricous*: popular name for the great black African vulture.

Page 169: *strom*: according to Davis, "the loan-word 'maelstrom' appears here in syncope as 'strom.' " ("Toward a 'Non-Vicious Circle,' " p. 139.) According to Césaire, much of the imagery in this poem is a response to the disaster caused by Mont Pelée's 1902 eruption; therefore our translation of "éclat" as "eruption."

Page 173: *Aguacero*: in Spanish, a brief sudden shower or downpour.

Page 177: *bille* (speck of coal): Césaire confirmed to Davis ("Toward a 'Non-Vicious Circle,' " p. 140) that "bille" here is "a fragmentary vocable for 'escarbille.' "

Page 187: *the Phoronidea would make roads with their tentacles*: Phoronidea are small, marine, wormlike animals, bearing numerous tentacles. Therefore our translation of "queues" as "tentacles."

Page 187: *the Trichomanes' crosiers*: Hearn describes Martinican tree-ferns as unrolling in a spiral from the bud and at first as assuming the shape of a crosier. He also notes that some of this species are called "archbishop-trees." (*Two Years*, p. 111.) It is possible that Césaire's reference to "bishop" at the beginning of this line is to evoke such a tree-fern, but we have been unable to locate anything called an archbishop-tree.

Page 197: *daba*: a short-handled African hoe.

Page 201: *paraschites*: in ancient Egypt a class of embalmers whose task, while preparing the mummy, was to make a lateral cut with a silex knife into the cadaver in order to extract the viscera.

Page 213: *tapaya*: popular name for an iguana of the Phrynosoma genus, comprising the horned toads.

Page 225: *The Light's Judgment*: in early editions of *Soleil cou coupé*, this is the last poem in the collection. For reasons that appear to be erroneous, in the *OC* the poem is placed as the opening piece in *Corps perdu*. We have taken the liberty of moving it back to its place in *Soleil cou coupé*.

Page 235: *souklyans*: a Dahoman sorcerer who has the ability to leave his skin to carry out his evil tasks. The word appears to be a variation on "soukougnan" or "soukongnan," all of which appear to be derived from *soukou* = moonless night, and *gnan* = master, i.e., a master of the moonless night, or sorcerer. (*Le vocabulaire du parler Créole*, pp. 167–168.)

Page 267: *rôlés* (forbeten): an archaic French word meaning "beaten." Our thanks to Professor Lee W. Patterson of the English Department at Johns Hopkins University who suggested the Middle English "forbeten."

Page 271: *Dalaba . . . Tinkisso*: Dalaba, Pita, Labé, and Mali are all towns on a south-north road which cuts through the Fouta Jallon mountains in central Guinea. The mountains end in the Tamgue range, which may be the reference here to Timbé. The Tinkisso is a tributary of the Niger which has its source in the Fouta Jallon mountains.

Page 275: *For Ina*: Ina is one of Césaire's daughters who has done extensive work on Caribbean anthropology and folklore. *Présence Africaine*, no. 121–122, 1982, contains her essay, "La triade humaine dans le conte antillais."

Page 275: *la mangle* (the coastal swamp): while the word "mangle" generally translates as "mangrove fruit," in this case, according to comments Césaire made in an interview conducted after the publication of *Ferrements* in 1960, the word refers to the swampy coastal fringe of Martinique. Césaire's response to this part of the interview deserves to be quoted here for it reveals his careful observation of Martinican nature. "I am an Antillean. I want a poetry that is concrete, very Antillean, Martinican. I must name Martinican things, must call them by their names. The cañafistula mentioned in "Spirals" is a tree; it is also called the drumstick tree. It has large yellow leaves and its fruit are those big purplish bluish black pods, used here also as a purgative. The balisier resembles a plantain, but it has a red heart, a red florescence at its center that is really shaped like a heart. The cecropias are shaped like silvery hands, yes, like the interior of a black's hand. All of these astonishing words are absolutely necessary, they are never gratuitous. . . . " (Hale, *Les Ecrits d'A. C.*, p. 406.)

Page 305: *Statue of Lafcadio Hearn*: the quoted lines in the first stanza appear to come directly from Hearn's book *Youma* (Alhambra: C. F. Braun and Co., 1951, pp. 151–152). They are shouted by a street medicine man who is trying to sell a potion of tafia, gunpowder, and crushed wasps, to laborers and fishermen.

In the second stanza, Yé and Nanie-Rosette are characters in some of the Martinican folktales that Hearn collected and published. He writes that Yé is the most curious figure in Martinican folklore, "a typical Bitaco—or mountain negro of the lazy kind." (*Two Years*, p. 401.) The reference to Yé in the poem comes from a tale in which to get food for his children, Yé clambers up a palm tree and accidentally kills the totem bird.

In another tale, Nanie-Rosette is depicted as a greedy child who spends the night feasting on the Devil's Rock, with the Devil and his entourage dancing about her.

An ajoupa is a Martinican hut made out of branches and leaves.

Page 307: *the bird with feathers*: the last two lines of this poem draw upon the consequences of Yé having killed and shared the totem bird with his family. The enchanted bird revives and demands that the family restore it to its very last feather. Kesteloot and Kotchy comment on the allegorical use of the folk tale in the poem in A. C. / *l'homme et l'oeuvre*, pp. 58–59.

Page 309: *tur-ra-mas*: an Australian boomerang made out of very hard wood.

Page 321: *Cavally Sassandra Bandama*: a series of three rivers which flow south in Ivory Coast into the Atlantic. The Cavally marks the frontier with Liberia.

Page 323: *Pachira*: a variation on "Pachirier," a tree from Guiana and the West Indies that resembles the horse chestnut tree.

Page 331: *Memorial For Louis Delgrès*: General Magloire Pélage was a Guadeloupan mulatto military leader who overthrew local French rule in 1801. Unlike Toussaint L'Ouverture, however, he took all possible means to demonstrate his loyalty to France, and when Richepanse prepared to invade Basse-Terre, Pélage attempted to get Delgrès to surrender. When handed Pélage's message, Delgrès tore it in pieces and denounced Pélage as a traitor.

Ignace, one of the black leaders at Basse-Terre, surrendered and then proceeded to kill himself. Gobert, the French general to whom he had surrendered, had his head cut off and exposed to view. See Shelby T. McCloy's *The Negro in the French West Indies*, (Lexington: University of Kentucky Press, 1966), pp. 106–110. McCloy's account of the death of Ignace, as well as where it took place, differs from Césaire's account of it in the poem.

Page 335: *une fripure de bagasses* (a shred of crushed sugarcane): "fripure" is a neologism formed by Césaire on "friperie," which in Martinique is the shed in which the sugarcane waits to be taken to the mill. According to Césaire, "fripure" is the residue of crushed sugarcane emptied of its vital juices.

Page 339: *In Memory Of A Black Union Leader*: Albert Cretinoir, who died from natural causes in Martinique in 1952.

Page 341: *quand mai dore en chabin* (when May gilds chabin-like): chabin is the European name for a kind of sheep crossbred by a ewe and a billygoat. Socially, in the West Indies, it refers to a mixed-race offspring.

Page 345: *au carne blanc coeur désinfecté* (in the white heart's tough antiseptic meat): Césaire confirmed our interpretation of this line. "Carne," a feminine noun, is used as an adjective for an otherwise masculine group of words.

Page 361: *cachaça*: in Spanish, "cachaza" is a kind of rum, or the first froth on cane juice when boiled to make sugar. Exu, elsewhere spelled Eshu, "is one of the names given to the loa who, in voodoo, and in Brazilian macumba, opens the paths or lifts the barriers between the world of men and the world of spirits." (Arnold, *Modernism and Negritude* p. 221.)

Page 361: *vatapá*: a Brazilian dish made of manioc meal mixed with fish or meat, and seasoned.

Page 361: *azulejo*: in Spanish, glazed tile painted with various colors or plain white.

Page 363: *Ethiopia* . . . : "Tedj" is a mead drink; "injera" is a pancakelike bread made from corn flour.
    "Saint-Guiorguis" is the Bieta Ghiorghis, the monolithic church at Lalibela.
    One of the names for the legendary Queen of Sheba is "Belkis Makeba" which in the context of the poem links her with the contemporary singer Miriam Makeba.
    The Galla are a southern Ethiopian people.

Page 369: *Boukman*: a black Haitian slave who became the leader of the ferocious revolts at Noé, Clément, Flaville, Gallifet, and Le Normand in 1791.

Page 371: *Dessalines*: Jean-Jacques Dessalines, a lieutenant trained by Toussaint L'Ouverture, who became governor of the South after the 1799 Haitian Revolution. Notorious for his hatred of whites, he commanded the assault in mid-November 1803 on Fort Breda, on Cap Haitien. Vertières was one of the fort's supporting positions.

Page 371: *Cabritos . . . bombaïa*: in Spanish, "cabritos" are young goats or kids.
    "Cantagallo" is a town in the state of Rio de Janeiro.
    "Botafogo" in Portuguese means "fire-spitting," and is a popular term for a troublemaker.
    "Bate" in Portuguese means "beating" or "shaking."
    "Favellas" are shanty slums.
    "Bombaïa" is a Haitian rallying cry associated with Boukman's voodoo ceremonies at Bois Cayman on the eve of the 1791 revolts.

Page 371: *moudang*: a variation on the word "Mondongue" or "Moudongue," an African people living at the Cameroon and Chad borders, or possibly a variant of "Mandingue," the large family of peoples in central West Africa (Bambara, Malinké, Soninké, Dyula, Wangara, etc.). Hearn comments that in Martinique "moudongue" is a very hard wood from which sticks, with magical power to inflict injury, were made. He adds that a Mondongue slave on a plantation was generally feared by his fellow blacks of other tribes to such an extent that the name became transformed into an adjective to denote anything formidable or terrible. (*Two Years*, p. 173.)

Page 375: *Decebalian*: Decebales was the name given to the King of Dacia. The Dacian Decebales fought the Roman Empire but eventually cooperated with it during the first century A.D. Probably a symbol of the colonization process for Césaire, who uses an adjective derived from the noun.

Page 375: *phlégréennes* (Flegreian): refers to the Campi Flegrei, a volcanic region in Campania, Italy, above the Bay of Naples, with many craters.

Page 385: *porana*: a climbing herb of tropical East Africa, Madagascar, Asia, and Australia, of the Convolvulaceae family.

Page 393: *poui*: a Trinidadian Créole word for the tree *Tabebuia Pallida*, with pink trumpet-shaped flowers.

Page 397: *parakimomène*: probably a misremembered Greek word, *parakinouménos*, a present middle/passive participle, meaning "very disturbed," or "very agitated."

Page 397: *couresse*: popular term for the nonvenomous Martinican water snake. When swimming, the *couresse* holds its head out of the water. "Proud as a couresse crossing a river" is a popular saying.

Page 397: *crabe-c'est-ma-faute* (through-my-fault crab): according to Hearn, "a crab having one very small and one very large claw, which latter it carries folded up against its body, so as to have suggested the idea of a penitent striking his bosom, and uttering the sacramental words of the Catholic confession, 'Through my fault, through my fault, through my most grievous fault.' " (*Two Years*, p. 141.)

Designer: Bob Cato
Title lettering: M. Manoogian
Compositor: Trend Western
Printer: Malloy Lithographers
Binder: Malloy/Dekker
Text: 10 pt. Electra
Display: Electra